WHERE TO STAY

Somewhere Special

ENGLAND 1997

Where to Stay in England 1997 *'Somewhere Special'*
1/96

Published by: **Jarrold Publishing,** Whitefriars, Norwich NR3 1TR, *in association with the* **English Tourist Board,** Thames Tower, Black's Road, Hammersmith, London W6 9EL *and* **Celsius**.

Managing Editor, ETB: Jane Collinson
Design, Compilation and Production: Celsius
Editorial Contributors: Tessa Lecomber, Hugh Chevallier
Photography (excluding line entries and where stated otherwise): Celsius, Britain on View, National Trust Photographic Library
Illustrations: Ian Penney (covers), Jeffy Salt, Mary Evans Picture Library
Cartography: Colin Earl
Typesetting: Celsius
Colour Origination: Spectrum LithoScan
Printed and bound in Great Britain

Display Advertisement Sales: Madison Bell Ltd, 3 St. Peter's Street, Islington Green, London N1 8JD. Telephone: (0171) 359 7737.

© English Tourist Board (except where stated), 1996

ISBN 0 7117 0872 X

Important:

The information contained in this guide has been published in good faith on the basis of information submitted to the English Tourist Board by the proprietors of the premises listed, who have paid for their entries to appear. Jarrold Publishing, the English Tourist Board and Celsius cannot guarantee the accuracy of the information in this guide and accept no responsibility for any error or misrepresentation. All liability for loss, disappointment, negligence or other damage caused by reliance in this guide, or in the event of bankruptcy, or liquidation, or cessation of trade of any company, individual or firm mentioned, is hereby excluded. Please check carefully all prices and other details before confirming a reservation.

The English Tourist Board

The Board is a statutory body created by the Development of Tourism Act 1969 to develop and market England's tourism. Its main objectives are to provide a welcome for people visiting England to take their holidays there; to encourage the provision of tourist amenities and facilities in England. The Board has a statutory duty to advise the Government on tourism matters relating to England and, with Government approval and support, administers the national classification and grading schemes for tourist accommodation in England.

Front cover: Hazel Bank (entry 19)
Back cover: Sproxton Hall (entry 77), The Nurse's Cottage (entry 350)

TO BEGIN

All you need to know about the guide and how to use it

*C*ontents

Welcome to the guide

SOMEWHERE SPECIAL IS THE GUIDE FOR THE DISCERNING TRAVELLER, FEATURING OVER FOUR HUNDRED HOTELS, GUESTHOUSES, B&BS AND INNS ALL OFFERING THEIR GUESTS THAT LITTLE BIT EXTRA. THE FORMAT IS EASY TO USE, WITH ATTRACTIVE, DETAILED ENTRIES CROSS-REFERENCED TO FULL-COLOUR MAPS, PLUS ARTICLES AND FEATURES AS WELL AS HELPFUL HINTS. WHATEVER YOUR BUDGET, AND WHETHER YOU WANT A SHORT GET-AWAY OR A LONGER BREAK, SOMEWHERE SPECIAL OFFERS A CHOICE OF ACCOMMODATION THAT PROMISES A WARM WELCOME AND A STAY THAT'S SPECIAL.

YOUR SURE SIGN OF WHERE TO STAY

As in other English Tourist Board *Where to Stay* accommodation guides, all accommodation included in this invaluable title has been classified under the Board's quality grading and classification scheme (see page 6). In *Somewhere Special*, however, you are promised something extra, for every single entry has achieved a top quality grading of HIGHLY COMMENDED or DE LUXE (see page 8). This means that whatever range of facilities are on offer, they are presented with exceptional care, individuality and quality of service.

QUALITY FIRST

Whether you're looking for no-holds-barred luxury on a grand scale, a short break in a small hotel with character or an intimate bed and breakfast that gives personal attention to perhaps only three or four guests, you're looking in the right guide. The criterion for inclusion in *Somewhere Special* is excellence rather than the range of facilities available – though of course you'll be able to see at a glance exactly what's on offer.

HOW TO CHOOSE

To help you choose somewhere to stay, each entry is illustrated by both a colour photograph and a detailed description. Also displayed are its quality grading, Crown classification and estimated 1997 prices. Facilities are indicated by clear, at-a-glance symbols – see the back flap for a key. You'll also find those important details such as meal times, number of bedrooms, parking spaces and which credit/debit cards are accepted, together with address, telephone and fax numbers.

REGIONAL DIVISIONS

To make finding somewhere special even easier, the guide is divided into four sections, each with its own map: England's North Country, England's Heartland, England's West Country and South and South East England. At the start of each section is a regional introduction followed by a detailed map, cross-referenced to the geographical list of accommodation. Features on topics as varied as the Grizedale Forest Sculpture Trail in Cumbria, and Lawrence of Arabia's actual and spiritual home in the depths of Dorset are interspersed throughout the entries to make perusal even more absorbing.

HIGHLY COMMENDED AND DE LUXE

Those establishments awarded a **HIGHLY COMMENDED** or **DE LUXE** grading represent only a small percentage of all Tourist Board quality-graded accommodation. So whether you're looking for somewhere large or small, you can expect to find accommodation of the very highest standard, accompanied by those personal touches which can transform a guesthouse, B&B, inn or hotel into *somewhere really special*.

Crown classifications and quality gradings

THE ENGLISH TOURIST BOARD'S ACCOMMODATION RATING SCHEME HAS BECOME RECOGNISED AS THE AUTHORITATIVE INDICATOR OF THE LEVEL OF SERVICE YOU CAN EXPECT TO FIND AT YOUR SELECTED GUESTHOUSE, B&B, INN OR HOTEL. OUR TEAM OF INSPECTORS HAS VISITED OVER 11,000 ESTABLISHMENTS THROUGHOUT ENGLAND TO CARRY OUT OBJECTIVE ASSESSMENTS OF THE FACILITIES AND SERVICES OFFERED AND THEIR OVERALL QUALITY STANDARD.

THE CROWN SYSTEM EXPLAINED

A system of Crown classifications may be applied to any type of establishment offering 'serviced' accommodation – hotels, guesthouses, inns, B&Bs and farmhouses. The number of Crowns is an indication of the range of facilities and services on offer – quite simply, the more Crowns, the wider the range of facilities available. There are six classification bands starting at LISTED, and then increasing in line with the facilities from ONE to FIVE CROWN. The Tourist Board lays down strict rules about how these Crown classifications are applied, stipulating, for example, that every classified establishment meets standards for the size of bed, type of bed linen and even the extent of illumination in each room. Assessment for higher bands of classification includes the provision of tourist information, the number – and location – of colour televisions, the use of 13-amp power outlets, the availability of room service and much, much more.

CROWN CLASSIFICATIONS – A QUICK GUIDE

Listed You can be sure that the accommodation will be clean and comfortable, but the range of facilities and services may be limited.

⬤ You will find additional facilities, including washbasin and chair in your bedroom and you will have use of a telephone.

〰〰 There will be a colour TV in your bedroom (or in a lounge) and you can enjoy morning tea/coffee in your bedroom. At least some of the bedrooms will have a private bath (or shower) and WC.

〰〰〰 At least half of the bedrooms will have private bath (or shower) en-suite. You will also be able to order a hot evening meal.

〰〰〰〰 Your bedroom will have a colour TV, radio and telephone, there will be lounge service until midnight and evening meals can be ordered up to 2030 hours. At least 90% of the bedrooms will have private bath and/or shower and WC en-suite.

〰〰〰〰〰 Every bedroom will have a private bath, fixed shower and WC en-suite. The restaurant will be open for breakfast, lunch and dinner (or you can take meals in your room from breakfast until midnight) and you will benefit from an all-night lounge service. A night porter will also be on duty.

QUALITY GRADINGS

A separate quality grading indicates the overall standard of services and facilities. In order to determine which of the four quality grades (APPROVED, COMMENDED, HIGHLY COMMENDED and DE LUXE) should be awarded, a highly-trained Tourist Board inspector assesses every aspect of the accommodation. Those establishments awarded a **HIGHLY COMMENDED** or **DE LUXE** grading represent only a small, select percentage of all Tourist Board quality-graded accommodation.

The rigorous and objective annual English Tourist Board inspection takes into account such factors as warmth of welcome, atmosphere, efficiency, as well as the quality of furnishings and equipment, and the standard of meals and their presentation. Consideration is also given to the style and nature of the accommodation. This means that all types of establishment, whatever their Crown classification, can achieve a high quality grade if the facilities and services they provide, even if limited in scope, are to a very high standard. You will therefore find that *Somewhere Special* features accommodation, from **LISTED** to **FIVE CROWN**, that have all been awarded a top quality grading of **HIGHLY COMMENDED** or **DE LUXE**. Since only a small percentage are awarded these top two gradings, you know that if your chosen accommodation is in this guide, it is clearly somewhere very special indeed.

AN INSPECTOR CALLS

Before a quality grading is awarded, one of over 55 Tourist Board inspectors visit the guesthouse, B&B, farmhouse, inn or hotel for an assessment. The inspector books in advance, but does not reveal his or her identity on arrival. Sadly for those contemplating a career move, the inspector does not have a lazy time; he or she is busy noting the standard of decor, the state of the grounds, the quality of the food and the courtesy of the staff. Once the bill has been paid the next morning, the inspector announces his or her identity to the management and tours the building. At the end of the tour, they discuss the conclusions, with the inspector making suggestions where helpful. Only after the visit does the inspector arrive at a conclusion for the quality grade – so the assessment is 100 per cent independent and reliable.

ACCESSIBILITY

It's all very well deciding exactly where you'd like to stay, but if you find difficulty in walking or are a wheelchair user, then you also need to know how accessible a particular establishment is. If you book your accommodation at an establishment displaying the Accessible symbol, there's no longer any guesswork involved. The National Accessibility Scheme forms part of the *Tourism for All* campaign that is being promoted by all three National Tourist Boards. The Tourist Boards recognise three categories of accessibility, based upon what are considered to be the practical needs of wheelchair users:

 CATEGORY 1: accessible to all wheelchair users including those travelling independently

 CATEGORY 2: accessible to a wheelchair user with assistance

 CATEGORY 3: accessible to a wheelchair user able to walk short distances and up at least three steps

Additional help and guidance for those with special needs can be obtained from: Holiday Care Service, 2 Old Bank Chambers, Station Road, Horley, Surrey RH6 9HW. Telephone (01293) 774535, Fax (01293) 784647, Minicom (01293) 776943.

How to use this guide

SOMEWHERE SPECIAL WILL ENABLE YOU TO FIND THAT SPECIAL PLACE TO STAY IN — WHICHEVER PART OF THE COUNTRY YOU ARE PLANNING TO VISIT. EVEN IF YOU ONLY HAVE A ROUGH IDEA OF WHERE YOU WISH TO GO, YOU CAN EASILY USE THIS GUIDE TO LOCATE A REALLY HIGH QUALITY PLACE TO STAY.

THE GUIDE IS DIVIDED into four distinct sections: England's North Country, England's Heartland, England's West Country and South and South East England. On page 12 you will find a comprehensive break-down of which county is in which region, together with an accompanying 'England-at-a-Glance' map. At the start of each section is a full-colour regional map which clearly plots by number the location of all the *Somewhere Special* entries, as well as the positions of major roads, towns, stations and airports. If you know the area you want to visit, first locate the possible establishments on the regional map and then turn to the appropriate pages in the regional section. The entries are listed by their geographical position, so you'll find that the places you're interested in are usually close to each other in the listing.

Each entry provides detailed information on the nature of the establishment together with the facilities provided and a colour photograph so that you can easily determine whether the place meets the criteria you have in mind. It also lists 1997 estimated prices, so you immediately know whether the entry falls within your price range.

THE ENTRIES IN MORE DETAIL

The entries are designed to convey as much information as possible in a clear, attractive and easy-to-read format. The first line contains the name of the inn, hotel, guesthouse or B&B, together with its Crown classification and quality grading. In *Somewhere Special,* of course, every entry will have a quality grading of either **HIGHLY COMMENDED** or **DE LUXE**. Below these come the full address and telephone number of the establishment and, where applicable, its fax number.

Each entry features a full-colour photograph of the establishment and a short description of its main attractions. These details have been supplied by the proprietors themselves and although this information has been checked for accuracy, you are advised to confirm all relevant details at the time of booking. At the foot of each entry comes the all-important practical information:

- A guide to 1997 prices for bed & breakfast and for half board, for both single and double rooms. Prices can sometimes change after the guide has gone to press, so please check when making a booking.

- Mealtimes for both lunch and evening meal, when available.

- The numbers of bedrooms and bathrooms, and whether the latter are en-suite, private or shared.

- The number of parking spaces.

- The range of any credit and charge cards accepted.

In the bottom right-hand corner of the entry is a list of symbols representing in greater detail the range of facilities and services offered. The key explaining exactly what these mean is conveniently located on the back of the cover flap, which can be kept open while you're browsing through the entries. The symbols cover everything from the provision of private shooting rights to whether or not there's a sauna for guests' use. Most importantly, they allow you to see at a glance whether any special requirements you may have can be met.

OTHER FEATURES OF THE GUIDE

As well as the entries – over 400 in all – you'll find many features on a wide variety of subjects scattered throughout the book. The four informative introductions to the regions appear on pages 13, 63, 113 and 155. At the back of the book (pages 193–197) you will find more detailed information about booking accommodation. You are strongly recommended to read this before committing yourself to any firm arrangements, bearing in mind the fact that all details have been supplied by proprietors themselves.

IN THIS GUIDE, ENGLAND IS DIVIDED INTO FOUR MAIN SECTIONS. A MAP OF THE AREA, SHOWING EACH ENTRY AND ITS NEAREST TOWN OR CITY, AS WELL AS NEARBY MAJOR ROADS OR MOTORWAYS, CAN BE FOUND AFTER THE REGIONAL INTRODUCTION.

England at a glance

ENGLAND'S NORTH COUNTRY

Cumbria, Durham, Northumberland, Tees Valley, Tyne & Wear, Cheshire, Greater Manchester, Lancashire, Merseyside, East Riding of Yorkshire, North, South & West Yorkshire and North & North East Lincolnshire.

ENGLAND'S HEARTLAND

Gloucestershire, Hereford & Worcester, Shropshire, Staffordshire, Warwickshire, West Midlands, Derbyshire, Leicestershire, Nottinghamshire, Northamptonshire, Bedfordshire, Cambridgeshire, Essex, Hertfordshire, Lincolnshire, Norfolk and Suffolk.

ENGLAND'S WEST COUNTRY

Bath & North East Somerset, Bristol, Cornwall, Devon, North Somerset, Somerset, South Gloucestershire, Western Dorset, Wiltshire and the Isles of Scilly.

SOUTH AND SOUTH EAST ENGLAND

London, Berkshire, Buckinghamshire, Eastern Dorset, Hampshire, Isle of Wight, Oxfordshire, East & West Sussex, Kent and Surrey.

England's North Country

England's Heartland

South and South East England

England's West Country

E N G L A N D

England's
North Country

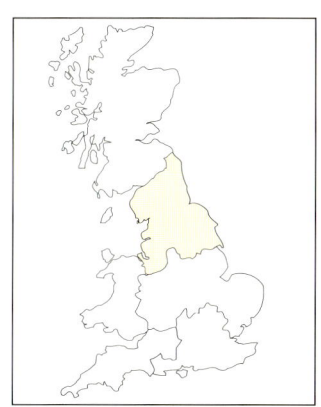

SCENICALLY, ENGLAND'S NORTH COUNTRY is hard to match, and amid the celebrated beauty spots, there remain many villages, towns and tracts of countryside known only to the discerning few. Cheshire, lying quietly in its south-western corner, gets the region off to a largely unexplored start. The Peckforton Hills, ten miles south-east of Chester, are a picturesque short chain of sandstone hills crowned by the spectacular Beeston Castle. Peppering the county are many excellent examples of one of England's most attractive building styles, the black and white 'magpie' houses especially favoured by 16th-century builders.

Heading north between the great cities of Liverpool and Manchester and on up the M6, visitors can choose whether to turn left for the delights of Blackpool – with its miles of beach, famous illuminated tower and vast range of leisure facilities – or right for the Forest of Bowland. This forgotten corner of Lancashire is made up of rounded hills, magnificent angling waters (the River Hodder is the best example) and glorious stone-built villages such as Chipping and Slaidburn. It's the sort of place you intend to visit for an afternoon, but end up staying a fortnight.

▶ Cragside

Cragside, perched on a rocky Northumberland hillside like some medieval Bavarian castle, was in fact

the most modern house of its day, the first in the world to be lit by water-generated electricity. Its creator, the Victorian inventor, engineer and gunmaker, William Armstrong, fitted the house with every labour-saving device possible, including a special water-powered engine to turn the spits in the kitchen. In around 1878, the first electric lights were installed to illuminate pictures in a new gallery; the electricity was generated by a stream running through the grounds. The splendid house, now in the care the National Trust, remains a testimony to Armstrong's extraordinary ingenuity.

▶ The mouseman of Kilburn

In the small town of Kilburn, on the southern fringes of the North York Moors, is a furniture-making company of international repute. It was established at the turn of the century by a local carpenter, Robert Thompson. He was inspired by the exquisite medieval wood-carvings in Ripon Cathedral to try to emulate the work of the medieval masters. By the time of his death in 1955 his exquisitely carved furniture had become world-famous. Thompson's reputation as the Kilburn 'mouseman' stems from his trademark, a little mouse, which was – and is – carved on every piece of furniture.

Any tour of the scenic highlights of England's North Country must pay deserved regard to the Lake District. Variations on the unbeatable theme of wind-ruffled lake sheltering beneath towering fell are everywhere. Almost 900 square miles of England's largest national park ensure countless views of breath-taking grandeur. Add to this perfect landscape whitewashed stone farmhouses with blue-green Cumbrian slate roofs and Lakeland's appeal is immediately evident. Understandable popularity and a road network made up of picturesque but decidedly narrow tracks mean that exploration is perhaps most rewarding early in the morning or out of season, but always on foot.

Not that it's difficult to escape the August crowds. Either take advantage of Cumbria's long and largely undeveloped coastline, or journey north and east beside Hadrian's Wall into the Northumberland national park. Whichever you choose, visitors melt like late-spring snow, soon to be replaced by the sound of innumerable seabirds or the eerie call of the curlew, emblem of the national park. Here in Northumberland, at the northern end of the Pennines, the landscape seems unforgivingly wild. This was frontier country, the 'debatable lands' where English and Scots fought bloody battles against the backdrop of the bleak and desolate moorland they were disputing. Almost every dwelling of any antiquity has been fortified to protect the inhabitants from centuries of cross-border raiders, and many pele towers can be visited today. Recreation of a more peaceful nature is provided nowadays throughout Northumberland, with options including boat trips to Holy Island (Lindisfarne) and the smaller Farne Islands where, in 1838, Grace Darling risked her life to rescue shipwrecked mariners.

If you're unlucky enough to hit upon a spell of wet weather, one of the best compensations is to spend the next fine day at one of the waterfalls in which the northern Pennines seem to specialise, always at their most dramatic after heavy rainfall. Upper Teesdale has two of the best, with Caldron Snout and High Force just four or five miles apart. To reach the Snout – the highest cascade in the land – you'll have to walk some distance from the car. Both High Force and mighty Aysgarth Force (in Wensleydale) are conveniently close to civilisation. Further up the dale access to spectacular Hardraw Force is through the Green Dragon pub, a useful excuse for a pint, should one be needed. The pub also lies on the route of England's premier long-distance footpath, the Pennine Way which, if followed in a northerly direction, leads on to Swaledale, dotted with an extraordinary number of picturesque stone barns. These add a further level of texture to a landscape already rich both in rock features and wild flowers – Muker boasts some of the best traditional hay meadows in the land.

The Yorkshire Dales and the nearby North York Moors are both large enough to be able to accommodate large numbers of visitors seeking solace in the glorious scenery. A quick survey of the ecclesiastical remains of hereabouts soon reveals that those in search of spiritual well-being have been coming to this part of the world for centuries. The magnificent abbeys of Fountains, Rievaulx, Jervaulx and, a little further afield, Bolton all selected their positions with care. The ecclesiastical, commercial and cultural centre of this area now lies a little further south in York. Walk the city's medieval walls and you're enjoying urban beauty at its zenith.

Roman remains survive across the region, some famous, others positively unfamiliar. Into the latter category falls windswept Blackstone Edge. Here, in the desolate country between Rochdale and Huddersfield and at a height of almost 1,500ft (457m), is the surprising location of the best-preserved stretch of Roman road in England. A feat of civil engineering on an even grander scale towers over the flatter fields surrounding the Humber Estuary. The suspension bridge with the world's longest span, the huge Humber Bridge, is a mere 1,800 years younger than the highway on Blackstone Edge. From the small town of Beverley, a few miles to the north, the twin piers of the bridge are clearly visible. This market town has mixed parentage; the marriage of a medieval core and Georgian elegance has nevertheless produced one of England's most beautiful progeny.

Left: Hardraw Force, near Hawes, North Yorkshire; inset: Alnwick Castle, Northumberland

▶ **Early Quakers**

George Fox (1624–91), the son of a Leicester weaver, became convinced after a series of revelations and visions that he should spread word of the 'inner light' of Christ's salvation.

Eschewing the rigid framework of the established church, he travelled the country, preaching out of doors to all who would listen. In the spring of 1652 over a thousand congregated on Firbank Fell, near Sedbergh, Cumbria, an occasion now seen as instrumental to the founding of Quakerism. A plaque marks the spot where Fox preached, while nearby is Brigflatts, one of the earliest Friends' meeting houses (1675), a serenely peaceful building (open to the public).

▶ **Beeston Castle**

Perched on its crag-top setting, Beeston Castle is the natural focal point of the modest Peckforton Hills. The castle commands staggering vistas over the Cheshire Plain to Liverpool and the Wirral, and on a clear day no fewer than eight separate counties are reputedly visible. As dramatic as the view is the 13th-century castle itself, although its history is less turbulent than its appearance might suggest.

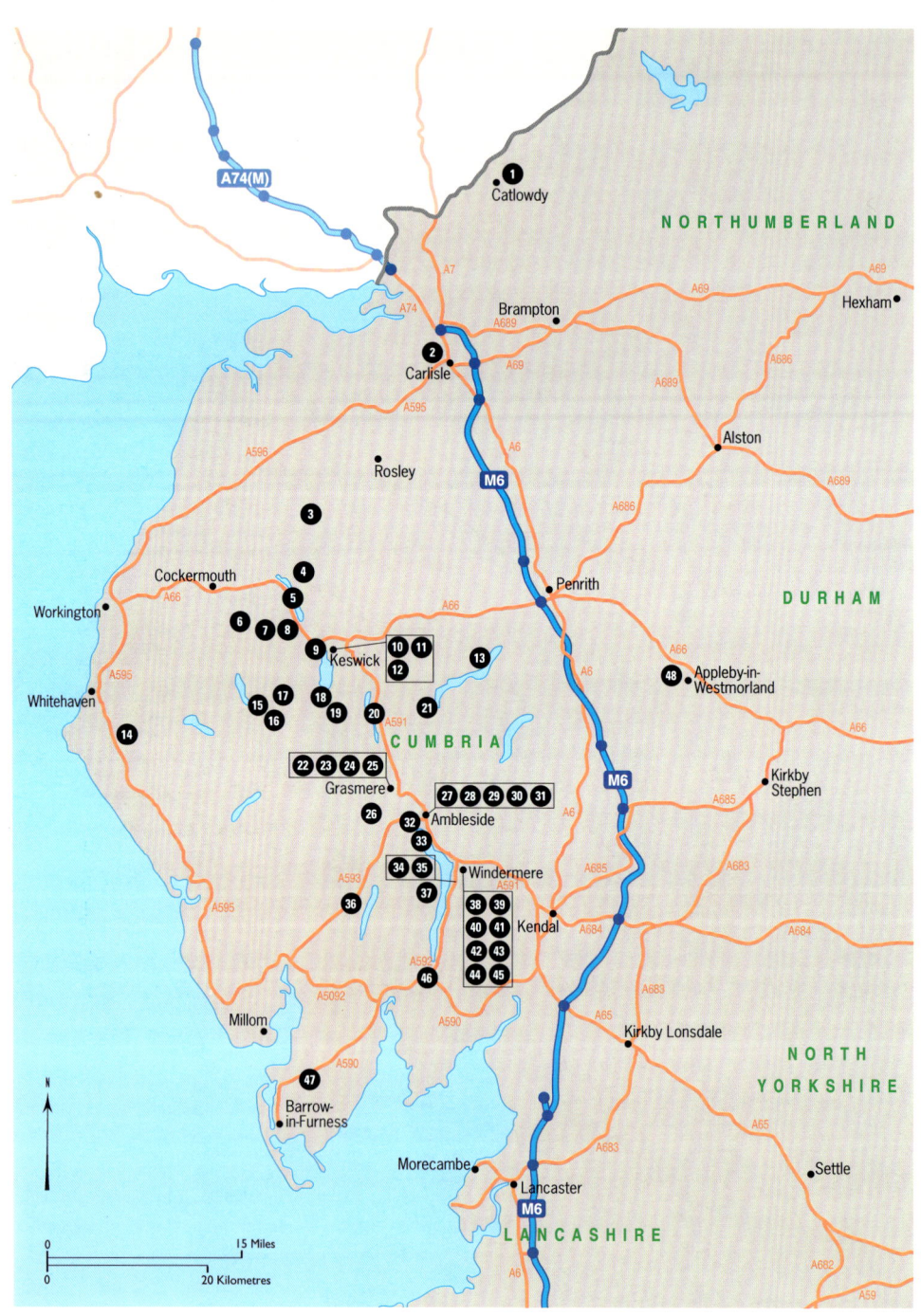

A74(M)

1 Catlowdy

N O R T H U M B E R L A N D

Hexham

A7

Brampton
A689

A69

A69

2 Carlisle

A595

A6

M6

Alston

A686

A689

Rosley

A596

Cockermouth

3

A66

4

5

6 **7** **8**

Workington

A595

Keswick

9

10 **11**

12

13

Penrith

D U R H A M

A66

A66

48 Appleby-in-Westmorland

Whitehaven

15 **17** **18**

16 **19**

20

A591

21

C U M B R I A

14

22 **23** **24** **25**

Grasmere

26

27 **28** **29** **30** **31**

A6

M6

Kirkby Stephen

A685

32 Ambleside

33

34 **35**

37

A593

Windermere
A591

A685

A683

36

A595

A592

38 **39**

40 **41**

42 **43**

44 **45**

Kendal

A684

A684

46

A5092

Millom

A590

A590

Kirkby Lonsdale

A65

N O R T H

Y O R K S H I R E

A683

47

Barrow-in-Furness

A65

Settle

Morecambe

Lancaster

M6

L A N C A S H I R E

A6

A59

A683

A682

0   15 Miles
0   20 Kilometres

40 Miles
60 Kilometres

N

Berwick-upon-Tweed 49
Cornhill-on-Tweed 50
Alnwick
A1
A697
A74(M)
A68
NORTHUMBERLAND
Catlowdy
Morpeth
A696
A19
Newcastle upon Tyne
TYNE & WEAR
Hexham 51
52
A69
A1
Carlisle
M6
A6
Penrith
A686
Durham
A1(M)
54
55
DURHAM
53
Workington
A596
A66
SEE FACING PAGE FOR ENTRIES IN CUMBRIA
TEES VALLEY
Middlesbrough
Whitby 73
A66
56
Darlington
71
72
A171
CUMBRIA
A595
A591
A6
A86
57
A19
74
Scarborough
Windermere
A590
M6
58
Leyburn
60
59
61
NORTH
Thirsk
77
78
79
75
Sgarborough
80
98
A65
62
63
YORKSHIRE
76
A170
A64
91
Lancaster
A683
64 65 66 67 68
A59
70
A1(M)
83 84 85 86
87 88 89 90
A165
99
69
Skipton
Harrogate
York
82
EAST RIDING
OF YORKSHIRE
100
97
A59
A650
81
M55
LANCASHIRE
M65
Bradford
Leeds
A64
92
Preston
A646
WEST
A1
M62
A19
Kingston upon Hull
A63
102
A565
YORKSHIRE
96
Pontefract
94
A15
NORTH LINCOLNSHIRE
Grimsby
103
101
Huddersfield
M18
M180
NORTH EAST LINCOLNSHIRE
M61
GREATER
105
M1
A635
93
MERSEYSIDE
MANCHESTER
104
Liverpool
M62
Manchester
A628
SOUTH
A1(M)
M53
95
YORKSHIRE
M56
108
Knutsford
106
A537
Sheffield
A61
Chester
M6
107
110
A556
109
A55
A34
CHESHIRE
A49
M1
M6

Colin Earl Cartography

17

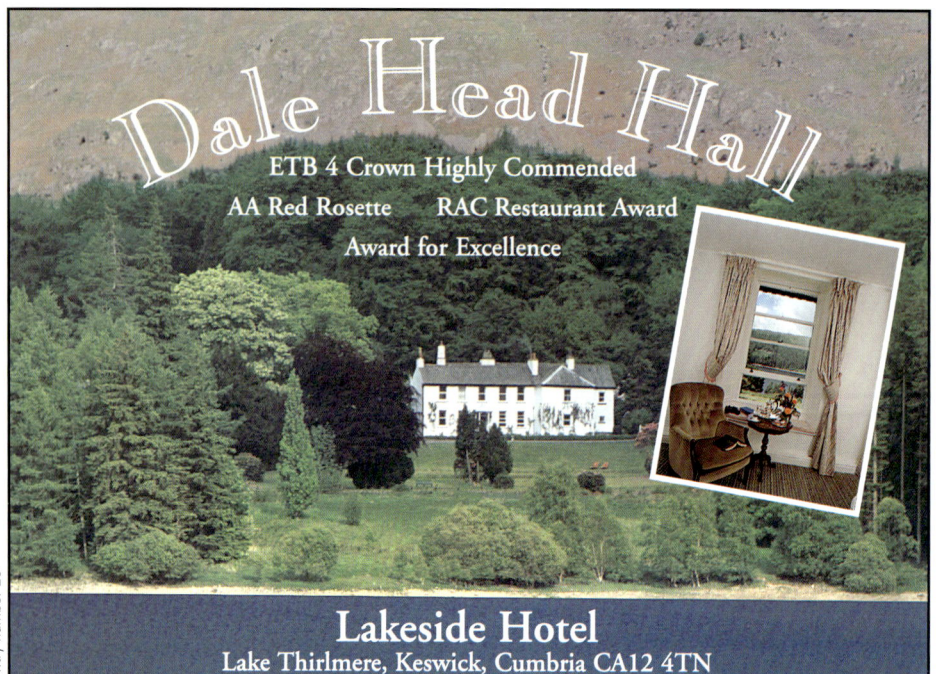

Dale Head Hall

ETB 4 Crown Highly Commended

AA Red Rosette   RAC Restaurant Award

Award for Excellence

Lakeside Hotel
Lake Thirlmere, Keswick, Cumbria CA12 4TN
Tel: 017687 72478

See entry number 20

KEY TO SYMBOLS

For ease of use, the key to symbols appears on the back of the cover flap and can be folded out while consulting individual entries. The symbols which appear at the end of each entry are designed to enable you to see at-a-glance what's on offer, and whether any particular requirements you have can be met. Most of the symbols are clear, simple icons and few require any further explanation, but the following points may be useful:

ALCOHOLIC DRINKS: Alcoholic drinks are available at all types of accommodation listed in the guide unless the symbol ⓤ (unlicensed) appears. However, even in licensed premises there may be some restrictions on the serving of drinks, such as being available to diners only.

SMOKING: Many establishments offer facilities for non-smokers, indicated by the symbol ✄. These may include no smoking bedrooms and parts of communal rooms set aside for non-smokers. Some establishments prefer not to accommodate smokers at all, and if this is the case it will be made clear in the establishment description in the guide entry.

PETS: The symbol ✖ is used to show that dogs are not accepted in any circumstances. Some establishments will accept pets, but we advise you to check this at the time of booking and to enquire as to whether any additional charge will be made to accommodate them.

① BESSIESTOWN FARM COUNTRY GUESTHOUSE 〰〰〰 HIGHLY COMMENDED

Catlowdy, Longtown, Carlisle, Cumbria CA6 5QP Tel (01228) 577219 Fax (01228) 577219

One of the nicest farm guesthouses, warm and welcoming, peaceful and quiet with pretty en-suite bedrooms and delicious home cooking using much locally grown produce, with country recipes and mouth-watering sweets. Delightful public rooms. Drinks licence. The indoor heated swimming pool is open mid-May to mid-September. An ideal year-round touring base or break on long journeys. Bessiestown is easily reached from junction 44 of the M6: take the A7 to Longtown, right at Bush Hotel, six-and-a-half miles to T-junction, right for one-and-a-half miles to Catlowdy.

Bed & Breakfast per night: single occupancy from £26.50–£29.50; double room from £42.00–£46.00
Half board per person: £32.00–£34.00 daily
Evening meal 1900 (last bookings 1600)

Bedrooms: 2 double, 1 twin, 1 triple
Bathrooms: 4 en-suite
Parking for 10
Cards accepted: Access, Visa, Amex

② NUMBER THIRTY ONE 〰〰〰 DE LUXE

31 Howard Place, Carlisle, Cumbria CA1 1HR Tel (01228) 597080 Fax (01228) 597080

This elegant city-centre town house has been restored by Philip and Judith into an interesting and comfortable home. All rooms provide private bath, shower and toilet. Philip holds cookery courses and serves imaginative traditional and vegetarian meals. He is an enthusiastic fell walker and guide, game fisherman and water colourist. His knowledge of the Lakes, Carlisle city, Hadrian's Wall and other interesting places to visit, all add to the pleasure of a stay here.

Bed & Breakfast per night: single room from £35.00–£40.00; double room from £40.00–£50.00
Half board per person: £32.50–£40.00 daily; £227.50–£280.00 weekly
Evening meal 1800 (last orders 1930)

Bedrooms: 1 single, 2 double
Bathrooms: 3 en-suite
Open: February–December

③ WOODLANDS COUNTRY HOUSE 〰〰〰 HIGHLY COMMENDED

Ireby, Cumbria CA5 1EX Tel (016973) 71791 or Fax (016973) 71482

Woodlands is an elegant Victorian house enjoying magnificent open views over the tranquil northern fells. Ireby, a truly unspoilt Cumbrian village, is an ideal base for exploring northern Lakeland. All our rooms are charmingly and comfortably appointed, and we offer freshly-prepared home cooking. Pauline and John Bibby offer a personal and caring service and a warm welcome. Residential licence. Non-smoking. Vegetarian alternatives. Open fires. Suitable for wheelchair users. ♿ CATEGORY 2

Bed & Breakfast per night: single room from £22.50–£27.50; double room from £45.00–£55.00
Half board per person: £35.00–£40.00 daily; £210.00–£225.00 weekly
Evening meal 1900 (last bookings 1600)

Bedrooms: 1 single, 3 double, 2 twin, 2 triple
Bathrooms: 8 en-suite
Parking for 12
Cards accepted: Access, Visa, Amex, Switch/Delta

④ RAVENSTONE LODGE   〰〰〰 HIGHLY COMMENDED

Bassenthwaite, Keswick, Cumbria CA12 4QG Tel (017687) 76629 or (017687) 76638 Fax (017687) 76629

A warm and friendly welcome awaits you at Ravenstone Lodge, our 19th-century stone-built property nestling at the foot of Ullock Pike, just four miles north of Keswick on the A591. The lodge is set in five acres of spectacular countryside with a private terrace, a large walled garden and ample off-the-road parking space. Enjoy the relaxed atmosphere of our stable dining room, bar and large Victorian-style conservatory.

Bed & Breakfast per night: single occupancy from £28.50–£30.50; double room from £53.00–£57.00
Half board per person: £40.00–£42.00 daily; £261.50–£274.50 weekly
Evening meal 1900 (last bookings 1800)

Bedrooms: 6 double, 2 twin, 1 family room
Bathrooms: 9 en-suite
Parking for 12
Cards accepted: Access, Visa, Switch/Delta

⑤ PHEASANT INN   〰 HIGHLY COMMENDED

Bassenthwaite Lake, Cockermouth, Cumbria CA13 9YE Tel (017687) 76234 Fax (017687) 76002

A tranquil, traditional, north Lake District inn, adjacent to Bassenthwaite Lake, and surrounded by gardens and woodland providing a wealth of wildlife. Three lounges feature antiques, beams, open fires and fresh flowers. Commended by major guides for high quality English food and service, Pheasant Inn also has twenty individually-decorated bedrooms with private facilities. Dogs welcome – kennels available. ⋔ CATEGORY 3

Bed & Breakfast per night: single room from £58.00–£60.00; double room from £74.00–£136.00
Half board per person: £56.00–£88.00 daily; £350.00–£460.00 weekly
Snack lunch available: 1230–1400 (afternoon teas 1600–1730)

Evening meal 1900 (last orders 2030)
Bedrooms: 5 single, 8 double, 7 twin
Bathrooms: 20 en-suite
Parking for 80
Cards accepted: Access, Visa

⑥ WINDER HALL   〰〰 HIGHLY COMMENDED

Low Lorton, Cockermouth, Cumbria CA13 9UP Tel (01900) 85107

Winder Hall is a listed manor house, circa 1630, on the River Cocker in the peaceful Lakeland village of Lorton. Six miles from Buttermere, eight from Keswick. The spacious accommodation is comfortably furnished to complement the Hall, with its stone-mullioned leaded windows, oak-panelled dining room, real fires and fell views. Traditional carved-oak four-poster bed. Mary and Derek Denman offer you a warm welcome and good service. Light refreshments available; good food at the local inn.

Bed & Breakfast per night: single occupancy from £27.00–£32.00; double room from £44.00–£60.00

Bedrooms: 3 double, 1 twin, 1 family room
Bathrooms: 5 en-suite
Parking for 5
Open: February–November

❼ COTTAGE IN THE WOOD

 HIGHLY COMMENDED

Whinlatter Pass, Keswick, Cumbria CA12 5TW Tel (017687) 78409

Situated in a superb location in the Whinlatter Forest Park, with wonderful views of the Skiddaw mountain range, our hotel offers quiet seclusion and the chance to savour first class cooking and fine wines in idyllic surroundings. Our en-suite rooms are very well appointed, two having four-poster beds for the romantically inclined, and all having hair dryers, clock radios, electric blankets and hot drink facilities. We would appreciate the opportunity to send you our brochure and tariff.

Bed & Breakfast per night: double room from
£50.00–£66.00
Half board per person: £41.00–£45.00 daily
Evening meal 1900 (last bookings 1830)

Bedrooms: 6 double, 1 twin
Bathrooms: 6 en-suite, 1 private, 1 public
Parking for 15
Open: March–November
Cards accepted: Access, Visa, Switch/Delta

❽ THWAITE HOWE HOTEL

 HIGHLY COMMENDED

Thornthwaite, Keswick, Cumbria CA12 5SA Tel (017687) 78281 Fax (017687) 78529

Situated in its own grounds, with superb views across the Derwent Valley to the Skiddaw range, our hotel is in a very peaceful position, but in easy reach of all the Lake District's attractions. Mary's delicious, award-winning home cooking is complemented by fine wines, or followed by one of Harry's cask-strength malt whiskies. Red squirrels feed in the garden daily and, together with guests, enjoy the friendly informal atmosphere.

Half board per person: £41.00–£46.25 daily;
£287.00–£302.75 weekly
Evening meal 1900 (last orders 1900)

Bedrooms: 5 double, 3 twin
Bathrooms: 8 en-suite
Parking for 12
Open: March–October
Cards accepted: Access, Visa, Switch/Delta

❾ DERWENT COTTAGE

HIGHLY COMMENDED

Portinscale, Keswick, Cumbria CA12 5RF Tel (017687) 74838

Gleaming silver, cut glass, five spacious en-suite bedrooms and elegant furnishings are all to be found at Derwent Cottage. This Lakeland house, dating from the 18th-century, stands in an acre of secluded gardens in the quiet village of Portinscale, one mile from Keswick. A four-course, candle light table d'hôte is served at 1900 each evening with classical music in the background. A residential licence is held and drinks and wine are available throughout the evening. We are a totally non-smoking establishment.

Bed & Breakfast per night: double room from
£48.00–£64.00
Half board per person: £41.00–£45.00 daily;
£255.00–£283.00 weekly
Evening meal 1900 (last orders 1900)

Bedrooms: 5 double
Bathrooms: 5 en-suite
Parking for 10
Open: March–October
Cards accepted: Access, Visa

10 SKIDDAW HOTEL

HIGHLY COMMENDED

Market Square, Keswick, Cumbria CA12 5BN Tel (017687) 72071 Fax (017687) 74850

Situated in the heart of Keswick, northern Lakeland's leading market town, the Skiddaw Hotel provides the perfect setting for that special break away from it all. Romantic packages are available which include lake-cruise picnics, Bucks Fizz breakfasts and candle-lit dinners. Free facilities exclusive to our residents include in-house saunas, mid-week golf and a leisure club with fully equipped gym and swimming pool. Special breaks are always available.

Bed & Breakfast per night: single room from
£34.00–£38.00; double room from £62.00–£70.00
Half board per person: £45.00–£53.00 daily
Lunch available: 1200–1430
Evening meal 1830 (last orders 2130 winter, 2200 summer)

Bedrooms: 10 single, 11 double, 11 twin, 8 triple
Bathrooms: 40 en-suite
Cards accepted: Access, Visa, Amex

11 THE GRANGE COUNTRY HOUSE HOTEL

HIGHLY COMMENDED

Manor Brow, Ambleside Road, Keswick, Cumbria CA12 4BA Tel (017687) 72500

The Grange Country House Hotel is set in its own grounds overlooking Keswick-on-Derwentwater and the surrounding mountains. An elegant Lakeland house built in the 1840s, The Grange is proudly owned by Duncan and Jane Miller. The hotel offers quality and comfort in a warm relaxing atmosphere, holds various awards and is featured in many of the leading guides. Lovely bedrooms, log fires and freshly prepared food. Unforgettable.

Bed & Breakfast per night: double room from
£62.00–£75.00
Half board per person: £46.00–£52.50 daily;
£315.00–£329.00 weekly
Evening meal 1930

Bedrooms: 7 double, 3 twin
Bathrooms: 10 en-suite, 1 public
Parking for 13
Open: March–November
Cards accepted: Access, Visa

12 RAVENSWORTH HOTEL

HIGHLY COMMENDED

29 Station Street, Keswick, Cumbria CA12 5HH Tel (017687) 72476

Ideally situated near the town centre and all its amenities, with the lake and lower fells just a short walk away. Tastefully furnished bedrooms are en-suite and have tea/coffee trays and colour TVs. Start your day with our hearty breakfast, enjoy the Lakes by day and then while away the evening in the Herdwick Bar or relax in the spacious lounge. Personally run for over eleven years, we now rank among the top small hotels in Keswick.

Bed & Breakfast per night: double room from
£30.00–£50.00

Bedrooms: 7 double, 1 twin
Bathrooms: 7 en-suite, 1 private
Parking for 5
Open: March–November
Cards accepted: Access, Visa

13 LEEMING HOUSE HOTEL

🌊🌊🌊🌊 DE LUXE

Watermillock, Ullswater, Penrith, Cumbria CA11 0JJ Tel (017684) 86622 Fax (017684) 86443

Leeming House, dating back to the early 1800s, is idyllically situated in twenty acres of woodland and gardens leading down to the shores of Ullswater, only eight miles from the M6 junction 40 at Penrith. Many of the luxurious bedrooms feature private balconies with breathtaking views over the gardens, lake and fells beyond. The hotel's graceful public rooms include a library and conservatory, with log fires during the winter months. This relaxing hotel has an excellent reputation for its fine food.

Half board per person: £69.00–£94.00 daily;
£435.00–£525.00 weekly
Lunch available: 1230–1345 restaurant; 1200–1430
conservatory
Evening meal 1930 (last orders 2045)

Bedrooms: 5 single, 21 double, 13 twin
Bathrooms: 39 private
Parking for 50
Cards accepted: Access, Visa, Diners, Amex,
Switch/Delta

14 THE ENNERDALE COUNTRY HOUSE HOTEL

🌊🌊🌊🌊 HIGHLY COMMENDED

Cleator, Cumbria CA23 3DT Tel (01946) 813907 Fax (01946) 815260

Situated at the top of the Lakes, between Whitehaven and Keswick, the Ennerdale is surrounded by fine countryside, whilst being close enough for visitors to explore the coast. A delightful country house hotel with an enviable reputation for food and hospitality. Relax by log fires in sumptuous leather sofas and partake afternoon tea in the Garden Room. Peace and tranquillity abound, with fine hospitality and quality standards being the order of the day.

Bed & Breakfast per night: single room from
£80.00–£90.00; double room from £90.00–£110.00
Half board per person: £98.50–£108.50 daily;
£619.50–£689.50 weekly
Lunch available: 1200–1400

Evening meal 1900 (last orders 2130)
Bedrooms: 3 single, 11 double, 8 twin
Bathrooms: 22 private
Parking for 80
Cards accepted: Access, Visa, Diners, Amex, Switch/Delta

15 BRIDGE HOTEL

🌊🌊🌊🌊 HIGHLY COMMENDED

Buttermere, Cockermouth, Cumbria CA13 9UZ Tel (017687) 70252 Fax (017687) 70252

An 18th-century coaching inn, beautifully situated between two lakes in Lakeland's loveliest valley. Superb unrestricted walking country and breathtaking scenery. Complimentary afternoon tea is served near the log fire in our very comfortable residents' lounge. Two well-stocked bars serve expertly-kept real ales. Four-poster beds. Dogs welcome. Special breaks offered throughout the year.

Bed & Breakfast per night: single room from
£33.50–£38.50; double room from £67.00–£77.00
Half board per person: £42.00– daily; £307.00 weekly
Lunch available: 1200–1430
Evening meal 1900 (last orders 2030)

Bedrooms: 2 single, 8 double, 12 twin
Bathrooms: 21 en-suite, 1 private
Parking for 60
Cards accepted: Access, Visa, Switch/Delta

16 PICKETT HOWE

 DE LUXE

Buttermere Valley, Cockermouth, Cumbria CA13 9UY Tel (01900) 85444 Fax (01900) 85209

National Winner of ETB's prestigious 'England for Excellence' Award. Nestling peacefully beneath rugged lakeland peaks, this 17th-century former farmhouse offers just eight non-smoking guests a unique holiday experience. Slate floors, oak beams and mullioned windows are enhanced by quality furnishings and antiques, the quaint bedrooms have jacuzzi baths and Victorian brass iron beds. The exceptional and extensive breakfast menu and well-balanced, beautifully presented dinners combined with caring, relaxed hospitality make Pickett Howe a perfect base for walking, touring or just relaxing!

Bed & Breakfast per night: double room £73.00
Half board per person: £58.00 daily; £378.00 weekly
Evening meal 1915

Bedrooms: 3 double, 1 twin
Bathrooms: 4 en-suite
Parking for 6
Open: March–November
Cards accepted: Access, Visa

Cumbrian Sports

LAKELAND CUSTOMS AND TRADITIONS remain strong amongst the people who live there despite the pressures of tourism. Nowhere is this more clearly demonstrated than in the many Cumbrian sporting events which occur throughout the year, several of which are unique to the region.

The high fells are not conducive to horse-riding – fox-hunting here is pursued on foot – but gentler Cartmel has one of England's most scenic racecourses. Racedays are held twice a year, during the spring and summer bank-holiday weekends, shaking the town out of its usual tranquillity. In early June, Appleby-in-Westmorland is also inundated by horses of a rather different breed, when it becomes the venue for the famous gypsy and horse fair.

Houndtrailing is roughly the Lakeland equivalent of greyhound racing, with betting an integral part of the sport. Here, though, the course is the fells, and obstacles such as stone walls and streams must be negotiated as the hounds tear after a scent of aniseed and turpentine. In fell-running contests men, too, hurtle over mountain tops. The aim is simple: to reach the summit and return to the bottom again faster than anyone else. Competitors climb arduously over rocks and through undergrowth to the peak, only to career back at terrifying speed.

Lakeland wrestling is a highly technical sport with skills and jargon all its own. The object is to push the opponent off balance; once a man's shoulder touches the ground he has lost the bout. The wrestlers' costume – white vest and hose with finely embroidered trunks (contests are sometimes held for the best outfit) – makes this the most picturesque of Lakeland sports.

Wrestling, hound-trailing and fell-running all take place at the many country shows held during summer and autumn. Of these the most famous are at Grasmere (mid-August) and Ambleside (July/August), but other towns often add their own variations to the main events. At Egremont's Crab Fair (celebrating the fruit, not the crustacean) usually held in late September, competitors attempt to scale a greasy pole to reach a leg of lamb, and afterwards vie to pull the most grotesque face possible in the world gurning championships. At Wasdale Head stories become ever taller in the biggest liar in the world competition, held in various pubs during the town's mid-October show. Details of all sporting events are available from the Cumbrian Tourist Board's information service (tel: 015394 44444).

⑰ SWINSIDE LODGE
 DE LUXE

Newlands, Keswick, Cumbria CA12 5UE Tel (017687) 72948 Fax (017687) 72948

Swinside Lodge is a delightful Victorian house in a beautiful and tranquil corner of the Lake District, just beneath Cat Bells and a five-minute stroll from the shores of Derwent Water. Relax in this most comfortable and elegantly furnished house where you can enjoy superb award-winning food served by friendly staff in the candle-lit dining room. The hotel, which is personally run, is totally no smoking and is unlicensed but please bring your own favourite wines. A warm welcome awaits you.

Bed & Breakfast per night: single occupancy from £43.00–£52.00; double room from £70.00–£100.00
Half board per person: £61.00–£78.00 daily
Evening meal 1930 (last orders 2000)

Bedrooms: 5 double, 2 twin
Bathrooms: 7 en-suite
Parking for 12
Open: February–November and Christmas

---

⑱ BORROWDALE GATES COUNTRY HOUSE HOTEL & RESTAURANT
HIGHLY COMMENDED

Grange-in-Borrowdale, Keswick, Cumbria CA12 5UQ Tel (017687) 77204 Fax (017687) 77254

Borrowdale Gates Hotel nestles peacefully in two acres of wooded gardens on the edge of the ancient hamlet of Grange. This charming Lakeland house is set amidst the breath-taking scenery of the Borrowdale valley with panoramic views of the countryside. The bedrooms, of which six are on the ground floor, are tastefully decorated and furnished. The award-winning restaurant offers fine food that is complemented by a carefully chosen wine list.

Half board per person: £47.50–£75.00 daily; £342.50–£437.50 weekly
Lunch available: 1215–1330 (last orders)
Evening meal 1900 (last orders 2045)

Bedrooms: 2 single, 10 double, 8 twin, 2 triple
Bathrooms: 22 en-suite, 1 public
Parking for 40
Open: February–December
Cards accepted: Access, Visa, Amex, Switch/Delta

---

⑲ HAZEL BANK
HIGHLY COMMENDED

Rosthwaite, Borrowdale, Keswick, Cumbria CA12 5XB Tel (017687) 77248

Standing on an elevated site overlooking the village of Rosthwaite, there are unsurpassed views of the Borrowdale Valley and central Lakeland peaks. The peaceful location makes Hazel Bank an ideal base for walkers, birdwatchers and lovers of the countryside, with direct access to many mountain and valley walks. The Victorian residence has been carefully and sympathetically converted to provide quality country house accommodation. Come and discover how enjoyable a stay in Borrowdale can be. Non-smokers only, please.

Half board per person: £40.00–£45.00 daily; £280.00 weekly
Evening meal 1900 (last orders 1900)

Bedrooms: 1 single, 2 double, 3 twin
Bathrooms: 6 en-suite
Parking for 12
Open: April–October
Cards accepted: Access, Visa, Switch/Delta

20 DALE HEAD HALL LAKESIDE HOTEL 〰〰〰〰 HIGHLY COMMENDED

Thirlmere, Keswick, Cumbria CA12 4TN Tel (017687) 72478 or 0800 454166 Fax (017687) 71070

With Helvellyn rising majestically behind, the hotel stands alone on the shores of Lake Thirlmere. At Dale Head Hall we offer a friendly home, a place of relaxation and beauty, set apart from the increasing pace of the modern world. Little can compare to a delicious dinner, prepared with love and care, particularly when wholesome ingredients come from the hotel's walled garden.

Bed & Breakfast per night: double room from
£75.00–£109.00
Half board per person: £62.00–£79.00 daily;
£329.00–£448.00 weekly
Evening meal 1930 (last orders 2030)

Bedrooms: 6 double, 2 twin, 1 triple
Bathrooms: 9 en-suite
Parking for 20
Cards accepted: Access, Visa, Amex, Switch/Delta

21 GLENRIDDING HOTEL 〰〰〰〰 HIGHLY COMMENDED

Glenridding, Penrith, Cumbria CA11 0PB Tel (017684) 82228 Fax (017684) 82555

Friendly, relaxing quality in the heart of the 'real' Lake District. Give the car a break – we have rambling, fishing, windsurfing, boating, tennis and trekking all within walking distance. Come and sample our good food, real ales and log fires, set overlooking Lake Ullswater surrounded by mountains. You'll be glad you did!

Bed & Breakfast per night: single room from
£64.00–£69.00; double room from £88.00–£94.00
Half board per person: £57.00–£74.50 daily;
£342.00–£357.00 weekly
Lunch available: 1200–1415

Evening meal 1900 (last orders 2030)
Bedrooms: 5 single, 20 double, 11 twin, 4 family rooms
Bathrooms: 40 en-suite
Parking for 30
Cards accepted: Access, Visa, Diners, Amex, Switch/Delta

22 THE GRASMERE HOTEL 〰〰〰〰 HIGHLY COMMENDED

Grasmere, Ambleside, Cumbria LA22 9TA Tel (015394) 35277 Fax (015394) 35277

An elegant Victorian Lakeland stone-built country house set in the quiet location of Grasmere village, in an acre of secluded natural gardens bordered by the River Rothay. Renowned for our cuisine, our beautiful restaurant offers a four-course dinner with a varied choice of culinary delights that are imaginatively presented with only fresh produce used. A place for all seasons, The Grasmere Hotel extends a warm welcome and all the comfort you could wish for.

Bed & Breakfast per night: single room from
£30.00–£45.00; double room from £60.00–£90.00
Half board per person: £35.00–£70.00 daily;
£200.00–£360.00 weekly
Evening meal 1930 (last orders 2030)

Bedrooms: 1 single, 9 double, 2 twin
Bathrooms: 11 en-suite, 1 private shower
Parking for 16
Open: February–December
Cards accepted: Access, Visa

23 RIVERSDALE

 HIGHLY COMMENDED

Grasmere, Cumbria LA22 9RQ Tel (015394) 35619

Quietly situated on the banks of the River Rothay and commanding fine views, this charming and attractive six-bedroomed Lakeland stone house is warm and welcoming, tastefully furnished to the highest standard and offers every comfort. A friendly relaxed atmosphere, combined with genuine and caring hospitality, an exceptional breakfast and excellent service assure our guests of a happy and memorable stay. Private parking.

Bed & Breakfast per night: double room from
£42.00–£54.00

Bedrooms: 3 double
Bathrooms: 2 en-suite, 1 private
Parking for 4

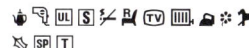

24 REDMAYNE

 HIGHLY COMMENDED

Keswick Road, Grasmere, Ambleside, Cumbria LA22 9QY Tel (015394) 35635

Traditionally built in Lakeland stone, Redmayne offers quiet relaxing accommodation and enjoys an elevated private position in three acres of natural hillside near to Wordsworth's Dove Cottage. Magnificent all-round panoramic views. Beautifully appointed en-suite rooms with colour television and tea/coffee-making facilities. Situated just five minutes walk from Grasmere village, Redmayne is an ideal base for exploring the whole of this superb National Park. Brochure on request. Private parking. Non-smoking.

Bed & Breakfast per night: double room from
£36.00–£48.00

Bedrooms: 1 double, 1 twin
Bathrooms: 2 en-suite
Parking for 2
Open: February–November

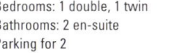

25 WOODLAND CRAG GUEST HOUSE

 HIGHLY COMMENDED

Howe Head Lane, Grasmere, Ambleside, Cumbria LA22 9SG Tel (015394) 35351

A warm welcome and an informal atmosphere are found in this delightful house, situated on the edge of Grasmere near Dove Cottage. Secluded but with easy access to all facilities, the accommodation has fine tastefully-decorated bedrooms, all with individual character and wonderful views of the lake, fells or gardens. Ideal for walking and centrally placed for the motorist (enclosed parking). All major outdoor activities are catered for nearby, including sailing, fishing, wind surfing and pony trekking. Totally non-smoking.

Bed & Breakfast per night: single room from
£23.00–£25.00; double room from £50.00–£54.00

Bedrooms: 2 single, 2 double, 1 twin
Bathrooms: 3 en-suite, 1 public
Parking for 5

26 LANGDALE HOTEL & COUNTRY CLUB 〰〰〰〰〰 HIGHLY COMMENDED

Great Langdale, Ambleside, Cumbria LA22 9JD For reservations Freephone 0500 051197 Fax (015394) 37694

The Langdale Estate is a haven of peace and tranquillity, an ideal touring base to discover and enjoy all that the Lake District has to offer. Founded on the site of an abandoned 19th-century gunpowder works, it is dotted with massive millstones and other carefully preserved reminders of its history. The hotel has two restaurants, a traditional Lakeland pub and leisure facilities. So much to do and so much to remember… the scenery, the comfort, the good food and the warm and friendly service.

Bed & Breakfast per night: single occupancy from
£90.00–£105.00; double room from £140.00–£170.00
Half board per person: £105.00–£120.00 daily;
£427.00–£504.00 weekly
Evening meal 1900 (last orders 2200)

Bedrooms: 41 double, 24 twin
Bathrooms: 65 en-suite
Parking for 120
Cards accepted: Access, Visa, Diners, Amex,
Switch/Delta

27 BORRANS PARK HOTEL 〰〰〰 HIGHLY COMMENDED

Borrans Road, Ambleside, Cumbria LA22 0EN Tel (015394) 33454 Fax (015394) 33003

Peacefully situated in the heart of Lakeland, Borrans Park is the place to enjoy award-winning traditional home cooking and experience a truly memorable sweet trolley. Choose a fine wine from the extensive personally-selected wine list and relax by the log fire or in the comfort of one of the four-poster bedrooms each with an en-suite spa bathroom. Special breaks are available all year. Complimentary membership of an exclusive nearby leisure club.
♦ CATEGORY 3

Bed & Breakfast per night: single occupancy from
£29.00–£49.00; double room from £58.00–£78.00
Half board per person: £45.00–£55.00 daily;
£255.00–£329.00 weekly
Evening meal 1900 (last bookings 1800)

Bedrooms: 9 double, 3 twin
Bathrooms: 12 en-suite
Parking for 20
Cards accepted: Access, Visa, Switch/Delta

28 LAUREL VILLA 〰〰〰 HIGHLY COMMENDED

Lake Road, Ambleside, Cumbria LA22 0DB Tel (015394) 33240

Centrally situated in the heart of the Lake District, this elegant Victorian house, once visited by Beatrix Potter, is now personally run by resident proprietors, and is within easy walking distance of the village of Ambleside and Lake Windermere. Spacious, luxurious rooms decorated in William Morris style, and all the bedrooms overlook the fells. Private car park.

Bed & Breakfast per night: single occupancy from £50.00;
double room from £60.00–£80.00
Evening meal 1900 (last bookings 1700)

Bedrooms: 7 double, 1 twin
Bathrooms: 8 en-suite
Parking for 10
Cards accepted: Access, Visa, Amex

29 ROWANFIELD COUNTRY GUESTHOUSE
🌊🌊 HIGHLY COMMENDED
Kirkstone Road, Ambleside, Cumbria LA22 9ET Tel (015394) 33686 Fax (015394) 31569

Set in idyllic tranquil countryside, three-quarters of a mile from Ambleside, Rowanfield enjoys fabulous panoramic lake and mountain views. This delightful period house with its country house decor is warm and welcoming. All bedrooms are en-suite, individually and tastefully furnished, with a special de luxe room available at a supplementary rate. The chef/patron, Philip Butcher, creates exciting evening meals from the finest fresh produce. Unlicensed, but own wine welcome. Superb central location for exploring the whole Lake District area. No smoking. ♠ CATEGORY 3

Bed & Breakfast per night: double room from £52.00–£56.00
Half board per person: £43.00–£45.00 daily; £261.00–£277.00 weekly
Evening meal 1900 (last bookings 1700)

Bedrooms: 5 double, 1 twin, 1 triple
Bathrooms: 7 en-suite
Parking for 8
Open: March–December
Cards accepted: Access, Visa, Switch/Delta

30 KIRKSTONE FOOT COUNTRY HOUSE HOTEL
🌊🌊🌊🌊 HIGHLY COMMENDED
Kirkstone Pass Road, Ambleside, Cumbria LA22 9EH Tel (015394) 32232 Fax (015394) 32232

Imagine a gracious and elegant 17th-century manor house, set in two acres of quiet and secluded flower-filled gardens. Kirkstone Foot is such a place. Three minutes' walking distance from the centre of Ambleside, the hotel is warm, homely and totally relaxing. Whether staying for a romantic escape, Valentine's Day, Christmas break, or even our speciality Wine Weekends, you are assured of a warm welcome, courteous service, award-winning cuisine and an extensive wine cellar – truly a unique Lakeland experience. ♠ CATEGORY 3

Bed & Breakfast per night: single occupancy from £43.00–£49.00; double room from £80.00–£92.00
Half board per person: £50.00–£65.00 daily; £336.00–£455.00 weekly
Evening meal 1930 (last orders 2030)

Bedrooms: 12 double, 1 twin, 1 triple
Bathrooms: 14 en-suite
Parking for 30
Open: February–December
Cards accepted: Access, Visa, Diners, Amex, Switch/Delta

31 ROTHAY MANOR HOTEL
🌊🌊🌊🌊 HIGHLY COMMENDED
Rothay Bridge, Ambleside, Cumbria LA22 0EH Tel (015394) 33605 Fax (015394) 33607

Rothay Manor, an elegant Regency house run by the Nixon family for over 25 years, stands in its own grounds a quarter mile from the head of Lake Windermere. The drawing rooms and candle-lit dining room still retain the relaxed atmosphere of a private house. Care, consideration and comfort are evident throughout. The menu is varied and meals are prepared and served with flair and imagination to the highest of standards, complemented by a comprehensive wine list. Residents have free use of a nearby Leisure Centre, with swimming pool, sauna, steam room and jacuzzi, and free fishing permits are also available.

Bed & Breakfast per night: single room from £78.00; double room from £118.00–£132.00
Half board per person: £86.00–£110.00 daily; £525.00–£665.00 weekly
Lunch available: 1230–1400 (1330 on Sundays)

Evening meal 1945 (last orders 2100)
Bedrooms: 2 single, 5 double, 3 twin, 5 triple, 3 family rooms
Bathrooms: 18 en-suite
Parking for 50   Open: February–December
Cards accepted: Access, Visa, Diners, Amex

32 NANNY BROW COUNTRY HOUSE HOTEL ≋≋≋≋ HIGHLY COMMENDED

Clappersgate, Ambleside, Cumbria LA22 9NF Tel (015394) 32036 Fax (015394) 32450

This elegant country house sits peacefully under Loughrigg Fell in five acres of gardens and woodland, with access onto the fell, and also enjoys spectacular views of the River Brathay. The hotel is noted for its award-winning restaurant with a warm and friendly atmosphere. There are log fires on chilly evenings and fresh flowers are attended to daily. Bedrooms are individually designed and furnished in traditional quality. Croquet, fishing, spa bath, solarium, leisure club facilities, dogs accepted. Personally managed by the resident owners Michael and Carol Fletcher.

Bed & Breakfast per night: single occupancy from £45.00–£65.00; double room from £90.00–£130.00
Half board per person: £60.00–£90.00 daily; £378.00–£598.00 weekly
Evening meal 1930 (last orders 2030)

Bedrooms: 11 double, 4 twin, 3 triple
Bathrooms: 18 en-suite
Parking for 22
Cards accepted: Access, Visa, Diners, Amex, Switch/Delta

33 WATEREDGE HOTEL ≋≋≋≋ HIGHLY COMMENDED

Waterhead Bay, Ambleside, Cumbria LA22 0EP Tel (015394) 32332 Fax (015394) 31878

Wateredge is a delightfully situated family-run hotel on the shores of Windermere, with gardens leading to the lake edge. It was developed from two 17th-century fishermen's cottages which are still part of the charm of the whole building. Relax in comfortable lounges overlooking the lake, or on our lakeside patio where teas and light lunches are served. In the evening, dine under oak beams and enjoy exquisitely cooked food. Cosy bar, pretty bedrooms and relaxed friendly service.

Bed & Breakfast per night: single room from £42.00–£56.00; double room from £66.00–£138.00
Half board per person: £53.00–£89.00 daily; £362.00–£595.00 weekly
Lunch available: 1200–1400 (light lunches)

Evening meal 1900 (last orders 2030)
Bedrooms: 3 single, 12 double, 8 twin
Bathrooms: 23 en-suite
Parking for 25   Open: February–December
Cards accepted: Access, Visa, Amex, Switch/Delta

34 FAYRER GARDEN HOUSE HOTEL ≋≋≋ HIGHLY COMMENDED

Lyth Valley Road, Bowness-on-Windermere, Cumbria LA23 3JP Tel (015394) 88195

Fayrer Garden House is beautifully situated in five acres of grounds overlooking Lake Windermere. The conservatory restaurant and elegant lounges all enjoy the vista over the lake. Ten rooms, each with four-poster or canopied beds and whirlpool baths en-suite, all overlook the lake. Enjoy candle-lit dinners featuring our award-winning food, with the pianist playing your favourite tune. Nearby leisure facilities are freely available for your use. This is somewhere special for someone very special.

Bed & Breakfast per night: double room from £55.00–£110.00
Half board per person: £39.50–£75.00 daily
Evening meal 1930 (last orders 2030)

Bedrooms: 1 single, 10 double, 3 triple
Bathrooms: 1 en-suite, 13 private
Parking for 20
Cards accepted: Access, Visa, Amex

35 LINTHWAITE HOUSE HOTEL

〰〰〰〰 DE LUXE

Crook Road, Windermere, Cumbria LA23 3JA Tel (015394) 88600 Fax (015394) 88601

Country house hotel, twenty minutes from the M6, situated in fourteen acres of peaceful hilltop grounds, overlooking Lake Windermere and with breathtaking sunsets. The eighteen rooms have en-suite bathrooms, satellite television, radio, telephone and tea/coffee making facilities. The restaurant serves modern British food using local produce complemented by fine wines. There is a tarn for fly-fishing, croquet, golf practice hole and free use of nearby leisure spa. Romantic breaks feature a king-size double bed with canopy, champagne, chocolates and flowers. English Tourist Board 'Hotel of the Year' 1994. ✝ CATEGORY 3

Bed & Breakfast per night: single room £90.00; double room from £120.00–£170.00
Half board per person: £69.00–£105.00 daily; £483.00–£735.00 weekly
Lunch available: 1230–1330

Evening meal 1915 (last orders 2045)
Bedrooms: 1 single, 13 double, 4 twin
Bathrooms: 18 en-suite
Parking for 30
Cards accepted: Access, Visa, Amex, Switch/Delta

Grizedale Forest Sculpture Trail

TWO HUNDRED YEARS AGO, the area between Lake Coniston and Windermere was a higgledy-piggledy mixture of hilly pasture and oak woodland; now stately rows of tall trees march across the landscape. This is Grizedale Forest, 6,000 acres of mixed woodland owned by the Forestry Commission. A walk through the forest offers a surprising and intriguing trail of discovery and the opportunity to contemplate some 80 or so large-scale sculptures dotted around it.

The sculptures are the result of an imaginative project, begun in 1977, to provide a stimulating working environment for sculptors. Through a scheme of short artists' residences, selected sculptors are invited to explore the forest and embody their responses to the environment in one or more works of art. The result is an enormously diverse collection of works all united by a common theme: the forest. Most are built from materials readily available in the landscape, principally wood and stone, and many are directly inspired by the shapes and forms which naturally occur there. Gordon Young's wooden carving of a fox, *Forest Denizen*, is one of several representations of the forest's indigenous wildlife. Another creation, *Taking a Wall for a Walk* by Andy Goldsworthy, could at first be taken for one of the many existing drystone walls which thread their way through the trees. Goldsworthy's wall, however, coils and twists sinuously between straight tree trunks, creating a satisfying arrangement of horizontal curves and vertical lines.

In some cases the similarity of these sculptures to the natural landscape increases the challenge of discovery. What might at first glance appear to be a log or a tumbled heap of rock reveals itself on closer inspection as a work of art. In fact, some now blend rather better into the landscape than their creators originally intended, as the elements gradually take their toll!

Most of the sculptures are found near the Silurian Way, a 9½-mile circular walk starting at the Grizedale Visitor Centre (tel: 01229 860010) where maps of the route may be purchased. There is no need to complete the entire trail, however, as plenty of short cuts lead back to the car-park, and each has its own complement of sculptures. At the Gallery in the Forest, near the Visitor Centre, displays give an insight into how sculptors choose their location and design their work. Also on site is the Theatre in the Forest (tel: 01229 860291), offering a year-round programme of varied arts events.

36 WHEELGATE COUNTRY HOUSE HOTEL

🍵🍵🍵 HIGHLY COMMENDED

Little Arrow, Coniston, Cumbria LA21 8AU Tel (015394) 41418

A delightful, 17th-century country house with a warm, relaxed atmosphere in a peaceful rural location, close to the heart of Lakeland. The hotel features exquisite individually-styled bedrooms and an enchanting oak-beamed lounge with log fire. In the intimate candle-lit restaurant the finest fresh local produce can be sampled. Breakfasts are delicious, comprising an extensive buffet of cereals/fruits followed by a hearty grill. Free leisure club facilities are provided. Quality service is guaranteed - a perfect and unforgettable experience. Smoking restricted to the bar.

Bed & Breakfast per night: single room from
£25.00–£34.00; double room from £50.00–£68.00
Half board per person: £44.00–£52.00 daily;
£245.00–£315.00 weekly
Evening meal 1930 (last orders 1930)

Bedrooms: 2 single, 6 double
Bathrooms: 8 en-suite
Parking for 8
Open: March–November
Cards accepted: Access, Visa, Amex

37 SAWREY HOUSE COUNTRY HOTEL

🍵🍵🍵 HIGHLY COMMENDED

Near Sawrey, Ambleside, Cumbria LA22 0LF Tel (015394) 36387 Fax (015394) 36010

Situated in three acres of grounds in the centre of the Lake District National Park, this family-run hotel offers a very special combination of elegance and comfort. It directly overlooks both Grizedale Forest and Esthwaite Water, nestling in the conservation hamlet which won the heart of Beatrix Potter, whose house 'Hilltop' lies nearby. We place special emphasis on our delicious five-course dinners, complemented with a well-stocked cellar offering reasonably priced wines.

Bed & Breakfast per night: single room from
£39.50–£50.00; double room from £79.00–£100.00
Half board per person: £52.50–£62.50 daily;
£330.00–£400.00 weekly
Lunch available: 1200–1400

Evening meal 1930 (last orders 2030)
Bedrooms: 1 single, 5 double, 2 twin, 2 triple
Bathrooms: 10 en-suite
Parking for 20   Open: February–December
Cards accepted: Access, Visa

38 HOLBECK GHYLL COUNTRY HOUSE HOTEL

🍵🍵🍵🍵 DE LUXE

Holbeck Lane, Windermere, Cumbria LA23 1LU Tel (015394) 32375 Fax (015394) 34743

Peacefully located in seven acres of grounds with breathtaking views across Lake Windermere. 19th-century hunting lodge, former home of Lord Lonsdale, with log fires and intimate candle-lit oak-panelled restaurant. Luxurious bedrooms with vases of fresh flowers, decanters of sherry and fluffy bathrobes. Young, caring staff offering genuine hospitality. Holbeck Ghyll is 'Something Special' for that eagerly awaited important anniversary or birthday celebration. Rated by all guide books in their highest category. Central Lakes location. Colour brochure and special breaks upon request.

Half board per person: £65.00–£110.00 daily;
£410.00–£693.00 weekly
Lunch available: 1200–1430
Evening meal 1900 (last orders 2045)

Bedrooms: 10 double, 3 twin, 1 triple
Bathrooms: 14 en-suite
Parking for 22
Cards accepted: Access, Visa, Diners, Amex

39 GILPIN LODGE COUNTRY HOUSE HOTEL & RESTAURANT 〰〰〰〰 DE LUXE

Crook Road, Windermere, Cumbria LA23 3NE Tel (015394) 88818 Fax (015394) 88058

Gilpin Lodge is an elegant, family-run country house hotel and restaurant set in twenty acres of gardens and woodlands. Two miles from Lake Windermere and near the golf course, it has sumptuous bedrooms, some with four-posters. Fresh flowers, antiques and pictures abound. The food at Gilpin Lodge is a pleasant obsession! The wine list features over one-hundred-and-seventy wines, and the service is attentive and friendly. Free use of nearby private leisure club.

Bed & Breakfast per night: single occupancy from £65.00–£85.00; double room from £80.00–£140.00
Half board per person: £55.00–£85.00 daily; £365.00–£555.00 weekly
Lunch available: 1200–1430

Evening meal 1900 (last orders 2045)
Bedrooms: 9 double, 1 twin, 1 triple
Bathrooms: 11 en-suite
Parking for 40
Cards accepted: Access, Visa, Diners, Amex, Switch/Delta

40 LINDETH FELL COUNTRY HOUSE HOTEL 〰〰〰〰 HIGHLY COMMENDED

Windermere, Cumbria LA23 3JP Tel (015394) 43286 or 44287 Fax (015394) 47455

In a uniquely beautiful garden setting above Lake Windermere, Lindeth Fell offers brilliant views, peaceful surroundings and superb modern English cooking – at highly competitive prices. Lawns are laid for tennis, croquet and putting, and Windermere Golf Club is one mile away. Good fishing is available free and interesting walks start from the door. Call for a brochure from the resident owners.

Half board per person: £57.50–£65.00 daily; £385.00–£430.00 weekly
Lunch available: 1300 (Sundays only)
Evening meal 1930 (last orders 2030)

Bedrooms: 2 single, 5 double, 5 twin, 2 triple, 1 suite
Bathrooms: 15 en-suite
Parking for 20
Open: March–November
Cards accepted: Access, Visa

41 THE BEAUMONT HOTEL 〰〰 HIGHLY COMMENDED

Holly Road, Windermere, Cumbria LA23 2AF Tel (015394) 47075 Fax (015394) 47075

Opened in 1992 and ideally situated for Windermere and Bowness, The Beaumont is an elegant Victorian House Hotel of a very high standard. All ten luxury bedrooms are en-suite with tea/coffee making facilities, hairdryers and colour television. Four-poster beds are available for that special occasion, with the option of a romantic presentation of wine, chocolates and flowers to order. Breakfasts are of the hearty kind to set you up for the day. Malcolm and Kathy play host to you in this warm and friendly setting. Totally non-smoking.

Bed & Breakfast per night: single room from £23.00–£40.00; double room from £46.00–£72.00

Bedrooms: 1 single, 7 double, 1 twin, 1 family room
Bathrooms: 10 en-suite
Parking for 10
Cards accepted: Access, Visa, Amex

42 THE ARCHWAY

 HIGHLY COMMENDED

13 College Road, Windermere, Cumbria LA23 1BU Tel (015394) 45613

Impeccable Victorian terraced guest house, beautifully restored and with a civilised and relaxing atmosphere. Lots of antiques and country furniture, interesting paintings and prints, good books, fresh flowers, super mountain views. Renowned for gourmet home cooking emphasising fresh organic ingredients brought together in imaginative and nutritionally-thoughtful menus (the breakfast fare offers everything from freshly squeezed fruit and vegetable juices and home made yoghurts to spicy apple griddle cakes – bread is wholemeal and home baked!) We are a no smoking house.

Bed & Breakfast per night: double room from
£44.00–£54.00
Half board per person: £34.50–£39.50 daily
Evening meal 1845

Bedrooms: 2 double, 2 twin
Bathrooms: 4 en-suite
Parking for 2
Cards accepted: Access, Visa, Amex

43 WOODLANDS

 HIGHLY COMMENDED

New Road, Windermere, Cumbria LA23 2EE Tel (015394) 43915 Fax (015394) 48558

Conveniently situated between Windermere and Bowness, The Woodlands is an excellent family-run hotel renowned for its high standard of cleanliness and comfort. All rooms are en-suite, with tea and coffee making facilities and televisions. Guests are welcome to relax in our lounge whilst enjoying a drink from the bar. Resident proprietors Juliet and Andrew Wood look forward to welcoming you to The Woodlands.

Bed & Breakfast per night: single room from
£22.00–£30.00; double room from £44.00–£60.00
Evening meal 1900

Bedrooms: 2 single, 10 double, 1 twin, 1 family room
Bathrooms: 14 en-suite
Parking for 14
Cards accepted: Access, Visa, Switch/Delta

44 CEDAR MANOR HOTEL

 HIGHLY COMMENDED

Ambleside Road, Windermere, Cumbria LA23 1AX Tel (015394) 43192 Fax (015394) 45970

Situated close to Windermere village and the lake, Cedar Manor Hotel is a haven for food lovers and those who enjoy the good things in life. Personally run by Lynn and Martin Hadley, the hotel has won many awards for food and service over the past twelve years. For those who like to work off the calories gained in the restaurant we have facilities at the nearby Spinnaker Club for their enjoyment.

Bed & Breakfast per night: single occupancy from
£39.50–£47.50; double room from £59.00–£75.00
Half board per person: £38.00–£51.00 daily;
£203.00–£315.00 weekly
Evening meal 1930 (last orders 2030)

Bedrooms: 9 double, 3 twin
Bathrooms: 12 private
Parking for 20
Cards accepted: Access, Visa

45 THE BURN HOW GARDEN HOUSE HOTEL & MOTEL 〰〰〰〰 HIGHLY COMMENDED

Back Belsfield Road, Windermere, Cumbria LA23 3HH   Tel (015394) 46226   Fax (015394) 47000

We offer comfort and superb service near the shore of Windemere, in spacious family chalets or elegant four-poster rooms all with private bathrooms, television, radio, and parking space. Many rooms have private balconies and four of the ground floor ones are suitable for wheelchairs. We serve first-class English and French cuisine and are acclaimed for our fine food. You also receive free use of a premier leisure club. It's that extra personal service that makes all the difference. ⚇ CATEGORY 3

Bed & Breakfast per night: single room from £48.00–£56.00; double room from £76.00–£99.00
Half board per person: £44.00–£69.00 daily; £230.00–£370.00 weekly
Lunch available: 1230–1300

Evening meal 1900 (last orders 2030)
Bedrooms: 2 single, 8 double, 8 twin, 8 triple
Bathrooms: 25 en-suite, 1 private
Parking for 30
Cards accepted: Access, Visa, Diners, Amex, Switch/Delta

46 SWAN HOTEL 〰〰〰〰 HIGHLY COMMENDED

Newby Bridge, Ulverston, Cumbria LA12 8NB   Tel (015395) 31681   Fax (015395) 31917

At the southern end of Lake Windermere, the Swan Hotel undoubtedly has one of the most picturesque locations in the whole of the Lake District, with views over the water and surrounding countryside. 36 en-suite bedrooms range from a suite, four de luxe doubles to high standard doubles, singles and twins. The public rooms are attractively decorated with comfortable bars as well as an elegant lounge which adjoins the traditional Tithe Barn Restaurant (no smoking) or less formal Mailcoach.

Bed & Breakfast per night: single room from £60.00–£87.50; double room from £92.00–£135.00
Half board per person: £62.00–£100.00 daily
Lunch available: 1145–1445
Evening meal 1900 (last orders 2130)

Bedrooms: 7 single, 13 double, 10 twin, 6 triple
Bathrooms: 36 en-suite
Parking for 106
Cards accepted: Access, Visa, Diners, Amex, Switch/Delta

47 CLARENCE HOUSE COUNTRY HOTEL AND RESTAURANT 〰〰〰〰 HIGHLY COMMENDED

Skelgate, Dalton-in-Furness, Cumbria LA15 8BQ   Tel (01229) 462508   Fax (01229) 467177

Clarence House is an elegant late Victorian mansion, luxuriously furnished to the taste of its owner, set in three acres of its own grounds overlooking a beautiful wooded valley. Seventeen centrally-heated bedrooms, luxuriously decorated, offer only the finest accommodation; dine in beautiful surroundings served by our friendly welcoming staff. Our à la carte, five-course speciality and famous carvery offer even the most discerning diner a superb choice. "Quite simply the best".

Bed & Breakfast per night: single occupancy from £45.00–£60.00; double room from £50.00–£75.00
Half board per person: £57.50–£78.50 daily; £388.50–£494.75 weekly
Lunch available: 1200–1430

Evening meal 1830 (last orders 2130)
Bedrooms: 14 double, 3 twin
Bathrooms: 17 en-suite
Parking for 40
Cards accepted: Access, Visa, Amex, Switch/Delta

48 APPLEBY MANOR COUNTRY HOUSE HOTEL 〰〰〰〰 HIGHLY COMMENDED

Roman Road, Appleby-in-Westmorland, Cumbria CA16 6JB Tel (017683) 51571 Fax (017683) 52888

Probably the most relaxing and friendly hotel you'll ever stay at! Set amidst breathtaking beauty, you'll find high-quality accommodation; satellite television and video films; a splendid indoor leisure club that has a small swimming pool, jacuzzi, steam-room, sauna and sunbed; magnificent lounges, and great food in the award-winning restaurant – all in a genuine country house. Golf, squash, horse-riding and all the delights of the Lake District and Yorkshire Dales are close by.

Bed & Breakfast per night: single occupancy from £61.50–£75.00; double room from £88.00–£118.00
Half board per person: £49.50–£84.50 daily; £297.00–£507.00 weekly
Lunch available: 1200–1400

Evening meal 1900 (last orders 2100)
Bedrooms: 14 double, 8 twin, 1 triple, 7 family rooms
Bathrooms: 30 en-suite
Parking for 50
Cards accepted: Access, Visa, Diners, Amex, Switch/Delta

Kielder Water and Kielder Forest

KIELDER WATER, the largest man-made lake in Europe, lies at the heart of Kielder Forest. With 150 million trees this is the biggest single wooded area in Britain. Until the mid-20th-century, visitors to this wild part of Northumberland – and there were few of them – would have had a very different prospect. The area may once have been carpeted with tall Scots pines, but these were felled long ago to make way for the sheep-farming and coal-mining economy of the valley of the River North Tyne. The first sitka spruces were planted in the late 1940s, when mining proved uneconomic and even hardy sheep struggled in the then harsh landscape.

Nowadays the Kielder area is Northumberland's most popular tourist attraction, drawing upwards of 100,000 visitors a year. The transformation is thanks largely to the controversial construction of the reservoir. Seventy homes were drowned and eight archaeological sites lost. However, a reliable water supply for the homes and industry of the North-East was created, and a host of recreational facilities soon followed Kielder Water's completion in 1982.

Watersports may be the most obvious attraction of the Kielder area, but there is also an imaginative array of activities available within the forest, and a huge range of tastes can now be indulged. Visitors may: fish for trout from bank or boat, or for salmon just downstream from the dam; hire canoes, dinghies, sailboards and motor boats from Leaplish Waterside Park; sail their own craft; receive expert tuition in yachting, windsurfing and rowing; there's even a separate 120-acre area devoted to waterskiing. Alternatively, they can cruise the lake on board the *Osprey*, complete with commentary, shop, bar and galley. The cruise is highly enjoyable in its own right, but many use the *Osprey* as a means of reaching the north shore to walk on glorious paths far from the nearest car. Experienced walkers can set aside a full day to complete the Kielder Water Challenge Walk. This strenuous route circumnavigates the reservoir's 27-mile shoreline in just 26 miles – possible if a few corners are cut – the equivalent of a full marathon. Shorter, waymarked walks, mountain-biking, bird-watching (and, if you're lucky, otter-watching), orienteering, horse-riding and a 12-mile forest drive are land-based options on offer throughout the year. Special events include husky-racing in March, several fishing competitions and the Kielder stages of the RAC Rally in November. Call 01434 240398 for more information.

⑨ MIDDLE ORD MANOR HOUSE
 〰〰 DE LUXE

Middle Ord Farm, Berwick-upon-Tweed, Northumberland TD15 2XQ Tel (01289) 306323

Mrs. Gray offers quality accommodation within her Grade II listed farmhouse on a working farm with a very comprehensvie breakfast menu served in a gracious dining room. Two residents' lounges (one no smoking) and secluded gardens. The en-suite bedrooms include a four-poster if desired. Northumbria Tourist Board 'Best Bed & Breakfast' Award, 1993 and 1994. English Tourist Board 'England for Excellence' Silver Award, 1994. Come and enjoy the ambience of such a high standard in our truly friendly home. Sorry, no children or pets.

Bed & Breakfast per night: double room from £50.00

Bedrooms: 2 double, 1 twin
Bathrooms: 3 en-suite, 1 public
Parking for 6
Open: April–October

㊿ THE COACH HOUSE
〰〰〰 HIGHLY COMMENDED

Crookham, Cornhill-on-Tweed, Northumberland TD12 4TD Tel (01890) 820293 Fax (01890) 820284

The Coach House offers warm, spacious bedrooms surrounding a sunlit courtyard. The large lounge, with peach leather furniture and fine pictures, overlooks a west-facing terrace. A flock of Soay sheep graze beneath the damson trees. Food is fresh and varied, reflecting modern ideas on healthy eating, with some Mediterranean influence. Local fish, game and meat are used, organically-reared where possible. Special diets catered for. Excellent facilities for disabled guests. Lovingly renovated to a high standard. ♿ CATEGORY 1

Bed & Breakfast per night: single room from £23.00–£34.00; double room from £46.00–£68.00
Half board per person: £38.50–£49.50 daily
Evening meal 1930 (last orders 1930)

Bedrooms: 2 single, 2 double, 5 twin
Bathrooms: 7 en-suite, 2 public
Parking for 12
Open: March–October
Cards accepted: Access, Visa

⑤① THE COURTYARD
〰〰 DE LUXE

Mount Pleasant, Sandhoe, Corbridge, Northumberland NE45 4LX Tel (01434) 606850 Fax (01434) 606632

A warm family welcome greets visitors to this lovingly restored and beautifully furnished country house, dating from 1730. Surrounded by open countryside, with wonderful panoramic views over Corbridge and Corstopitum Roman Fort – both two miles away – and the lovely Tyne valley. All rooms have exposed oak beams, en-suite bath/shower rooms, colour TVs, central heating and tea/coffee facilities, with one having an antique four-poster bed. Evening meals are offered at prior notice. Residential licence. No smoking, children or credit cards.

Bed & Breakfast per night: single occupancy from £40.00–£60.00; double room from £50.00–£70.00

Bedrooms: 1 double, 1 twin, 1 triple
Bathrooms: 3 en-suite
Parking for 6

52 TOWN BARNS

Off Trinity Terrace, Corbridge, Northumberland NE45 5HP Tel (01434) 633345

Set in the heart of the beautiful Tyne Valley and once the home of Catherine Cookson, a warm welcome awaits you at Town Barns, an impressive detached stone house enjoying uninterrupted views yet only two minutes from the village centre. A double staircase accesses a balcony off which are three luxurious bedrooms (en-suite/private facilities, television, tea and coffee makers). Explore Hadrian's Wall, the Roman Sites and the Metro Centre, or relax in the superb lounge overlooking the heated indoor swimming pool (seasonal). Totally non-smoking. Proprietor: Dorothy Wilson.

Bed & Breakfast per night: single occupancy £25.00; double room from £40.00–£44.00

Bedrooms: 2 double, 1 triple
Bathrooms: 2 en-suite, 1 private
Parking for 5
Open: March–October

53 BEE COTTAGE FARM

Castleside, Consett, Durham DH8 9HW Tel (01207) 508224

A working farm set in peaceful surroundings with access to quiet pleasant walks with unspoilt views. Visitors are welcome to help with the animals that are mainly calves, goats, etc. The farm is ideally situated for visits to Beamish Museum, Durham Cathedral, Hadrian's Wall or as an overnight break in a long journey. There are some ground floor rooms, a tearoom open daily between 1300 and 1800, and an evening meal is available. No smoking. Dogs by arrangement. You will be made very welcome.

Bed & Breakfast per night: single room from £25.00; double room from £44.00
Half board per person: from £35.50 daily
Evening meal 1930 (last orders 2000)

Bedrooms: 1 single, 3 double, 2 twin, 1 triple, 2 family rooms
Bathrooms: 1 en-suite, 2 private, 5 public
Parking for 20

54 GREENHEAD COUNTRY HOUSE HOTEL

Fir Tree, Crook, Durham DL15 8BL Tel (01388) 763143

Greenhead Hotel is perfectly situated at the centre of rural Durham countryside at the foot of Weardale, just fifteen minutes from Durham city, surrounded by open fields and woodlands. The tranquillity of Greenhead is complemented by the fact that only private resident guests are catered for (no public bars or discos). The accolades, describing why Greenhead offers something special in the way of service and accommodation, can be seen in our full colour brochure.

Bed & Breakfast per night: single occupancy from £35.00–£40.00; double room from £50.00–£60.00
Evening meal 1800 (last bookings 1700)

Bedrooms: 4 double, 2 twin
Bathrooms: 6 private
Parking for 15
Cards accepted: Access, Visa

55 ELDON HOUSE

 HIGHLY COMMENDED

East Green, Heighington, Darlington, Durham DL5 6PP Tel (01325) 312270

This is a 17th-century house with spacious bedrooms, overlooking the village green, with a large garden and tennis court. There is ample parking. Easy to find and convenient, it is situated six miles from Darlington railway station, twelve miles from Teeside Airport, three miles from A1(M), and three miles from Newton Aycliffe.

Bed & Breakfast per night: single occupancy from £27.00–£32.00; double room from £40.00–£45.00

Bedrooms: 3 twin
Bathrooms: 1 en-suite, 2 private
Parking for 6

Beamish Open Air Museum

UNTIL A COUPLE OF YEARS AGO, time stood still at Beamish. Wherever you went – the chapel, the drift mine, the Co-op or any of the other buildings – it was always 1913, the year before the slaughter of World War I. In 1995, however, the North of England Open Air Museum, as it is properly called, opened Pockerley Manor, and time wound back to the 1820s, a period when England was still jubilant after victory in the Napoleonic Wars. Visitors can now choose whether they wish to become Georgians living during the reign of George IV (1820–30) or George V (1910–36) – or both.

The museum's history is shorter, though it can claim to be the first regional open air museum in England, admitting the public in 1971. Since then this award-winning complex has gone from strength to strength. A fundamental part of Beamish's *modus operandi* is that it lives up to its name as an 'open air museum', so you will find no exhibits behind glass cases. Instead every object is in an appropriate setting, and it is the combined effect of intriguing artefacts and a range of authentic surroundings that makes Beamish so appealing.

There is no shortage of attractions; arriving at Beamish, most visitors jump aboard the picturesque electric trams and head for the Town, where all manner of buildings vividly recreate life in 1913. Have a drink at the Sun Inn (rescued from nearby Bishop Auckland) and notice the traditional beer engine used to serve your pint. Visit the dentist's surgery at No. 3 Ravensworth Terrace and be thankful for the dental advances the intervening years have brought. Give your 1990s dentist some more work by buying the traditional wares of the Jubilee confectioners. Read the headlines of 1913 in the Newspaper office, drop in at the Beamish Motor and Cycle Works or go for lessons at the Music Teacher's – all of these, and more, are on offer. Returning towards the entrance you can visit the fairground before calling in at Home Farm to see an exhibition of cheese-making. There's also the chance to go underground at the drift mine or seek a more uplifting experience at the Wesleyan Chapel. Costumed interpreters are on hand at all these sights. The costumes are of course from an earlier century at Pockerley, a beautiful fortified manor house beside which the museum is currently restoring the formal and kitchen gardens.

Beamish, open throughout the year except for the second half of December, lies about 9 miles south-west of Newcastle upon Tyne. Special events (tel: 01207 231811) are held during summer months.

56 HEADLAM HALL HOTEL

〰〰〰〰 HIGHLY COMMENDED

Headlam, Gainford, Darlington, Durham DL2 3HA Tel (01325) 730238 Fax (01325) 730790

Set in four acres of formal gardens and surrounded by its own rolling farmland, Headlam Hall offers twenty six tastefully furnished en-suite bedrooms. These include two suites, three family rooms and ten four-poster bedrooms; leisure facilities available for guests include an indoor heated swimming pool, sauna, snooker room, tennis court and fishing. The restaurant serves traditional English and Continental cuisine of the highest standards. Secluded yet easily accessible from main transport links, Headlam Hall is a family business offering value and individuality.

Bed & Breakfast per night: single occupancy from £55.00–£83.00; double room from £70.00–£98.00
Half board per person: £49.00–£54.00 daily
Lunch available: 1200–1400
Evening meal 1930 (last orders 2200)

Bedrooms: 16 double, 6 twin, 4 triple
Bathrooms: 26 en-suite
Parking for 60
Cards accepted: Access, Visa, Diners, Amex, Switch/Delta

57 OLD BREWERY GUEST HOUSE

〰〰〰 HIGHLY COMMENDED

29 The Green, Richmond, North Yorkshire DL10 4RG Tel (01748) 822460 Fax (01748) 825561

Nestling on the green just off the town centre, close to the River Swale and with marvellous views of the castle high above, The Old Brewery Guest House has a really attractive location. Once an old inn, it has been fully re-furbished in a luxurious Victorian style capturing the essence of a bygone age, whilst retaining all the modern comforts. Pre-theatre snacks for the early Georgian Theatre Royal bookings, packed lunches and evening dinners are available.

Bed & Breakfast per night: single occupancy from £29.50; double room from £39.00–£41.00
Half board per person: £31.50–£32.50 daily; £220.50–£227.50 weekly
Evening meal 1930 (last bookings 1730)

Bedrooms: 4 double, 1 twin
Bathrooms: 4 en-suite, 1 private

58 HELM COUNTRY HOUSE

〰〰〰 HIGHLY COMMENDED

Askrigg, Leyburn, North Yorkshire DL8 3JF Tel (01969) 650443

Idyllically situated with 'the finest view in Wensleydale'. Experience the comfort, peace and quiet of our 17th-century hillside Dales farmhouse. Each charmingly furnished bedroom has en-suite facilities and many special little touches. Period furniture, oak beams and log fires create the ideal atmosphere in which to relax and share our passion for really good food. We offer a superb choice of breakfasts, home-made bread and preserves, exceptionally good dinners and an inspired selection of wines. Totally non-smoking.

Bed & Breakfast per night: double room from £56.00–£64.00
Half board per person: £42.50–£47.50 daily; £297.50 weekly
Evening meal 1900 (last orders 1900)

Bedrooms: 2 double, 1 twin
Bathrooms: 3 en-suite
Parking for 5
Open: January–November

59 SIMONSTONE HALL

≋≋≋ HIGHLY COMMENDED

Hawes, North Yorkshire DL8 3LY Tel (01969) 667255 Fax (01969) 667741

This elegant ten-bedroomed country house hotel, dating from 1733, is set deep in the Yorkshire Dales enjoying unsurpassed views of Wensleydale and a unique atmosphere of tranquillity, luxury and indulgence. Let yourself be pampered and enjoy the fresh air of the Dales, the space, the grace, comforts and good food – all of which make it ideal for relaxing and shedding the cares of modern day living.

Bed & Breakfast per night: single occupancy from £39.20–£61.60; double room from £70.00–£110.00
Half board per person: £55.00–£75.00 daily; £346.50–£472.50 weekly
Lunch available: 1200–1400

Evening meal 1900 (last orders 2030)
Bedrooms: 7 double, 3 twin
Bathrooms: 10 en-suite
Parking for 22
Cards accepted: Access, Visa, Switch/Delta

60 HAYLOFT SUITE

≋≋ HIGHLY COMMENDED

Foal Barn, Spennithorne, Leyburn, North Yorkshire DL8 5PR Tel (01969) 622580

A two-hundred-year-old barn, set around a picturesque garden courtyard in a tranquil village by the River Ure, this cottage suite is for the exclusive use of one party of up to four people and offers privacy, peace and comfort. Climb old stone steps to the private entrance to your own beamed lounge with an open fire. A freshly-cooked breakfast of your choice will be served. Two miles from Leyburn market town and the historical town of Middleham.

Bed & Breakfast per night: single occupancy £23.00; double room £46.00

Bedrooms: 1 double, 1 twin
Bathrooms: 1 private
Parking for 4

61 MILLERS HOUSE HOTEL

≋≋≋≋ HIGHLY COMMENDED

Middleham, Wensleydale, North Yorkshire DL8 4NR Tel (01969) 622630 Fax (01969) 623570

An award-winning luxury hotel set in the historic village of Middleham in the heart of Herriot's Yorkshire Dales where the owners emphasise personal care and attention to detail. The renowned restaurant uses quality local produce, including homegrown herbs and vegetables, and provides an original selection of dishes, including vegetarian choices. Elegant, individually-furnished en-suite rooms, including a luxury four-poster, are decorated in keeping with the Georgian period. Gourmet Wine Weekends, Racing Breaks, and Christmas and New Year celebrations are a must. Yorkshire & Humberside Tourist Board 'Hotel of the Year' runner-up.

Bed & Breakfast per night: single room £39.00; double room from £77.00–£90.00
Half board per person: £55.50–£64.50 daily; £340.00–£420.00 weekly
Evening meal 1915 (last orders 2030)

Bedrooms: 1 single, 3 double, 3 twin
Bathrooms: 6 en-suite, 1 private
Parking for 8
Open: February–December
Cards accepted: Access, Visa, Switch/Delta

62 HUSBANDS BARN

 HIGHLY COMMENDED

Stainforth, Settle, North Yorkshire BD24 9PN Tel (01729) 822240

Give yourself a special treat in a newly converted barn, restored to a very high standard and run as part of a working farm. Three en-suite rooms with colour TVs, tea and coffee making facilities, hair dryers, plus a lounge with open fire – all with exposed beams. The dining room has lovely views over the surrounding countryside. An ideal base for walking or touring the Yorkshire Dales. Close to the Settle–Carlisle railway, the Three Peaks and the village pub! Sorry, no children under twelve, no pets and no smoking.

Bed & Breakfast per night: double room from
£40.00–£50.00

Bedrooms: 2 double, 1 twin
Bathrooms: 3 en-suite
Parking for 5

Yorkshire Dales Barns

THE BEAUTY OF THE YORKSHIRE DALES derives in large part from the natural magnificence of the landscape: nature generously gave this central stretch of the Pennine chain dramatic limestone outcrops and clear, fast-running rivers. But man, too, has added to the splendour of the Dales. The trees may have been cleared long ago, but in their stead on the lower slopes came hay-meadows full of as many as 40 species of herb, bounded by drystone walls of simple beauty. In the northern Dales such as Swaledale and Arkengarthdale, almost every field has its own barn, each one adding to the glorious impression these valleys create.

These barns – it is estimated that there are over a thousand in Swaledale and Arkengarthdale alone – are a sign of a vanishing form of agriculture. In the 17th-, 18th- and 19th-centuries, when most of these barns were built, farms were small and numerous. Many who tended the land also worked in the local lead and coal mines, and so had little time to devote to farming. The summer harvest of the hay crop was the most labour-intensive time of year, and the hard-pressed farmers evolved an agricultural system which allowed a more even spread of work. They built their barns – almost all using the drystone method of construction with stones sloping outwards to take the rain away – in the fields where the hay was growing. Storing the hay in the nearby barns was therefore a simple task. Since the cows spent the winter in the same barn as their foodstuff, it was easy both to feed the cattle and to fertilise the same field with their manure. The *quid*

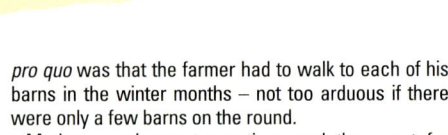

pro quo was that the farmer had to walk to each of his barns in the winter months – not too arduous if there were only a few barns on the round.

Modern employment practices and the quest for efficiency have meant that farms are now few and large. This no longer fits in with the traditional system, and many outlying field barns have become redundant. In Swaledale and Arkengarthdale a conservation scheme run by the national park has saved countless from dereliction; some are still used by their owners while others have found new life as 'bunkhouse barns'. These offer basic accommodation to walkers and are often on or near long-distance footpaths. At Hazel Brow, Low Row, visitors may go inside a traditional Dales barn as part of the open farm scheme (tel: 01748 886224 for more details).

63 YORKE ARMS HOTEL

≋≋≋≋ HIGHLY COMMENDED

Ramsgill, Harrogate, North Yorkshire HG3 5RL Tel (01423) 755243 Fax (01423) 755243

Nestling in tranquil Nidderdale, the Yorke Arms offers a high standard of accommodation and cuisine. We are open throughout the year and offer special rates for country breaks when the reservation is for more than two nights. Bar lunches and suppers are available daily, the restaurant opens each evening and also offers traditional sunday lunches. Functions are catered for according to numbers.

Bed & Breakfast per night: single room from
£40.00–£45.00; double room from £70.00–£110.00
Half board per person: £45.00–£65.00 daily
Lunch available: 1200–1400
Evening meal 1900 (last orders 2100)

Bedrooms: 3 single, 3 double, 5 twin, 2 triple
Bathrooms: 13 en-suite
Parking for 30
Cards accepted: Access, Visa, Switch/Delta

---

64 GRANTS HOTEL AND CHIMNEY POTS RESTAURANT

≋≋≋≋ HIGHLY COMMENDED

Swan Road, Harrogate, North Yorkshire HG1 2SS Tel (01423) 560666 Fax (01423) 502550

Award-winning, privately-owned Victorian town house hotel situated in the heart of Harrogate. Affiliated to the Academy Health and Leisure Club. Chimney Pots Restaurant provides an imaginative menu in an elegant, air-conditioned atmosphere and is a firm favourite with local gourmets. Close to the Yorkshire Dales, Herriot Country, the ancient city of York and the Royal Armouries in Leeds – an ideal base for touring, with lots to see and do.

Bed & Breakfast per night: single room from
£54.00–£94.50; double room from £80.00–£154.00
Half board per person: £71.50–£112.00 daily; £322.00
weekly
Lunch available: 1200–1330

Evening meal 1830 (last orders 2130)
Bedrooms: 13 single, 10 double, 17 twin, 2 triple
Bathrooms: 42 en-suite
Parking for 23
Cards accepted: Access, Visa, Diners, Amex, Switch/Delta

---

65 DELAINE HOTEL

≋≋≋ HIGHLY COMMENDED

17 Ripon Road, Harrogate, North Yorkshire HG1 2JL Tel (01423) 567974 Fax (01423) 561723

Set in beautiful award-winning gardens, with the convenience of the town centre and Valley Gardens only a few minutes' walk away. We offer our guests a warm welcome and take pride in ensuring you have a pleasant and enjoyable stay with the personal attention of the owners, Rupert and Marian Viner. Excellent freshly-prepared meals. Very pretty en-suite bedrooms, two of which are situated in the Coach House – one on the ground floor.

Bed & Breakfast per night: single room from
£35.00–£40.00; double room from £50.00–£56.00
Half board per person: £38.00–£41.00 daily
Evening meal 1830 (last orders 1900)

Bedrooms: 1 single, 5 double, 2 twin, 2 triple
Bathrooms: 10 en-suite
Parking for 14
Cards accepted: Access, Visa, Amex

66 BALMORAL HOTEL & HENRY'S RESTAURANT 🌊🌊🌊 HIGHLY COMMENDED

Franklin Mount, Harrogate, North Yorkshire HG1 5EJ Tel (01423) 508208 Fax (01423) 530652

Keith and Alison Hartwell, the owners and managers, have built a reputation for providing a rather special hotel with the most desirable accommodation in Harrogate: nine four-poster bedrooms and three suites. Henry's, the award-winning restaurant, is open to non-residents and has an extensive cellar. It is ideal for business/conference dinners as it is only a three-minute walk from the Conference and Exhibition Centre. Car park available.

Bed & Breakfast per night: single room from £50.00–£83.50; double room from £65.00–£165.00
Half board per person: £50.00–£201.00 daily
Evening meal 1900 (last orders 2100)

Bedrooms: 5 single, 11 double, 4 twin
Bathrooms: 20 en-suite, 1 public
Parking for 20
Cards accepted: Access, Visa, Amex, Switch/Delta

The Pennine Way

THE PENNINE WAY, best-known and perhaps most spectacular of England's many long-distance footpaths, was officially born on 24 April 1965. At a dignified ceremony held on Malham Moor within the Yorkshire Dales National Park, a gathering of ramblers and mountaineers listened to speeches from the great and the good. One of the speakers on that notable occasion was Tom Stephenson, without whom the Pennine Way would never have been created.

An inveterate walker, he entered journalism in 1933 when he was appointed the 'open-air correspondent' of the *Daily Herald*. Two years later he was apparently asked by a couple of energetic American women to devise a walking route up the Pennine ridge. Having risen to the challenge, Tom Stephenson decided to take the idea further, and set about creating a single right of way stretching from the southern edge of the Peak District up to the border with Scotland. The problems were huge, but determination won the day.

The result is a 256-mile footpath through England's toughest territory. It has become the rambler's Everest, a two- or three-week test of endurance that no serious walker can ignore. Indeed the path has fallen victim to its own popularity, and some stretches are badly erod-

ed. Cobbles, duckboards and new routes have, with limited success, all been employed to overcome the problem. Traffic tends to be heaviest near the southern end of the route – the Peak District is the most visited national park in Britain – and if you're not intending to walk all 256 miles from Edale to Kirk Yetholm at one go, you may wish to consider sampling the attractions of the Way from the Yorkshire Dales. The 60-odd miles through the Dales offer a great variety of scenery. The path enters the area in gentle fashion in Lothersdale – a quiet valley little frequented by visitors – before following the River Aire up to the geological splendours of Malham. From here the brooding silhouettes of Pen-y-ghent, Ingleborough and Whernside soon dominate the landscape before Wensleydale and its superb waterfall (Hardraw Force) is reached. It's then up and over to the lush meadows of Swaledale before the bleaker ascent to the remote Tan Hill Inn. Walking the Pennine Way in the Dales often has the distinct advantage of allowing ramblers to use public transport, an option largely unavailable in the remoter Durham and Northumberland countryside. If you are attempting any stretch of the Pennine Way, always ensure you are equipped for a sudden and marked deterioration in the weather.

67 ACACIA LODGE

21 Ripon Road, Harrogate, North Yorkshire HG1 2JL Tel (01423) 560752 Fax (01423) 503725

Acacia Lodge is a warm, lovingly restored and charming small family-run hotel with pretty gardens in a select, central conservation area, just a short stroll from Harrogate's fashionable shops, many restaurants and attractions. It retains all of its original character, with fine furnishings, beautiful antiques and old paintings. All bedrooms are en-suite and luxuriously furnished with every comfort to facilitate the most discerning guest. Award-winning breakfasts are served in the oak-furnished dining room and guests can relax in the beautiful lounge, which has an open fire and a library of books. Private floodlit parking for all. A non-smoking establishment.

Bed & Breakfast per night: single occupancy from £32.00–£48.00; double room from £48.00–£58.00

Bedrooms: 1 double, 2 twin, 3 triple
Bathrooms: 6 en-suite
Parking for 7

---

68 RUSKIN HOTEL AND RESTAURANT

1 Swan Road, Harrogate, North Yorkshire HG1 2SS Tel (01423) 502045 Fax (01423) 506131

A truly outstanding small Victorian hotel set in lovely mature gardens (with car park) in a quiet conservation area, only five minutes stroll from the town, magnificent gardens and conference/ exhibition halls. Beautifully appointed and decorated, antique furnished en-suite bedrooms, including a four-poster and ground floor room. Gracious and relaxing drawing room with fine antiques, open fire and interesting books. Renowned for superb breakfasts and excellent English/French cuisine served in the delightful Victorian-style restaurant with bar. Our warmth and hospitality ensure your stay is 'something special'.

Bed & Breakfast per night: single room from £39.00–£54.00; double room from £59.00–£85.00
Half board per person: £53.00–£68.00 daily
Evening meal 1900 (last orders 2100)

Bedrooms: 2 single, 3 double, 2 triple
Bathrooms: 7 en-suite
Parking for 10
Cards accepted: Access, Visa

---

69 DEVONSHIRE ARMS COUNTRY HOUSE HOTEL

Bolton Abbey, Skipton, North Yorkshire BD23 6AJ Tel (01756) 710441 Fax (01756) 710564

Surrounded by the Yorkshire Dales' peace and beauty, Chatsworth antiques add to the country house atmosphere, which is complemented by refreshingly good service and an award-winning restaurant. As well as a choice of outdoor activities, themed or activity breaks, the Devonshire Club offers a range of leisure, health, beauty and therapy facilities. The Devonshire is '92, '93 and '94 Yorkshire & Humberside Tourist Board 'Hotel of the Year' and a '93 English Tourist Board Silver Award winner. ⬆ CATEGORY 3

Bed & Breakfast per night: single occupancy from £105.00–£120.00; double room from £150.00–£250.00
Half board per person: £180.00–£275.00 daily
Evening meal 1900 (last orders 2145)

Bedrooms: 22 double, 19 twin
Bathrooms: 41 en-suite
Parking for 150
Cards accepted: Access, Visa, Diners, Amex

70 THE BOAR'S HEAD COUNTRY HOTEL 🜲🜲🜲 HIGHLY COMMENDED
Ripley Castle Estate, Harrogate, North Yorkshire HG3 3AY Tel (01423) 771888 Fax (01423) 771509

Overlooking the cobbled village square, this elegant country hotel is at the heart of the historic Ripley Estate. De luxe bedrooms with king-size beds are individually designed and decorated, and the award-winning restaurant offers the best English cuisine and a fine wine selection. The bistro and pub specialise in bar meals and serve a range of hand-pulled Yorkshire and guest beers. 'Somewhere Special' guests enjoy admission to the glorious walled gardens and grounds of Ripley Castle. 🜊 CATEGORY 3

Bed & Breakfast per night: single occupancy from £80.00–£95.00; double room from £105.00–£125.00
Half board per person: £70.00–£80.00 daily
Lunch available: 1200–1430
Evening meal 1900 (last orders 2130)

Bedrooms: 5 double, 20 twin
Bathrooms: 25 en-suite
Parking for 43
Cards accepted: Access, Visa, Diners, Amex, Switch/Delta

71 JUDGES AT KIRKLEVINGTON 🜲🜲🜲🜲 HIGHLY COMMENDED
Kirklevington, Yarm, Tees Valley TS15 9LW Tel (01642) 789000 Fax (01642) 782878

Hidden within twenty two acres of rhododendron gardens and mature woodlands, with access to the A19. The charm and elegance of this family-owned and managed country house hotel is reflected throughout the twenty one comfortable bedrooms, all individually furnished to the highest standards. The renowned Judges Restaurant offers superb and varied cuisine with an opportunity to relax afterwards in the comfortable surroundings of the bar and lounge. Warming log fires burn in winter.

Bed & Breakfast per night: single room from £99.00; double room from £135.00
Half board per person: £70.00 daily; £706.00 weekly
Lunch available: 1230–1400
Evening meal 1930 (last orders 2200)

Bedrooms: 3 single, 7 double, 11 twin
Bathrooms: 21 en-suite
Parking for 100
Cards accepted: Access, Visa, Diners, Amex, Switch/Delta

72 MANOR HOUSE FARM 🜲🜲 HIGHLY COMMENDED
Ingleby Greenhow, Great Ayton, North Yorkshire TS9 6RB Tel (01642) 722384

A charming old farm (part c1760) set idyllically in 168 acres of parkland and woodland at the foot of the Cleveland Hills in the North York Moors National Park. Wildlife surrounds the farmhouse. The environment is tranquil and secluded, and the accommodation is warm and welcoming. Guests have their own entrance, dining room and lounge with library. Evening dinners are prepared meticulously and the hosts are proud of their reputation for fine food and wines.

Half board per person: £36.50–£41.00 daily; £255.50 weekly
Evening meal 1900 (last bookings 1600)

Bedrooms: 1 double, 2 twin
Bathrooms: 1 en-suite, 2 private
Parking for 6
Cards accepted: Access, Visa, Switch/Delta

73 DUNSLEY HALL

≋≋≋ HIGHLY COMMENDED

Dunsley, Whitby, North Yorkshire YO21 3TL Tel (01947) 893437 Fax (01947) 893505

An elegant country hall in four acres of grounds, three miles north of Whitby in the North Yorkshire Moors National Park. Warm and relaxing, friendly service and good food. All the rooms are en-suite with toiletries and hairdryers, full central heating and open fires; there is also an indoor heated swimming pool, sauna/solarium, gym, tennis court and putting green. An ideal touring centre for the heritage coast, moors and Captain Cook country. Renowned cuisine. Full conference facilities.

Bed & Breakfast per night: single room from £55.00–£65.00; double room from £85.00–£130.00
Half board per person: £65.00–£85.00 daily
Lunch available: 1230–1400
Evening meal 1900 (last orders 2100)

Bedrooms: 1 single, 15 double, 4 twin
Bathrooms: 20 en-suite
Parking for 40
Cards accepted: Access, Visa, Amex, Switch/Delta

---

74 BURR BANK COTTAGE

≋≋≋ HIGHLY COMMENDED

Cropton, Pickering, North Yorkshire YO18 8HL Tel (01751) 417777 Fax (01751) 417789

A quarter mile from the village and set in forty five acres, with wonderful views over Cropton Forest and Moors. Comfortable and spacious ground-floor accommodation. Noted for personal attention to detail. Will provide an interesting, peaceful holiday with easy access to the coast, Moors, Wolds, Howardian Hills and York. Much to do and see using Burr Bank as your home for a while. We hope you enjoy our part of Yorkshire as much as we do. No smoking.

Bed & Breakfast per night: single occupancy £21.00; double room £42.00
Half board per person: £33.00 daily; £210.00 weekly
Evening meal 1900 (last orders 1900)

Bedrooms: 1 double, 1 twin
Bathrooms: 2 en-suite
Parking for 10

---

75 WREA HEAD COUNTRY HOTEL

≋≋≋≋ HIGHLY COMMENDED

Barmoor Lane, Scalby, Scarborough, North Yorkshire YO13 0PB Tel (01723) 378211 or (01723) 371780

Situated in fourteen acres of wooded and landscaped gardens, Wrea Head retains all the character and charm of a traditional country house, and offers peace and luxurious surroundings, ideal for long or short breaks. The award-winning Four Seasons restaurant offers outstanding cuisine, complemented by a first class wine list. All bedrooms are individually furnished to the highest standard, with de luxe and suites available.

Bed & Breakfast per night: single room from £57.50–£67.50; double room from £95.00–£165.00
Half board per person: £57.50–£82.50 daily; £300.00–£450.00 weekly
Lunch available: 1200–1400

Evening meal 1900 (last orders 2115)
Bedrooms: 4 single, 8 double, 6 twin, 1 triple, 2 family rooms
Bathrooms: 21 en-suite
Parking for 101
Cards accepted: Access, Visa, Diners, Amex, Switch/Delta

At-a-glance symbols are explained on the flap inside the back cover

76 OLD FARMHOUSE COUNTRY HOTEL & RESTAURANT 👑👑👑 HIGHLY COMMENDED

Raskelf, York YO6 3LF Tel (01347) 821971 Fax (01347) 822392

An old farmhouse, this small comfortable hotel is ideally situated for the Moors, Dales and York, which is just fourteen miles south. A warm welcome from the resident chef/proprietors, who will provide you with huge Yorkshire breakfasts, home baked bread, splendid dinners, a speciality English cheese board, fine wines, malt whiskies and en-suite rooms with central heating, television, direct dial phone and hospitality tray. Short Winter Breaks at reduced rates available. Ring for a brochure and sample menu.

Bed & Breakfast per night: single occupancy from £27.00–£31.00; double room from £46.00–£54.00
Half board per person: £38.00–£42.00 daily; £266.00–£280.00 weekly
Evening meal 1900 (last orders 2030)

Bedrooms: 6 double, 2 twin, 2 triple
Bathrooms: 10 en-suite
Parking for 12
Open: February–December

77 SPROXTON HALL 〰〰 HIGHLY COMMENDED

Sproxton, Helmsley, North Yorkshire YO6 5EQ Tel (01439) 770225 Fax (01439) 771373

Relax in the tranquil atmosphere and comfort of our 17th-century Grade II listed farmhouse. Magnificent views over idyllic countryside on a 300-acre working farm, one mile south of the market town of Helmsley. Lovingly and tastefully furnished, giving the cosy elegance of a country home. Restful, oak-beamed drawing room with log fire. Enjoy a hearty breakfast in a most attractive dining room. Extremely comfortable, centrally heated double and twin bedrooms. En-suite or private bathrooms, tea making facilities, remote control colour television. Guests' laundry facilities. Delightful country garden to relax in. No smoking.

Bed & Breakfast per night: double room from £38.00–£48.00

Bedrooms: 2 double, 1 twin
Bathrooms: 1 en-suite, 2 private, 1 public
Parking for 10

78 GREENACRES COUNTRY GUEST HOUSE 👑👑 HIGHLY COMMENDED

Amotherby, Malton, North Yorkshire YO17 0TG Tel (01653) 693623 Fax (01653) 693623

A quiet country guesthouse set in over two-and-a-half acres of gardens and woodlands, with an indoor heated swimming pool. All the bedrooms are en-suite with colour television, tea making and hairdryers. Situated in central Ryedale, it is an ideal base for York, the North Yorkshire Moors and the east coast. Colour brochure and details on request. Closed mid-November to March.

Bed & Breakfast per night: single room from £24.25–£27.50; double room from £48.50–£55.00
Half board per person: £35.00–£39.75 daily; £232.50 weekly
Evening meal 1900 (last orders 1900)

Bedrooms: 1 single, 3 double, 3 twin, 1 triple, 1 family room
Bathrooms: 9 en-suite
Parking for 15
Open: March–November
Cards accepted: Access, Visa

79 NEWSTEAD GRANGE

〰〰〰 HIGHLY COMMENDED

Norton, Malton, North Yorkshire YO17 9PJ Tel (01653) 692502 Fax (01653) 696951

The Grange is an elegant Georgian country house set in two-and-a-half acres of gardens and grounds with delightful views of the North Yorkshire Moors and Wolds. The style of the house is tastefully enhanced by antique furniture, open log fires burn in cooler weather and the bedrooms are individually furnished. The proprietors personally prepare the award-winning meals with produce from the organic kitchen garden and fresh local produce to a very high standard. Totally non-smoking.

Bed & Breakfast per night: single occupancy from £32.50–£41.00; double room from £57.00–£72.00
Half board per person: £41.00–£51.00 daily; £265.00–£290.00 weekly
Evening meal 1930 (last orders 1930)

Bedrooms: 4 double, 4 twin
Bathrooms: 8 en-suite
Parking for 15
Open: February–November
Cards accepted: Access, Visa

---

80 THE DOWNCLIFFE HOUSE HOTEL

〰〰〰 HIGHLY COMMENDED

The Beach, Filey, North Yorkshire YO14 9LA Tel (01723) 513310 Fax (01723) 516141

Tastefully refurbished to recapture its former Victorian glory, but with all the comforts expected by today's discerning customer: luxury en-suite bedrooms with panoramic sea views; attractively designed restaurant and bar overlooking Filey Bay; extensive breakfast choice and evening meals prepared from the finest produce ...and most of all, peace and quiet. If you want to get away from it all and relax, this is the place to be!

Bed & Breakfast per night: single room from £27.00–£35.00; double room from £54.00–£70.00
Half board per person: £37.00–£49.00 daily; £245.00–£280.00 weekly
Evening meal 1830 (last orders 2100)

Bedrooms: 1 single, 6 double, 1 twin, 1 triple, 1 family room
Bathrooms: 10 en-suite
Parking for 10
Open: February–December
Cards accepted: Access, Visa, Switch/Delta

---

81 THE MANOR COUNTRY HOUSE

〰〰〰 HIGHLY COMMENDED

Acaster Malbis, York YO2 1UL Tel (01904) 706723 Fax (01904) 706723

Family-run manor house in rural tranquillity, with private lake, set in five-and-a-half acres of beautiful mature grounds on the banks of the River Ouse. Fish in the lake, cycle or walk. Close to race-course and only a ten-minute car journey from the city – or take the leisurely river bus (Easter to October). Conveniently situated to take advantage of the Dales, Moors, Wolds and splendid coastline. Cosy lounge and licensed lounge bar with open fire. Conservatory dining room with Aga-cooked food.

Bed & Breakfast per night: single occupancy from £36.00–£40.00; double room from £45.00–£56.00
Evening meal 1900 (last orders 2030)

Bedrooms: 5 double, 2 twin, 3 triple
Bathrooms: 10 en-suite
Parking for 15

82 YORK PAVILION HOTEL

 HIGHLY COMMENDED

45 Main Street, Fulford, York YO1 4PJ Tel (01904) 622099 Fax (01904) 626939

Situated just two miles from the city centre, this privately-owned and run Georgian hotel, with the atmosphere of an English country house, offers charming relaxed and unpretentious accommodation. Quality food cooked with fresh local ingredients and an extensive wine list at sensible prices. The bedrooms are all individually designed with en-suite bathrooms. Car parking within mature grounds.

Bed & Breakfast per night: single occupancy from £84.00–£94.00; double room from £106.00–£120.00
Half board per person: £57.00–£65.00 daily
Lunch available: 1230–1400
Evening meal 1830 (last bookings 1400)

Bedrooms: 22 double, 10 twin, 2 family rooms
Bathrooms: 34 en-suite
Parking for 45
Cards accepted: Access, Visa, Diners, Amex, Switch/Delta

---

83 ARNDALE HOTEL

 HIGHLY COMMENDED

290 Tadcaster Road, York YO2 2ET Tel (01904) 702424

A delightful Victorian house overlooking York's famous race-course with beautiful enclosed walled gardens giving a country house atmosphere within the city. The spacious elegant lounge, complete with antiques, fresh flowers, paintings and a small bar, exudes the charm of a bygone age. The outstanding, thoughtfully-equipped bedrooms are all en-suite. Many bathrooms are Victorian with modern whirlpool baths. Antique half-tester/four-poster beds give an aura of nostalgic luxury. Substantial English breakfast. Large enclosed walled car park.

Bed & Breakfast per night: double room from £49.00–£59.00

Bedrooms: 7 double, 2 twin, 1 triple
Bathrooms: 10 en-suite
Parking for 20

---

84 DEAN COURT HOTEL

 HIGHLY COMMENDED

Duncombe Place, York YO1 2EF Tel (01904) 625082 Fax (01904) 620305

Superbly situated in the shadow of York Minster, the hotel has an unrivalled position in the heart of York. This historic city's main attractions are within walking distance and many tours to Castle Howard, the Moors and Dales can be arranged by the hotel. Renowned for very friendly service, it boasts an elegant restaurant offering excellent modern food and a delightful Tea-room Conservatory as well as comfortable lounges. Secure car park with valet parking service.

Bed & Breakfast per night: single room from £75.00–£85.00; double room from £110.00–£145.00
Half board per person: £57.00–£69.50 daily
Lunch available: 1230–1400
Evening meal 1900 (last orders 2130)

Bedrooms: 18 single, 8 double, 10 twin, 3 triple, 2 family rooms
Bathrooms: 41 en-suite
Parking for 30
Cards accepted: Access, Visa, Diners, Amex, Switch/Delta

85 4 SOUTH PARADE

 HIGHLY COMMENDED

York YO2 2BA Tel (01904) 628229 Fax (01904) 628229

Robin and Anne McClure welcome you to their home, with hospitality that is professional but personal. Everything is done to make you feel comfortable and relaxed by providing fine food in a luxurious and homely atmosphere. Number 4 is part of an elegant Georgian terrace in a private cobbled street in the centre of York. Beautifully restored with three impeccably furnished guest rooms, Edwardian-style en-suite facilities, original working fireplaces, fresh flowers and bowls of fruit.

Bed & Breakfast per night: single occupancy from
£63.00–£73.00; double room from £73.00–£93.00

Bedrooms: 1 double, 2 twin
Bathrooms: 3 en-suite, 1 public
Parking for 3

---

86 EASTONS

 HIGHLY COMMENDED

90 Bishopthorpe Road, York YO2 1JS Tel (01904) 626646

A former Victorian wine merchant's residence, ideally located three hundred yards from the city walls. William Morris decor, period furniture, marble fireplaces, original paintings, imaginative and generous 'Victorian sideboard' breakfast menu – kippers, kidneys, kedgeree and more. Fully equipped en-suite bedrooms. Eastons provides a standard of style and comfort not normally associated with bed and breakfast, but which is in accord with the standard of excellence that the owners strive for. Yorkshire & Humberside Tourist Board 'Bed & Breakfast of the Year' Winner, 1996.

Bed & Breakfast per night: single occupancy from
£31.00–£46.00; double room from £37.00–£66.00

Bedrooms: 7 double, 2 twin, 1 family room
Bathrooms: 10 en-suite
Parking for 8
Cards accepted: Access, Visa

---

87 JUDGES LODGING

 HIGHLY COMMENDED

9 Lendal, York YO1 2AQ Tel (01904) 623587 or (01904) 638733 Fax (01904) 679947

This early Georgian townhouse, built c1710 and formerly the residence of the Assize court judges, is a Grade I listed building of architectural and historical importance. Set in the very heart of the city, it provides an excellent base to explore the historic city of York. The hotel has thirteen en-suite individually furnished rooms, some with four-poster beds, and its own secure private parking for residents. Enjoy lunch and dinner in the elegant brasserie.

Bed & Breakfast per night: single room from
£70.00–£75.00; double room from £95.00–£135.00
Half board per person: £85.00–£90.00 daily;
£350.00–£525.00 weekly
Lunch available: 1145–1415

Evening meal 1830 (last orders 2130)
Bedrooms: 2 single, 6 double, 3 twin, 2 triple
Bathrooms: 13 en-suite
Parking for 12
Cards accepted: Access, Visa, Diners, Amex, Switch/Delta

88 HOLMWOOD HOUSE HOTEL

≋≋ HIGHLY COMMENDED

112-114 Holgate Road, York YO2 4BB   Tel (01904) 626183 Fax (01904) 670899

Close to the city walls, an elegant listed Victorian town house offering a feeling of home with a touch of luxury. All the en-suite bedrooms are different in size and decoration, some with four-poster beds and one has a spa bath; all rooms are non-smoking. Imaginative breakfasts are served to the sound of gentle classical music. The inviting sitting room, with its open fire, highlights the period style of the house. Car park. On the A59.

Bed & Breakfast per night: single occupancy from £35.00–£55.00; double room from £45.00–£70.00
Half board per person: from £47.50 daily

Bedrooms: 10 double, 1 twin, 1 triple
Bathrooms: 12 en-suite
Parking for 9
Cards accepted: Access, Visa, Amex, Switch/Delta

89 CURZON LODGE AND STABLE COTTAGES

≋≋ HIGHLY COMMENDED

23 Tadcaster Road, Dringhouses, York YO2 2QG Tel (01904) 703157

A charming, early 17th-century former farmhouse and stables in a conservation area overlooking York's 'Knavesmire' race-course, close to the historic heart of the city. Once a home of the Terry 'chocolate' family, guests are now invited to share the relaxed atmosphere in ten comfortably furnished en-suite rooms, some with four-posters or period brass beds. Country antiques, books, magazines, maps, local information, fresh flowers and sherry in our cosy sitting room contribute to the traditional English house ambience. Friendly and informal. Delicious breakfasts. Enclosed parking within grounds.

Bed & Breakfast per night: single room from £30.00–£40.00; double room from £45.00–£60.00

Bedrooms: 1 single, 4 double, 3 twin, 1 triple, 1 family room
Bathrooms: 10 en-suite
Parking for 16
Cards accepted: Access, Visa

90 THE GRANGE HOTEL

≋≋≋≋ HIGHLY COMMENDED

1 Clifton, York YO3 6AA Tel (01904) 644744 Fax (01904) 612453

Exclusive classical Regency townhouse, situated close to the heart of this historic city, within easy walking distance of York Minster and the ancient walls. Elegantly furnished in country house style, with fresh flowers and open fires in the cooler months, The Grange is the perfect place to relax and unwind. Enjoy a leisurely lunch or intimate dinner in one of our three restaurants. Choose from the classical Ivy, the Dom Ruinart Seafood Bar or the informal Brasserie – each venue offering its own distinctive atmosphere, excellent service and a superb choice of food and wine.

Bed & Breakfast per night: single room £95.00; double room from £105.00–£185.00
Half board per person: £75.00–£115.00 daily
Lunch available: 1200–1400
Evening meal 1800 (last orders 2230)

Bedrooms: 3 single, 9 double, 17 twin, 1 triple
Bathrooms: 30 en-suite
Parking for 26
Cards accepted: Access, Visa, Diners, Amex, Switch/Delta

91 THE OLD RECTORY

≋≋≋ HIGHLY COMMENDED

Cowlam, Driffield, East Riding of Yorkshire YO25 0AD   Tel (01377) 267617   Fax (01377) 267403

A Victorian rectory set in the traditional Riding of East Yorkshire. Enjoy the unspoilt market towns and historic houses, as well as the Minster cities of York and Beverley. We offer classic good food, log fires and elegant en-suite rooms in the heart of the unspoilt countryside and within easy reach of the coast. For our brochure and sample menus of our four-course dinners, please ring 01377 267617.

Bed & Breakfast per night: double room from
£51.00–£55.00
Half board per person: £42.00–£44.00 daily
Evening meal 1900–2000

Bedrooms: 1 double, 2 twin
Bathrooms: 2 en-suite, 1 private
Parking for 11

The Humber Bridge

WHEN DANIEL DEFOE was travelling the length and breadth of early 18th-century England, he spent four unpleasant hours crossing the Humber from Barton to Hull. He complained that the boat was open to the elements, and that the weather frequently made the journey extremely perilous. When the railways arrived in 1848 and moved the ferry terminus to nearby New Holland, Barton's very *raison d'être* had gone. For well over a hundred years the world seemed to pass Barton-upon-Humber by.

The town's fortunes looked up, however, in 1959 when Parliament granted permission for the construction of a road bridge over the Humber. Fourteen long years later work began and, after various setbacks, the Humber Bridge opened to traffic on 24 June 1981. The estimate for the construction of both bridge and approach roads was £28 million; at £98 million the actual cost was three-and-a-half times the original prediction. Although the bridge is still burdened with debt, Barton-upon-Humber has recently enjoyed something of a boom, making the most of its new-found proximity to Hull.

With a central span of almost a mile (4,626ft) and a total length of approaching a mile and a half, it remains the longest single unsupported section of any bridge in the world, though longer spans are currently under construction. Just as remarkable as the bridge's length are the string of other statistics that such civil-engineering projects always foster. The concrete weighs in at 470,000 tons, while the whole structure totals a staggering half a billion tons. The carriageway reaches a height of 100ft above high water, with the towers another 400ft taller. Despite their weight, these towers are hollow, each one containing an electric lift within one of its twin 'legs'. The two cables that support the entire carriageway are made from 15,000 parallel galvanised drawn-steel wires, each of a diameter of about one-fifth of an inch. There are now about six million vehicle crossings a year, roughly twice as many as when the bridge first opened.

Facilities for the visitor include viewing areas at both ends of the bridge; the northern end also has a tourist information centre (tel: 01482 640852) and country park. Views of and from the bridge are magnificent, and you can choose whether to enjoy them by driving, cycling or walking across.

92 MANOR HOUSE

Newbald Road, Northlands, Walkington, Beverley, East Riding of Yorkshire HU17 8RT Tel (01482) 881645 Fax (01482) 866501

The Manor House is set amidst rolling countryside and landscaped gardens within easy reach of Beverley. Serious "foodie" restaurant with friendly efficient service. The area is surrounded by historic houses, local museums and many other tourist attractions, with Scarborough and York being easily accessible.

Bed & Breakfast per night: single occupancy from £73.50–£83.50; double room from £83.50–£117.00
Evening meal 1930 (last orders 2115)

Bedrooms: 6 double, 1 family room
Bathrooms: 7 en-suite
Parking for 50
Cards accepted: Access, Visa, Switch/Delta

Wakefield Rhubarb

IN SPRING, SUPERMARKETS throughout the country are stocked with a crop which was once the pride of many a cottage garden and is now undergoing something of a renaissance in restaurant popularity – rhubarb. The chances are that the succulent pink stalks which end up in your shopping basket were pulled from a plant growing somewhere near Wakefield, for this is where a large proportion of the country's rhubarb is grown.

A hundred years ago an area stretching between Wakefield, Leeds and Morley, often known as the 'rhubarb triangle', was the world centre of rhubarb growing. At the height of its popularity in the 1930s over 4,000 acres were under cultivation. Today that figure is only 750 acres, but Wakefield still prides itself on being the country's rhubarb capital. The national rhubarb collection is kept just north of 'the triangle' at the Harlow Carr Botanic Gardens, near Harrogate, and consists of 150 or so different varieties.

Although regarded as one of the most English of desserts, rhubarb probably originated in China, where it has been used for medicinal purposes for almost 5,000 years. Its purgative properties are well-known, but it has also been claimed as a miracle cure for a whole variety of other ailments, from poisonous animal bites to venereal disease. It only took off as a culinary delicacy in England in the early 19th-century.

Rhubarb is technically a vegetable rather than a fruit in that, like celery, the stalks of the plant are consumed. The first, tender shoots of the spring have the sweetest flavour and so the practice has developed of covering the plants in winter and surrounding them with warm straw to 'force' them into early growth. Much of Wakefield's rhubarb is grown in forcing sheds, now artificially heated to bring the crops to fruition as early as Christmas. Some growers still insist on picking by candle light to ensure maximum darkness for the crop.

It is possible to arrange group tours of the rhubarb growing areas and forcing sheds by calling 01924 305841. The dedicated horticulturalist may inspect the national rhubarb collection at Harlow Carr Gardens (tel: 01423 565418) while the acres of rhubarb plants growing to the north of Wakefield, fleshy leaves dark, glossy and shoulder-high by late spring, are visible for all to see.

93 BRIGGATE LODGE INN

 HIGHLY COMMENDED

Ermine Street, Broughton, Brigg, Scunthorpe, North Lincolnshire DN20 0NQ Tel (01652) 650770 Fax (01652) 650495

Superbly located for all business and pleasure needs. Nestling amid an idyllic landscape of two hundred acres of wooded parkland, the hotel is a haven for those who enjoy being pampered. Easily accessible from the motorway system, Lincoln, Hull and York are within easy reach. International cuisine is served in the elegant Beech Tree Restaurant. Extensive table d'hôte and à la carte menus are available daily. For those who prefer more casual dining, the Buttery and Grill is open all day, every day, for drinks and bar meals. Forest Pines, a new 27-hole Championship Golf Course set in mature woodland, is now open for fantastic golfing breaks.

Bed & Breakfast per night: single room from
£45.00–£74.00; double room from £55.00–£82.00
Half board per person: £60.50–£89.50 daily;
£335.50–£539.50 weekly
Lunch available: 1200–1400 (plus bar meals all day)

Evening meal 1900 (last orders 2200)
Bedrooms: 2 single, 41 double, 7 twin
Bathrooms: 50 en-suite
Parking for 220
Cards accepted: Access, Visa, Diners, Amex, Switch/Delta

94 WENTBRIDGE HOUSE HOTEL

HIGHLY COMMENDED

Wentbridge, Pontefract, West Yorkshire WF8 3JJ Tel (01977) 620444 Fax (01977) 620148

Dating from 1700 and situated in twenty acres of the beautiful Went Valley among century-old trees, Wentbridge House is within easy reach of the M62 and A1. A traditional open fireplace and a fine collection of Meissen porcelain welcome you to the cocktail bar. The Fleur de Lys Restaurant, with its international ambience and Master Sommelier, attracts cosmopolitan lovers of food and wine. Individually furnished bedrooms include the Oakroom with its Mouseman four-poster bed.

Bed & Breakfast per night: single room from
£65.00–£85.00; double room from £75.00–£95.00
Half board per person: £57.25–£67.25 daily
Lunch available: 1215–1400
Evening meal 1930 (last orders 2130)

Bedrooms: 2 single, 12 double, 4 twin
Bathrooms: 18 en-suite
Parking for 100
Cards accepted: Access, Visa, Diners, Amex

95 WHITLEY HALL HOTEL

HIGHLY COMMENDED

Elliott Lane, Grenoside, Sheffield, South Yorkshire S30 3NR Tel (0114) 245 4444 Fax (0114) 245 5414

Whitley Hall dates from the 16th-century and is a lovely country house standing in its own thirty acres of gardens, woodland and lakes. Privately owned as a hotel for over twenty five years, we offer accommodation, food and service of the highest quality and in the best English tradition. This popular country hotel is ideally situated between the Yorkshire Dales and Derbyshire Peak District and only a few minutes from Sheffield's theatres, sports facilities and magnificent Meadowhall shopping complex.

Bed & Breakfast per night: single room from
£62.00–£78.00; double room from £83.00–£99.00
Half board per person: £61.00–£98.00 daily
Lunch available: 1200–1400
Evening meal 1900 (last orders 2130)

Bedrooms: 2 single, 8 double, 7 twin, 1 family room
Bathrooms: 18 en-suite
Parking for 100
Cards accepted: Access, Visa, Diners, Amex,
Switch/Delta

96 MOORFIELD HOUSE

 HIGHLY COMMENDED

Oxford Road, Gomersal, Cleckheaton, West Yorkshire BD19 4HD Tel (01274) 870611 or 0850 460959

An elegant Victorian residence set in secluded gardens and adjoining open farmland, yet close to the M62/M1, Leeds, Bradford, Dewsbury and Huddersfield. Joan and Bryan Webb look forward to welcoming you to their small but delightful hotel, with its warm, peaceful and friendly atmosphere. Their dining room offers home cooking of the highest standard, using fresh and home-grown produce. All bedrooms are beautifully furnished. Private car park. Jaegar Mill Shop within one mile.

Bed & Breakfast per night: single room from £35.50–£39.50; double room from £53.00–£58.00
Half board per person: £38.50–£51.50 daily; £250.00–£325.00 weekly
Evening meal 1900 (last orders 2030)

Bedrooms: 1 single, 2 double
Bathrooms: 3 en-suite
Parking for 8
Cards accepted: Access, Visa

97 FIVE RISE LOCKS HOTEL

 HIGHLY COMMENDED

Beck Lane, Bingley, West Yorkshire BD16 4DD Tel (01274) 565296 Fax (01274) 568828

Built for a wealthy Victorian mill owner, the house stands in mature gardens overlooking the Aire valley, yet is only a few minutes' walk away from the Five Rise Locks and Bingley town centre. Each en-suite bedroom has a unique view and has been individually designed and furnished. Enjoy home cooking prepared with intelligence and imagination and wines from a well-chosen list in elegant, yet comfortable, surroundings. Experience Haworth – the Brontës, Esholt village, steam trains, museums and tranquil, vast open spaces.

Bed & Breakfast per night: single occupancy from £32.50–£50.00; double room from £46.00–£60.00
Half board per person: £34.00–£57.00 daily
Evening meal 1930 (last orders 2030)

Bedrooms: 7 double, 2 twin
Bathrooms: 9 en-suite
Parking for 15
Cards accepted: Access, Visa, Switch/Delta

98 NEW CAPERNWRAY FARM

HIGHLY COMMENDED

Capernwray, Carnforth, Lancashire LA6 1AD Tel (01524) 734284 Fax (01524) 734284

An ideal London-to-Scotland stop, three miles from Junction 35/M6 in beautiful countryside, between the Lake District and Yorkshire Dales. High quality accommodation in an award-winning 17th-century Grade II listed former farmhouse, renowned for its warm hospitality, peace, comfort and excellent candle-lit dinners (unlicensed, please bring own wine). Delightful, fully-equipped, non-smoking bedrooms with private or en-suite facilities. Personally conducted tours to the Lake District, Yorkshire Dales and Hadrian's Wall. Brochure available. ETB's 1993 Best Bed & Breakfast in Lancashire. North West Tourism Award for Excellence: 'Bed & Breakfast of the Year' 1994.

Bed & Breakfast per night: single occupancy from £37.00–£42.00; double room from £54.00–£64.00
Half board per person: £46.50–£51.50 daily
Evening meal 1930

Bedrooms: 2 double, 1 twin
Bathrooms: 2 en-suite, 1 private
Parking for 4
Cards accepted: Access, Visa

99 MIDDLE HOLLY COTTAGE

≋≋≋ HIGHLY COMMENDED

Middle Holly Lane, Forton, Preston, Lancashire PR3 1AH Tel (01524) 792399

Originally a coaching inn on the main route north into Scotland, the cottage was re-designed and refurbished in 1990 from a working farm to provide superior accommodation for tourist and business people alike. The cottage has a quiet, peaceful, countryside outlook, is close to the historic city of Lancaster, on the fringe of the wonderful Forest of Bowland, is only minutes from nearby coastal resorts and thirty minutes away from the Lake District.

Bed & Breakfast per night: single room from £26.50–£32.50; double room from £39.50–£45.50
Evening meal 1800 (last orders 2030)

Bedrooms: 1 single, 2 double, 1 twin, 1 triple
Bathrooms: 5 en-suite
Parking for 10
Cards accepted: Access, Visa

Lowry's Lancashire

THE LANCASHIRE ARTIST Laurence Stephen Lowry (1887–1976) has become immortalised as the painter of matchstick men. He did indeed paint figures in a stylised, rather stick-like manner, but he painted much more besides. Above all he was a painter of the industrial scene, realising early in his career that no other artist in the world had seen this as a fit subject for serious art, and tackling it in his own inimitable and very distinctive style.

Lowry lived all his life in the industrial north, never moving far from Manchester, and living longest at Pendlebury on the city's north-western fringe. He was an enigmatic, reclusive character, living with his parents until they died, and maintaining a close secrecy in artistic circles about his working life as a clerk and rent collector. As Lowry said of himself and his family, 'We were cold fish'. Lowry showed little interest in art as a boy, but from the age of 18 took evening classes at the Manchester Municipal College where his drawing skills soon attracted attention.

From the start he drew his subject matter from his immediate environment: his family and home, holidays at the seaside with his parents, and above all his local area. Pendlebury was a district of looming coal mines and cotton mills which swallowed workers at the start of each day and spat them out at the end. At first repulsed by these scenes, Lowry eventually became fascinated by them. His most famous paintings are often composites of places he knew: factory gates, belching chimneys, towering mills, all populated by workers reduced and dehumanised into tiny stylised figures, dwarfed by the vast industrial monuments around them.

By the 1920s Lowry's paintings were attracting critical acclaim from an art establishment who found them a refreshing alternative to abstraction. One of the first galleries to appreciate his talent was close to home, at Salford. As his success grew it frequently exhibited his work and over the years the Salford Art Gallery (tel: 0161-736 2649) bought many of his paintings and drawings. He donated still more, and today the Salford collection is the best in the world. Over 150 of his works are on permanent display there, and together they convey the great range of his work, from early art-school drawings to the lesser known seascapes and 'lonely landscapes' of his later years.

100 OLDE DUNCOMBE HOUSE

 HIGHLY COMMENDED

Garstang Road, Bilsborrow, Preston, Lancashire PR3 0RE Tel (01995) 640336

A traditional, family-run, cottage-styled bed and breakfast offering a high standard of accommodation with all the rooms en-suite, plus many extra facilities and ideal for business people and tourists. Situated alongside the tranquil Lancaster Waterway, you can enjoy the picturesque scenery on our exclusive charter boat with a full bar for a simple cruise or a champagne buffet party (maximum 12 people). Charter boat not included in bed and breakfast price. All rooms can be used for single occupancy.

Bed & Breakfast per night: single room from £29.50–£35.00; double room from £39.50–£49.50
Evening meal 1800 (last orders 2030)

Bedrooms: 2 single, 4 double, 2 twin, 1 triple
Bathrooms: 9 en-suite
Parking for 12
Cards accepted: Access, Visa, Amex

101 HERON LODGE

HIGHLY COMMENDED

8 Bolton Road, Edgworth, Bolton, Greater Manchester BL7 0DS Tel (01204) 852262 Fax (01204) 852262

Beautiful Victorian house, in its own grounds, with views of the garden and river. Nestling in the Jumbles Country Park on the West Pennine Moors. With original beams and inglenook fireplace. For comfort, we offer Victorian brass beds covered with pretty lace linen. Traditional furniture. En-suite bathrooms. Ideal for business or pleasure. Within easy reach of Blackburn, Bolton, Bury and Manchester. Easy access to motorways.

Bed & Breakfast per night: single occupancy from £26.00–£32.00; double room from £40.00–£50.00

Bedrooms: 2 double, 1 twin
Bathrooms: 2 en-suite, 1 private, 1 public
Parking for 6

102 STUTELEA HOTEL AND LEISURE CLUB

HIGHLY COMMENDED

Alexandra Road, Southport, Merseyside PR9 0NB Tel (01704) 544220 Fax (01704) 500232 E-mail stutelea@cybase.co.uk

A charming hotel offering excellent cuisine and hospitality, recently refurbished to a high standard and some rooms now have balconies overlooking gardens. Extensive leisure facilities including swimming pool, jacuzzi, sauna, steam room, gymnasium, solariums, treatment room and games room. Two licensed bars, restaurant, library, lift, gardens, and car park. "Lets Go" special short breaks: £90.00 per person DB&B any two days, sharing twin or double room.

Bed & Breakfast per night: single room from £50.00–£55.00; double room from £75.00–£80.00
Half board per person: £45.00 daily; £315.00 weekly
Evening meal 1900 (last orders 2100)

Bedrooms: 2 single, 8 double, 9 twin, 3 triple
Bathrooms: 22 en-suite, 4 public
Parking for 16
Cards accepted: Access, Visa, Diners, Amex, Switch/Delta

103 **PRESCOTT'S FARM** RESTAURANT AND COUNTRY MOTEL ♛♛♛ HIGHLY COMMENDED
Lees Lane, Dalton, Wigan, Lancashire WN8 7RB Tel (01257) 464137

Originally a 16th-century farmhouse, each of our bedrooms has a separate entrance from the cobbled path opposite the restaurant that serves classical Italian and French cuisine in a delightful atmosphere. Personally supervised by the proprietors, we are ideally located in two acres of peaceful gardens and orchards, and have five luxury en-suite bedrooms. Seven minutes from Junction 27/M6.

Bed & Breakfast per night: single room £45.00; double room from £65.00–£70.00
Lunch available: 1200–1330
Evening meal 1830 (last orders 2200)

Bedrooms: 2 single, 2 double, 1 twin
Bathrooms: 5 en-suite
Parking for 25
Cards accepted: Access, Visa, Amex

The National Lawnmower Collection

THE NAMES OF ROLLS ROYCE, Hawker Siddley, Royal Enfield and Daimler all speak eloquently of English engineering excellence. One might expect to see examples of their achievements collected together in, perhaps, the Science Museum. But it comes as something of a surprise to the uninitiated that all these companies have, in their time, produced lawnmowers, and that there is a small museum dedicated to the display of these grass-cutting machines.

The British Lawnmower Museum (tel: 01704 501336) resides in the seaside resort of Southport, Merseyside, perhaps better known for its annual flower show (the largest summer flower show in the country) and its 7-mile beach. The museum's prized exhibits include machines dating from the early 19th-century, mowers once belonging to Nicholas Parsons and to Prince Charles, another capable of cutting a 2-inch wide strip, and what is believed to be the only hand-powered rotary lawnmower in existence. Also on view is the world's largest collection of toy mowers as well as one of the oldest surviving racing lawnmowers (built by the curator).

104 VICTORIA AND ALBERT HOTEL

 HIGHLY COMMENDED

Water Street, Manchester M3 4JQ Tel (0161) 832 1188 Fax (0161) 834 2484

We are a luxury hotel situated in the city centre of Manchester. The hotel has 156 luxuriously appointed bedrooms, plus two superb but completely different restaurants. Close by are all the amenities that Manchester has on offer: shops, theatres and tourist attractions. What better place to combine pleasure with business, or indeed just have the pleasure of staying at the Victoria and Albert. ⚹ CATEGORY 1

Bed & Breakfast per night: single room from
£85.00–£146.95; double room from £95.00–£168.90
Lunch available: 1200–1400
Evening meal 1900 (last orders 2200)

Bedrooms: 14 single, 96 double, 22 twin
Bathrooms: 132 en-suite
Parking for 167
Cards accepted: Access, Visa, Diners, Amex

105 YORK HOUSE HOTEL

HIGHLY COMMENDED

York Place, Off Richmond Street, Ashton-under-Lyne, Lancashire OL6 7TT Tel (0161) 330 5899 Fax (0161) 343 1613

Situated in a peaceful tree-lined cul-de-sac, close to the A635/A6107 junction.This very well-maintained family-run hotel has thirty-four well kept en-suite bedrooms set around a courtyard and a garden that has won two 'Britain in Bloom' competitions. The hotel's restaurant has an excellent reputation. Keith Absolom has owned the hotel for over twenty two years and the care and attention to his guests is to be found throughout the hotel.

Bed & Breakfast per night: single room from
£49.00–£58.00; double room from £72.00–£75.00
Half board per person: £66.00–£75.00 daily
Lunch available: 1200–1345
Evening meal 1900 (last orders 2130)

Bedrooms: 8 single, 19 double, 5 twin, 2 triple
Bathrooms: 34 en-suite
Parking for 36
Cards accepted: Access, Visa, Diners, Amex,
Switch/Delta

106 STANNEYLANDS HOTEL

HIGHLY COMMENDED

Stanneylands Road, Wilmslow, Cheshire SK9 4EY Tel (01625) 525225 Fax (01625) 537282

A strikingly handsome country house hotel set in beautiful gardens. With open fires and oak-panelled dining rooms, hospitality abounds on every hand. Stanneylands offers the very finest of English and International cuisine, prepared and served with pride and care. Ideally located for visiting Styal Mill, Jodrell Bank, Tatton Park and Bramall Hall.

Bed & Breakfast per night: single room from
£40.00–£115.00; double room from £60.00–£115.00
Lunch available: 1230–1430
Evening meal 1900 (last orders 2230)

Bedrooms: 7 single, 11 double, 14 twin
Bathrooms: 32 en-suite
Parking for 80
Cards accepted: Access, Visa, Diners, Amex,
Switch/Delta

107 BRERETON HOUSE

DE LUXE

Mill Lane, Brereton, Holmes Chapel, Cheshire CW4 8AU Tel (01477) 534511 Fax (01477) 544149

Award-winning Brereton House is a country haven of luxury and comfort with superbly equipped en-suite bedrooms, all individually furnished and decorated to a high standard. Crystal and candle light set the atmosphere for delicious and imaginative meals served in the elegant dining room. Set in gardens amidst open farmland, yet only a few minutes from Junctions 17 and 18/M6, Brereton House is well situated for touring many Cheshire and National Trust attractions. Strictly no smoking.

Bed & Breakfast per night: single room from £35.00–£50.00; double room from £55.00–£70.00
Half board per person: £51.00–£66.00 daily
Evening meal 2000 (last bookings 1930)

Bedrooms: 1 single, 4 double, 1 twin
Bathrooms: 6 en-suite
Parking for 6
Cards accepted: Access, Visa, Diners, Amex

108 THE PARK ROYAL INTERNATIONAL HOTEL

HIGHLY COMMENDED

Stretton Road, Stretton, Cheshire WA4 4NS Tel (01925) 730706 Fax (01925) 730740

This luxury hotel was awarded Cheshire Hotel of the Year 1994/5. Ideally situated with easy access to historic Chester, Manchester, Granada Studios, Liverpool's Albert Dock and set in its own breathtaking gardens. The hotel has 96 de luxe bedrooms and the Harlequin Restaurant, renowned in the locality for its food and comfortable lounges, will enhance your break in Cheshire. To follow in Spring 1997 is a superb leisure complex and health & beauty spa.
 CATEGORY 3

Bed & Breakfast per night: single room from £45.00–£90.45; double room from £65.00–£109.40
Half board per person: £61.45–£123.35 daily
Lunch available: 1200–1430
Evening meal 1900 (last orders 2200)

Bedrooms: 2 single, 61 double, 29 twin, 2 triple, 2 family rooms
Bathrooms: 96 en-suite
Parking for 400
Cards accepted: Access, Visa, Diners, Amex, Switch/Delta

109 GROVE HOUSE

 HIGHLY COMMENDED

Holme Street, Tarvin, Cheshire CH3 8EQ Tel (01829) 740893 Fax (01829) 741769

A warm welcome awaits you in a relaxing, spacious, comfortable home with a long-established Cheshire family. Ideal situation for Chester, Oulton Park, North Wales, Liverpool, the Potteries and Manchester Airport (where guests can be met by prior arrangement). Hosts happy to help with sight-seeing suggestions. Attractive walled garden, listed trees and ample off-road parking. Traditional English breakfast served in family dining room. In winter an open coal fire burns in the elegant drawing room. Excellent evening meals available within two miles. North West Tourist Board "Place to Stay" Award.

Bed & Breakfast per night: single room from £20.00–£35.00; double room from £46.00–£56.00

Bedrooms: 1 single, 1 double, 1 twin
Bathrooms: 1 en-suite, 1 public
Parking for 6

⑪⓪ GREEN BOUGH HOTEL AND RESTAURANT 〜〜〜〜 HIGHLY COMMENDED
60 Hoole Road, Chester CH2 3NL Tel (01244) 326241 Fax (01244) 326265

A family-run hotel in Victorian property, providing a personal yet professional service in a homely relaxed atmosphere; tastefully decorated with many antiques, ornaments and flower arrangements recreating a period ambience with an ornately carved oak fireplace and half-panelling. A no smoking restaurant serves fresh produce cooked to order with mainly traditional British dishes; vegetarians are catered for at breakfast and dinner. The bedrooms are individually styled containing Victorian, Edwardian and antique brass-cast beds. Ground floor and no smoking bedrooms available.
↟ CATEGORY 3

Bed & Breakfast per night: single room from £36.00–£44.00; double room from £52.00–£60.00
Half board per person: £38.50–£42.50 daily
Evening meal 1900 (last orders 2030)

Bedrooms: 2 single, 14 double, 1 twin, 3 triple
Bathrooms: 20 en-suite
Parking for 21
Cards accepted: Access, Visa, Amex, Switch/Delta

Walking Chester's walls

THE ROMANS ARRIVED in Chester in AD79, but almost two thousand years on, Cestrians (the city's inhabitants) and visitors still walk on magnificent walls containing Roman masonry. Indeed strolling along the 2-mile circuit of the fortifications high above the hubbub of city life now makes an intriguing couple of hours. This is a far cry from their original purpose, for the Roman walls protected their north-western base (Deva) from the warlike tribes of North Wales. In the Middle Ages, too, the city relied time and again on its stout defences, which in many places follow the course of the Roman fortifications.

During the Civil War (1642–9) the walls fared badly. Chester had been a Royalist stronghold, and only after a siege lasting 18 months and ceaseless bombardment of the defences did the city finally fall. The walls were rebuilt in the reign of Queen Anne (1702–14) for recreational rather than strategic purposes.

In walking the walls you are, quite literally, tracing the history of the city. Beside Newgate lie the remains of Deva's amphitheatre, the largest in Britain. Just east of Northgate are some of the best preserved sections of Roman military wall in northern Europe. This masonry, like all the walls, is hewn from the local sandstone. Built of the same fabric – and a short clockwise stroll from the thirteen courses of Roman blocks – is Chester Cathedral. Founded in 1092, this was originally the Benedictine Abbey of St Werburgh but, after the Dissolution of the Monasteries, became the cathedral in 1541. Other relics of medieval Chester include three towers, all to be found on the walls. When constructed in the 1100s Bonewaldesthorne's Tower stood in the River Dee,

guarding water traffic. By the 14th-century silting meant that the new Water Tower was built 100ft away, where the river then flowed. In time this, too, became stranded. The older tower now houses a *camera obscura* giving a fine panorama of the city. The Water Tower and King Charles's Tower both contain exhibitions on local history.

Above all else, though, this is a walk where the views change with every pace. At one moment it's Chester's own Bridge of Sighs over which condemned prisoners were taken to receive the last rites, the next a panorama of the nearby Clwyd Mountains. Then it's the Roodee, England's oldest racecourse (and the only one where horses run anti-clockwise), the deep cleft of the Shropshire Union Canal cut through sandstone, magnificent Georgian townhouses and, of course, Chester's unique Rows – medieval shopping malls on two levels. Tourist Information Centre (01244) 351609 or 317962.

England's Heartland

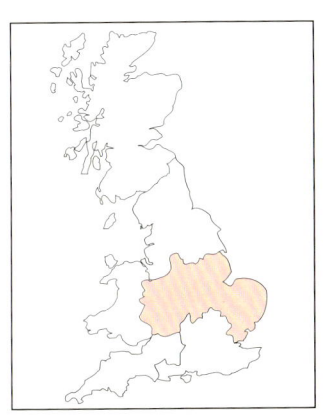

WITH A COASTLINE as tortuous as England's, there can be no one place at the very centre of the country. Such argument naturally does nothing to prevent various claimants, the best-known being Meriden, outside Coventry. The villagers propose that the medieval cross on their village green is the very *umbilicus Angliæ*, the navel of England. Given that, broadly speaking, England is inclined from a flatter east to a hillier west, travellers bound for the Welsh Marches should perhaps expect to be moving uphill as they leave Meriden.

This theory, by no means water-tight, roughly holds true in one respect: the border country of Shropshire, Hereford and Worcester, and Gloucestershire is as hilly as this region becomes (Derbyshire aside). If rolling countryside tending here and there towards the dramatic is what you crave, then the Welsh Marches are hard to beat. The little-explored Forest of Dean nestles in the south-western corner of the region, its isolated feel caused in part by the broad River Severn, and in part by its distinct industrial heritage; no other nearby region of England has relied upon coal for its livelihood. The Forest is still very wooded, and there are countless paths to be followed. One, starting near Speech House in the heart of the Forest, is a sculpture trail created with great imagination.

Until a reorganisation of local government in 1974, tiny Rutland, with a mere 97,000 acres, was England's smallest county. Although swallowed up by Leicestershire, its name and spirit lived on – in the district council, the Rutland County Show, the Rutland County Museum in Oakham and the peaceful, horseshoe-shaped reservoir, Rutland Water. Its landscape is most attractive: rolling green wolds divided by drystone walls and dotted with small woods and glorious villages (four of the prettiest are Croxton Kerrial, Great Casterton, Lyddington and Oakham, the former county town). The good news for Rutlanders is that in yet another reorganisation in 1997 Rutland will once again assume its county status.

▶ **Cheese-rolling at Coopers Hill**

Every Spring Bank Holiday at Cooper's Hill near Gloucester, a man in a white coat and top hat begins one of England's more eccentric customs by hurling a round Double Gloucester down a precipitous slope. He then gives the signal for the assembled local youth to hurtle down in hot pursuit. The race between mature cheese and youthful athleticism is invariably won by the former, but the winner is the first person to reach the bottom, and such prowess is rewarded with the cheese itself.

The most attractive route out of the Forest leads up the Wye Valley to Symonds Yat. This famous beauty spot becomes popular in season, but dawdling aimlessly in the lanes west of Hereford and Ross-on-Wye can often be just as rewarding. The scenery is superb, while discovering a hidden treasure such as the exquisitely carved Romanesque church at Kilpeck is a highlight of any excursion. On clear days the ancient Malvern Hills are often visible to the east. Further north are hill ridges striving to be mountains. These include the intriguingly named Stiperstones, Wenlock Edge, Long Mynd and Caradoc Hills, all comfortably exceeding 1,000ft (305m). The Clee Hills, north-east of the beautiful medieval town of Ludlow, edge towards 1,800ft (549m), and must be mountains in all but name.

Venturing back toward Meriden once again is the county of Warwickshire, which just manages to snatch a morsel of the northerly Cotswolds from its neighbours. The hills where these counties meet can still be pretty steep (see panel on Cooper's Hill), though not quite the altitude of the Shropshire hills. Countless Cotswold attractions include several superlative gardens and endless villages of mellow limestone. To the east lies the ridge of Edgehill, another magnificent vantage point. If the northern slopes seem to have a certain atmosphere, it might be because in 1642 this was the site of the first battle of the Civil War.

Heading some distance due north, the traveller reaches the Peak District, the high point of the region scenically, geologically and literally. England's first national park serves a densely populated catchment area and can suffer from pressure of numbers. Avoid the best-known honey-pots in high season, though, and the wild beauty of the area is easily appreciated. At 2,088ft (636m) Kinder Scout is the highest point in the national park, and the first scalp for those going north on the long trek up the Pennine Way. If you are content with spectacular upland scenery at a slightly lower altitude, try the Staffordshire section of the park. With fewer visitors than elsewhere, this superb terrain – ideal for walking and rock-climbing – is immensely rewarding.

As you leave the Peak behind, the mountains recede into the distance. Ahead are the massive oaks of Sherwood Forest and the historic fox-hunting territory of the Vale of Belvoir. The landscape remains restless, and in Charnwood Forest north of Leicester, two eerie crags, Beacon Hill and Bardon Hill, rise up from the ploughland. These little-visited viewpoints – it's a mile's walk to Bardon Hill's 912ft (278m) summit – look down on medieval abbeys and old quarries worked for their granite for a thousand years. South from here are the unsung towns and villages of Rutland and Northamptonshire. Many are a match for their more famous Cotswold cousins, but receive a fraction of the visitors. Oundle, Gretton, Rockingham, Rothwell and Oakham are a few of the wide choice. Rutland's motto, *Multum in parvo* (much in little), admirably sums up the wide range of sights in this tiny county. Just over into Lincolnshire is the dazzling town of Stamford.

The Great North Road leads south from Stamford and at St Neots crosses the River Great Ouse. This long, meandering river rises near Banbury and on its unhurried journey to the Wash flows through Bedford. The town's walks and riverside gardens are glorious, and there can be few better ways of passing a lazy summer afternoon than by hiring a boat on the Ouse.

Leaving Bedford bound for Essex, the traveller is still, in theory, descending towards England's eastern coast. In the way are the whimsically named East Anglian Heights, although they turn out to be little obstacle, for this is one of the flatter parts of the country. East Anglia may have no mountains, but it has a fine coastline running from Southend's mile-and-a-third-long pier to Hunstanton, the only west-facing resort on the east coast. In between are curiosities such as a tide mill at Woodbridge and the remnants of a vanished medieval town at Dunwich; the rest has been washed away by the relentless force of the North Sea. Inland, too, there is much to see. Essex has perhaps the oldest town in the land at Colchester, The Rodings (a group of eight attractive villages each containing the affix 'Roding') and Dedham, an unspoilt village at the heart of Constable country. Suffolk has gentle undulating farmland with a tradition of cider-making around Debenham, and one of the most sublime villages in Lavenham. Norfolk boasts a site of ancient pilgrimage in Walsingham, the Broads (an incomparable wetland habitat ideal for bird-watching) and acres of aromatic lavender.

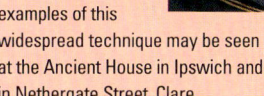

▶ Pargeting

One of Suffolk's most charming architectural features, pargeting came about as a cost-cutting measure rather than the extravagant display of craftsmanship and expense it now seems. Poor-quality timber frames could be disguised by means of plaster which, to make a virtue out of a necessity, could be 'combed' into swirling designs or modelled into elaborate relief. The term 'pargeting' came from the old French *pargeter* – to throw over – because the plaster was thrown over the timber frame. Some of the most extravagant examples of this widespread technique may be seen at the Ancient House in Ipswich and in Nethergate Street, Clare.

Left: Great Yarmouth, Norfolk; inset: Globe Inn, Linslade, Bedfordshire

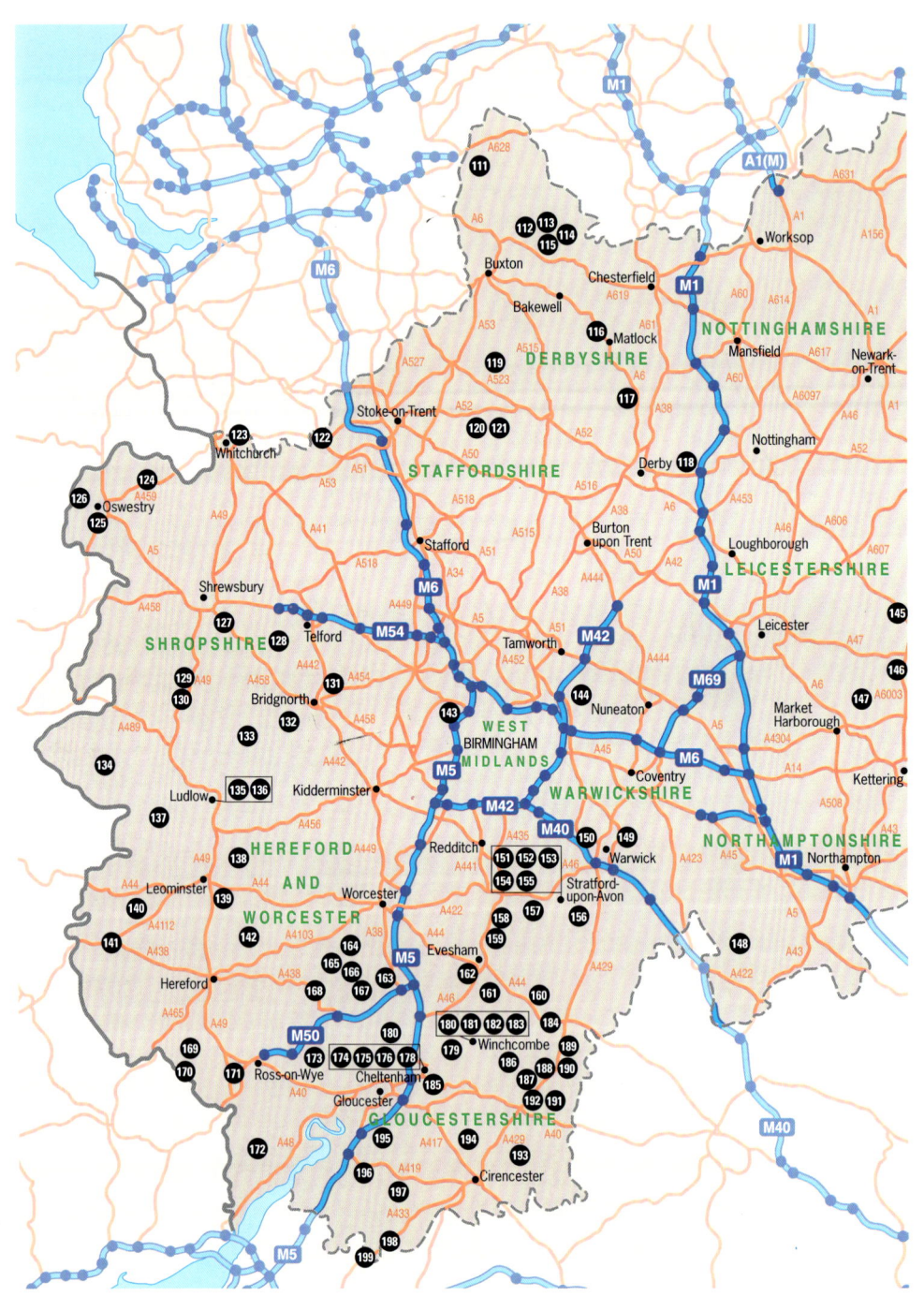

England's Heartland

0 ___ 30 Miles
0 ___ 40 Kilometres

N

LINCOLNSHIRE

Louth 200
Lincoln
Horncastle
Skegness
Sleaford
Boston
Grantham
Spalding
King's Lynn

NORFOLK

Wells-next-the-Sea
Cromer 207
206
205
Swaffham 203
Norwich 209 210 211
208
Great Yarmouth
204
212
Lowestoft
213 214
Wisbech
Peterborough

CAMBRIDGESHIRE

Ely
Thetford
Diss
215
217
216
Wellingborough
Huntingdon
218 220
219 221
Bury St-Edmunds
Newmarket

SUFFOLK

226
Cambridge
Bedford

BEDFORDSHIRE

222
Ipswich
Sudbury
224 223
Felixstowe
Harwich
M1
Luton
Stevenage
M11

HERTFORDSHIRE

Braintree
Colchester 225
A1(M)
Bishop's Stortford
St Albans 228

ESSEX

Chelmsford
Clacton-on-Sea
M25
M25
227
Rickmansworth
Basildon
Southend-on-Sea

Colin Earl Cartography

201 202 A606

67

111 WIND IN THE WILLOWS HOTEL

HIGHLY COMMENDED

Derbyshire Level, off Sheffield Road (A57), Glossop, Derbyshire SK13 9PT Tel (01457) 868001 Fax (01457) 853354

"Not so much an hotel, more a delightful experience" as someone said. A delightful combination of antiques, wood pannelling, log fires and homely atmosphere, but with true professionalism, so you don't feel overwhelmed. All rooms have en-suite facilities of the highest standards and all bedrooms vary. Some half-tester beds, four-poster and brass beds – all antiques. The dining room is open to residents and guests of residents, offering fine English food, all freshly prepared.

Bed & Breakfast per night: single occupancy from £57.00–£75.00; double room from £75.00–£95.00
Evening meal 1930 (last bookings 1600)

Bedrooms: 9 double, 3 twin
Bathrooms: 12 en-suite
Parking for 20
Cards accepted: Access, Visa, Diners, Amex

112 YE OLDE NAGS HEAD

HIGHLY COMMENDED

Castleton, Derbyshire S30 2WH Tel (01433) 620248 Fax (01433) 621604

A privately owned and personally-run 17th-century coaching house with fresh flower arrangements in abundance and antique paintings and furniture. Each bedroom is individually designed to very high standards: three are four-posters and one has a whirlpool bathroom. In the winter, log fires blaze in a bar/lounge area that serves traditional ales and an extensive menu of hot and cold food. Our elegant restaurant with first-class cuisine is open to residents and non-residents for breakfast, luncheon and dinner.

Bed & Breakfast per night: single occupancy from £52.50–£69.50; double room from £79.50–£99.50
Half board per person: £77.45–£94.45 daily; £542.15–£661.15 weekly
Lunch available: 1200–1400

Evening meal 1900 (last orders 2200)
Bedrooms: 6 double, 2 twin
Bathrooms: 8 en-suite
Parking for 16
Cards accepted: Access, Visa, Diners, Amex, Switch/Delta

113 UNDERLEIGH HOUSE

HIGHLY COMMENDED

Off Edale Road, Hope, Derbyshire S30 2RF Tel (01433) 621372 Fax (01433) 621372

A 19th-century, farmhouse-styled home with countryside views, privately situated one-and-a-half miles from the village centre. Stone-flagged floors and oak beams, along with quality furnishings, create the ambience, and each excellent en-suite room has many extras including a resident teddy bear. Renowned for hearty breakfasts and gourmet houseparty dinners cooked by the owner/chef. Winner of national garden competition. Underleigh is ideally situated for exploring the area on foot or by car. No children under 12 yrs. Sorry, no pets – we have our own!!

Bed & Breakfast per night: single occupancy from £35.00–£38.50; double room from £54.00–£60.00
Half board per person: £37.00–£45.00 daily; £260.00–£270.00 weekly
Evening meal 1930

Bedrooms: 3 double, 2 twin
Bathrooms: 5 en-suite
Parking for 5
Cards accepted: Access, Visa, Switch/Delta

114 STONEY RIDGE

HIGHLY COMMENDED

Granby Road, Bradwell, Derbyshire S30 2HU Tel (01433) 620538

Our lovely home is set in the heart of the Peak District National Park with good views overlooking the Hope Valley. Stoney Ridge provides the ideal base for hill-walking to visit well-dressings, country shows, sheepdog trials and more. Nearby are Castleton's caverns, Chatsworth House and Haddon Hall. Enjoy a swim in our twenty-eight by twelve foot heated indoor pool followed by breakfast on our balcony on sunny mornings.

Bed & Breakfast per night: single occupancy £28.00; twin room £48.00; double room £50.00

Bedrooms: 2 double, 2 twin
Bathrooms: 3 en-suite, 1 private, 1 public
Parking for 8
Cards accepted: Access, Visa, Switch/Delta

115 MAYNARD ARMS HOTEL

HIGHLY COMMENDED

Main Road, Grindleford, Derbyshire S30 1HP Tel (01433) 630321 Fax (01433) 630445

Established in 1898 in the heart of the Peak National Park, the Maynard Arms is an idyllic location for pleasure or business. Superior bedrooms have views over the Derwent Valley. The best local produce is served for both lunch (1200–1400) and dinner (1900–2130) accompanied by our extensive wine list, in the Padley Restaurant overlooking the hotel gardens. The Longshaw Bar satisfies the heartiest of appetites between 1200–1400 and 1900–2130, also serving traditional hand-pulled beers.

Bed & Breakfast per night: single room from £49.00–£55.00; double room from £65.00–£85.00
Lunch available: 1200–1400
Evening meal 1900 (last orders 2130)

Bedrooms: 1 single, 8 double, 2 twin
Bathrooms: 11 en-suite
Parking for 80
Cards accepted: Access, Visa, Amex

116 RIBER HALL

HIGHLY COMMENDED

Matlock, Derbyshire Tel (01629) 582795 Fax (01629) 580475

Enjoy pure tranquillity in the welcoming atmosphere of a bygone age in this historic Derbyshire country house. Experience English classical and French provincial cuisine in this old manor house recently nominated as 'One of the most romantic hotels in Britain' and featured in all major hotel and restaurant guides.

Bed & Breakfast per night: single occupancy from £85.00–£99.00; double room from £105.00–£150.00
Half board per person: from £110.00 daily
Lunch available: 1200–1330 (last orders)
Evening meal 1900 (last orders 2130)

Bedrooms: 11 double
Bathrooms: 11 en-suite
Parking for 50
Cards accepted: Access, Visa, Diners, Amex, Switch/Delta

117 DANNAH FARM COUNTRY GUESTHOUSE 〰〰〰 HIGHLY COMMENDED

Bowman's Lane, Shottle, Derby, Derbyshire DE56 2DR Tel (01773) 550273 or (01773) 550630 Fax (01773) 550590

A lovely 18th-century farmhouse on a mixed working farm, elegantly converted and combining first-class accommodation with superb food; perfectly situated to enjoy the myriad delights of Derbyshire and wonderful walking country with many historic houses and places of interest nearby. All the bedrooms (including a romantic four-poster suite) have the attention to detail that makes a stay extra special. Fully licensed. We have it all – from pot-bellied pigs to award winning food. 'Best of Tourism' award; East Midlands Tourist Board 1994 'Bed & Breakfast of the Year' award; short-listed for 1994 ETB 'England for Excellence' award.

Bed & Breakfast per night: single room from £35.00–£55.00; double room from £64.00–£85.00
Half board per person: £79.00–£90.00 daily; £300.00–£350.00 weekly
Evening meal 1800 (last orders 2000)

Bedrooms: 1 single, 4 double, 2 twin, 1 triple
Bathrooms: 6 en-suite, 1 private
Parking for 20
Cards accepted: Access, Visa

The Wise Men of Gotham

TODAY GOTHAM is perhaps best known as the fictional home of Batman, but to our ancestors the name of this Nottinghamshire village was synonymous with folly. Tradition has it that early in the 13th-century King John wished to establish a hunting lodge in or near Gotham. The Gothamites, unhappy at the likely cost of a royal neighbour, set about discouraging the king's visit. The scheme they hit on was to assume collective idiocy; when John's officers arrived, they were greeted by villagers hopping backwards on one leg, wearing their clothes back to front and lighting lanterns in broad daylight. The ploy had the desired effect, but to this day the Gothamites are paying the price, for their village name remains a by-word for stupidity.

Soon the antics of the ironically named 'Wise Men of Gotham' were hugely popular, and the *Merie Tales of the Mad Men of Gotam* became a 16th-century bestseller. One of the better-known tales has the 'wise men' constructing a hedge around a tree favoured by a cuckoo in a vain attempt to prevent the bird from flying away. Another recounts how a Gotham merchant noticed that his round cheeses would roll downhill. Telling them to follow him to market, he was dismayed when he spent market day behind an empty stall. He then set off towards York, having drawn the natural conclusion that the cheeses were doubtless going too fast to stop in Nottingham market.

The village still bears the scars of its lunatic residents, for the present-day visitor may see Cheese Hill, named after the uncooperative rounds of Cheddar,

as well as Cuckoo Bush Hill, Cuckoo Bush Mound and the Cuckoo Bush Inn (complete with sign illustrating bird, bush and blockheads) which all clearly celebrate the legendary escapade. And as for the Batman connection, it seems that Washington Irving, the American writer of short stories, may well have had the Nottinghamshire villagers in mind when he christened New York 'Gotham City', a name later picked up by the author of the comic-strip hero.

⑪⑧ RISLEY HALL HOTEL

〰〰〰〰 HIGHLY COMMENDED

Derby Road, Risley, Draycott, Derbyshire DE72 3SS Tel (0115) 939 9000 Fax (0115) 939 7766

At junction 25 of the M1, midway between the cities of Nottingham and Derby, Risley Hall Country House Hotel is set amongst five acres of historic period gardens and offers the highest standards of fine foods, wine and uniquely designed bedrooms. The Garden Restaurant offers the highest standard of English and continental food with extensive table d'hôte, à la carte and vegetarian menus available. Beautiful setting for wedding receptions, conferences and other special celebrations. Afternoon teas. Sunday lunches. Public bar. Leisure centre.

Bed & Breakfast per night: single occupancy from £50.00–£80.00; double room from £60.00–£95.00
Half board per person: £65.00–£95.00 daily; £472.50–£693.00 weekly
Evening meal 1830 (last orders 2130)

Bedrooms: 16 double
Bathrooms: 16 en-suite
Cards accepted: Access, Visa, Amex, Switch/Delta

---

⑪⑨ BUTTERTON MOOR HOUSE

〰〰 HIGHLY COMMENDED

Parsons Lane, Butterton, Leek, Staffordshire ST13 7PD Tel (01538) 304506 Fax (01538) 304506

A lovingly restored 17th-century farmhouse nestling in the hills overlooking the Manifold Valley. Original beams, paintings, antiques and interesting ornaments, combined with superb facilities, make this a beautiful setting. An indoor heated pool, snooker and darts room, a cosy lounge with games and videos all help to provide a relaxing end to a day spent walking or sightseeing. An ideal base for exploring the Peak District. A peaceful and enjoyable stay is guaranteed.

Bed & Breakfast per night: single occupancy from £35.00; double room from £45.00–£50.00

Bedrooms: 2 double, 1 twin
Bathrooms: 3 en-suite, 1 public
Parking for 9

---

⑫⓪ BANK HOUSE

〰〰 HIGHLY COMMENDED

Farley Road, Oakamoor, Stoke-on-Trent, Staffordshire ST10 3BD Tel (01538) 702810 Fax (01538) 702810

A luxurious, elegant and peaceful licensed country home offering the highest standards of food and comfort, a third-of-a-mile south of the village. Each en-suite or private-bath bedroom has a beautiful view of the picturesque Churnet Valley, England's little Rhineland. Within the Staffordshire Moorlands, next to the National Park, one mile from Alton Towers, and amidst superb countryside for walking, it is also convenient for visiting the Potteries, Derbyshire Dales, numerous great houses, gardens and other attractions. Heart of England Tourist Board nominee for 'England for Excellence' Award 1994.

Bed & Breakfast per night: single room £40.00; double room from £50.00–£70.00
Half board per person: £42.00–£55.00 daily; £250.00–£330.00 weekly
Evening meal 1930 (last orders 2130)

Bedrooms: 1 single, 1 double, 1 twin
Bathrooms: 2 en-suite, 1 private
Parking for 8
Cards accepted: Access, Visa

121 RIBDEN FARM

 **HIGHLY COMMENDED**

Oakamoor, Stoke-on-Trent, Staffordshire ST10 3BW Tel (01538) 702830 Fax (01538) 702830

Built in 1745, this lovely old stone farmhouse has an abundance of crooked walls, sloping ceilings and oak beams. One room has a four-poster bed. Rooms with tea/coffee and biscuits, clock radios, colour television, toiletries, bath and hand towels. Separate dining room and guests' own television lounge with pay-phone. Large garden with patios and furniture. Safe off-road parking. Five minutes from Alton Towers and ideally situated for visiting the Peak District and Potteries. Local pubs serving good food.

Bed & Breakfast per night: double room from
£38.00–£42.00

Bedrooms: 2 double, 1 triple, 3 family rooms
Bathrooms: 5 en-suite, 1 private
Parking for 3
Cards accepted: Access, Visa, Diners, Switch/Delta

Brewers of Burton-upon-Trent

THE SMELL OF HOPS AND MALT pervades the town of Burton-upon-Trent, the centre of British brewing. No fewer than three major breweries are here: Carlsberg Tetley, Marston's and Bass. The historic reason for their presence is the mineral-rich water drawn from local sources and found to be especially suitable for brewing beer; the old wells with romantic sounding names – Nile and Cairo, The Hay, Andressey – are still tapped. Today, however, the water has to be completely purified before being used in lager (more popular than beer these days) and, if needed for beer-making, the all-important minerals, calcium and magnesium salts, now have to be added afresh!

The history of the industry dates back to medieval times when ales were brewed here by the monks of Burton Abbey. Despite the dissolution of the monastery in the 16th-century, brewing continued in Burton, and was well-established when William Bass set up his brewery in the 18th-century. When the Trade Marks Act was introduced in 1875 Bass, with its famous red triangle, was the first company to register; it is said that a loyal company employee spent an uncomfortable night outside the registrar's office in order to be first in the queue.The Bass family gave the town some of its finest buildings including the Town Hall, St Paul's Institute and St Paul's Church. Michael Arthur Bass, who became Lord Burton in 1886, also paid for the development of Kind Edward's Place and the building of the Ferry Bridge.

Today Bass still dominates the town. It also has an exciting museum (tel: 01283 511000) which throws light on the company's historic role in the brewing history of Burton-upon-Trent. Exhibits include items from its transport fleet, such as its famous Daimler (shaped like a beer bottle) and its four splendid shire horses (the company once used more than 90 shire horses to deliver its beer). Bass also offers tours of the modern brewery (pre-booking is advised, tel: 01283 511000) where the complicated stages in the brewing process – malting, milling, mashing, boiling, cooling, fermenting and canning – can be observed firsthand. Here, too, visitors can familiarise themselves with the arcane terminology of brewing. Intriguing words such as barm, grist, mash, shive, sparging, trub and wort are all part of the brewer's vocabulary.

At Carlsberg Tetley (tel: 01283 502197) brewery tours are on offer to groups and may include hospitality in their historic old vaults, once used as cellars. Marston's, too, offers tours of its traditional Victorian brewery for groups of between 12 and 30 (tel: 01283 507434).

122 HERRIOTTS GUEST HOUSE

 HIGHLY COMMENDED

London Road, Woore, Cheshire CW3 9SF Tel (01630) 647556

Barbara and Graham King run this small, high-quality country guesthouse which is set in picturesque gardens, overlooking open countryside, in an award-winning village with olde worlde pubs. We offer three tastefully furnished, en-suite bedrooms. Ideal location for short breaks – Bridgemere Garden World, Stapeley Water Gardens, Chester, Potteries, Shrewsbury, Ironbridge, canal locks at Audlem and the delightful town of Nantwich. Complemented by home cooking, with evening meals available and special diets catered for. Non smoking, private parking, brochure available.

Bed & Breakfast per night: single occupancy from £23.00–£26.00; double room from £30.00–£40.00
Half board per person: £25.00–£30.00 daily; £164.50–£196.00 weekly
Evening meal 1900 (last bookings 1000)

Bedrooms: 1 double, 1 twin, 1 triple
Bathrooms: 3 en-suite, 1 public
Parking for 4

123 DEARNFORD HALL

 HIGHLY COMMENDED

Whitchurch, Shropshire SY13 3JJ Tel (01948) 662319 Fax (01948) 662319

Discerning guests will discover elegant country-house charm combined with spacious accommodation at 17th-century Dearnford Hall, which has been lovingly restored by its present owners, Charles and Jane Bebbington. An angling utopia (fly only) situated adjacent to Shropshire's premier trout fishery where fifteen acres of pure spring-fed water help to create a tranquil atmosphere. A relaxed, rural retreat with a friendly welcome, Dearnford is the perfect base for exploring Shropshire, Cheshire and North Wales.

Bed & Breakfast per night: single occupancy from £30.00–£40.00; double room from £60.00–£70.00

Bedrooms: 2 double
Bathrooms: 2 en-suite
Parking for 6

124 GREENBANKS

 HIGHLY COMMENDED

Coptiviney, Ellesmere, Shropshire SY12 0ND Tel (01691) 623420 Fax (01691) 623420

Greenbanks is an attractive and comfortable red brick Victorian house set within its own 20 acres. It is peacefully situated in the tranquillity of this totally rural area, yet well placed for Shrewsbury, Oswestry, Wrexham, Chester and Llangollen. The great houses and gardens of Chirk, Erddig and Powis are nearby. Spacious bedrooms with en-suite or private bathrooms, television and tea/coffee making facilities. Imaginative four-course dinners by prior arrangement. Extensive garden. Tennis court.

Bed & Breakfast per night: single occupancy from £27.00–£30.00; double room from £54.00–£60.00
Half board per person: £44.00–£47.00 daily; £308.00–£329.00 weekly

Bedrooms: 2 twin
Bathrooms: 1 en-suite, 1 private, 1 public
Parking for 4
Cards accepted: Visa

125 THE HAWTHORNS

 HIGHLY COMMENDED

Weston Lane, Oswestry, Shropshire SY11 2BG Tel (01691) 657678

A warm welcome awaits you at our very quiet Victorian detached town house in the old border market town of Oswestry, near the Berwyn mountain range and the glorious Vale of Llangollen. Relax in the reading room prior to retiring to your en-suite bedroom. In the morning enjoy a fresh fruit compote, followed by a generous cooked breakfast.

Bed & Breakfast per night: single occupancy £19.00; double room £34.00

Bedrooms: 1 double, 1 twin
Bathrooms: 2 en-suite, 1 public
Parking for 6

126 PEN-Y-DYFFRYN COUNTRY HOTEL

 HIGHLY COMMENDED

Rhyd-y-Croesau, Oswestry, Shropshire SY10 7DT Tel (01691) 653700 Fax (01691) 653700

Once a Georgian rectory, now an award-winning country hotel in the most peaceful of situations in the lovely Shropshire Hills, midway between Shrewsbury and Chester. Full of character with a delightfully informal atmosphere, the hotel has eight bedrooms (including one on the ground floor), all with lovely hill views and en-suite bathrooms. Our renowned restaurant, which is fully licensed, utilises the best local produce. Guests return again and again.

Bed & Breakfast per night: single room from £40.00–£47.00; double room from £62.00–£70.00
Half board per person: £45.00–£49.50 daily; £270.00–£300.00 weekly
Evening meal 1900 (last orders 2100)

Bedrooms: 1 single, 3 double, 3 twin, 1 triple
Bathrooms: 8 en-suite
Parking for 38
Cards accepted: Access, Visa, Amex, Switch/Delta

127 UPPER BROMPTON FARM

HIGHLY COMMENDED

Brompton, Cross Houses, Shrewsbury, Shropshire SY5 6LE Tel (01743) 761629

Our delightful Georgian farmhouse with extensive lawns and gardens is a haven of peace, comfort and elegance. Five minutes from Shrewsbury – 'England's finest Tudor town' – and fifteen minutes from Ironbridge – 'the birthplace of industry' – we are ideally situated for exploring Housman's Shropshire. Our three guest bedrooms have en-suite facilities and are furnished to the highest standard with many welcoming touches. The two double rooms have four-poster beds and wonderful views to the Shropshire Hills. Breakfast in the sun-filled dining room. Relax in front of an open fire.

Bed & Breakfast per night: single occupancy from £36.00–£40.00; double room from £48.00–£54.00
Half board per person: £42.00–£45.00 daily; £260.00–£275.00 weekly
Evening meal 1830

Bedrooms: 2 double, 1 twin
Bathrooms: 3 en-suite
Parking for 10

128 BRIDGE HOUSE

Buildwas, Telford, Shropshire TF8 7BN Tel (01952) 432105

A charming 17th-century Grade II listed period residence, set close to the beautiful Ironbridge Gorge. Our character home offers guests a comfortable relaxing stay with a breakfast to be remembered.

Bed & Breakfast per night: single occupancy from £28.00–£30.00; double room from £45.00–£50.00

Bedrooms: 2 double, 1 twin, 1 triple
Bathrooms: 4 en-suite
Parking for 12

---

129 JINLYE

Castle Hill, All Stretton, Church Stretton, Shropshire SY6 6JP Tel (01694) 723243 Fax (01694) 723243

A beautifully situated country guest house set in the lovely Shropshire Highlands. A stroll from the house can provide some of the most stunning views in England. Delightfully furnished in period decor, offering luxurious and peaceful accommodation. Inglenook fireplaces and comfortable lounges. All of our spacious en-suite rooms have magnificent views. For a romantic interlude, our Wedding Suite is furnished around a splendidly carved 17th-century French wedding bed. Ground floor rooms. Excellent home cooking. Licensed. Traditional Christmas breaks. Colour brochure. CATEGORY 3

Bed & Breakfast per night: double room from £44.00–£68.00
Half board per person: £37.00–£51.00 daily; £245.00–£335.00 weekly
Evening meal 1900

Bedrooms: 4 double, 4 twin
Bathrooms: 8 en-suite
Parking for 10

---

130 MYND HOUSE HOTEL

Little Stretton, Church Stretton, Shropshire SY6 6RB Tel (01694) 722212 Fax (01694) 724180

Set in an idyllic rural hamlet with thatched church, hills, and walks in all directions. Ludlow, Shrewsbury and Ironbridge are within a half-hour's drive. Visit romantic monasteries, castles and churches. Interesting range of themed breaks available. Small informal hotel and restaurant, all bedrooms en-suite, two suites available, one with four-poster bed. Four-course à la carte dinners featuring cuisine of the Marches and the best of rural Italy and France. Outstanding cellar offering over three hundred wines in bottles and over two hundred in halves.

Bed & Breakfast per night: single room from £40.00–£45.00; double room from £60.00
Half board per person: £55.00–£75.00 daily
Evening meal 1930 (last orders 2115)

Bedrooms: 1 single, 3 double, 3 twin
Bathrooms: 7 en-suite
Parking for 16
Open: February–December
Cards accepted: Access, Visa, Amex, Switch/Delta

131 OLD VICARAGE HOTEL

 DE LUXE

Worfield, Bridgnorth, Shropshire WV15 5JZ Tel (01746) 716497 Fax (01746) 716552

An Edwardian vicarage set in two acres of grounds on the edge of a conservation village in glorious Shropshire countryside, close to Ironbridge Gorge, Severn Valley Railway and Welsh border towns. With an award-winning dining room and cellar, the Old Vicarage is personally run by Peter and Christine Iles. Two night leisure breaks available at any time of the year which include free passport tickets to the Ironbridge Gorge museums. CATEGORY 2

Bed & Breakfast per night: single occupancy from £68.50–£89.50; double room from £97.00–£135.00
Half board per person: £73.50–£97.50 daily; £486.50–£577.50 weekly
Evening meal 1930 (last orders 2130)

Bedrooms: 8 double, 5 twin, 1 triple
Bathrooms: 14 en-suite
Parking for 30
Cards accepted: Access, Visa, Diners, Amex

---

132 MIDDLETON LODGE

 HIGHLY COMMENDED

Middleton Priors, Bridgnorth, Shropshire WV16 6UR Tel (01746) 712228

An imposing stone building in a one-acre garden with spacious bedrooms overlooking Brown Clee Hill, Middleton Lodge is within easy reach of many places of interest, including Severn Valley Railway, Ironbridge, and the historic towns of Ludlow, Shrewsbury, Much Wenlock, Bridgnorth and Church Stretton.

Bed & Breakfast per night: single occupancy from £25.00–£35.00; double room from £50.00–£60.00

Bedrooms: 2 double, 1 twin
Bathrooms: 2 en-suite, 1 private
Parking for 4

---

133 SPRING COTTAGE

 HIGHLY COMMENDED

Abdon, Craven Arms, Nr Ludlow, Shropshire SY7 9HU Tel (01746) 712551

Peacefully nestling into the western slopes of the majestic Brown Clee – 1,200ft above the beautiful Corvedale – this charming country house offers luxurious accommodation, a most delicious and varied cuisine and warm and welcoming hospitality. The house, with its magnificent views over undulating pasture and distant Welsh hills, is a haven of peace and tranquillity, perfect for relaxing and letting the world go by, yet the historic towns of Ludlow, Shrewsbury and Ironbridge are just a short drive away.

Bed & Breakfast per night: single room from £22.50–£29.50; double room from £45.00–£49.00
Half board per person: £37.50–£42.50 daily; £245.00–£280.00 weekly
Evening meal 1830 (last orders 2100)

Bedrooms: 1 single, 1 double, 1 twin
Bathrooms: 1 en-suite, 1 private
Parking for 8

134 COCKFORD HALL

〰〰 DE LUXE

Cockford Bank, Clun, Craven Arms, Shropshire SY7 8LR Tel (01588) 640327 Fax (01588) 640881

Stay in the tranquil comfort of Cockford Hall. Relax and enjoy this idyllic rural area in the midst of "Housman's Country". The lovingly restored farmhouse nestles in twenty acres on a wooded hillside above the historic village of Clun and is surrounded by an inspirational landscape of gentle rolling hills, patchwork fields and hidden valleys. The charm of Cockford Hall, with many features of architectural and historic interest, has been preserved and now combines traditional hospitality with state-of-the-art facilities.

Bed & Breakfast per night: single occupancy from £35.00–£40.00; double room from £50.00–£65.00
Half board per person: £53.00–£60.00 daily; £350.00–£400.00 weekly
Evening meal 1900 (last orders 2100)

Bedrooms: 1 double, 1 twin
Bathrooms: 2 en-suite
Parking for 6

135 THE FEATHERS AT LUDLOW

〰〰〰〰 HIGHLY COMMENDED

Bull Ring, Ludlow, Shropshire SY8 1AA Tel (01584) 875261 Fax (01584) 876030

Ludlow has been described as the most beautiful and historic small town in England, enjoying the beauty of the incomparable Welsh Marches. An outstanding landmark, this lovely Jacobean building is a hotel with an excellent reputation for fine traditional food and comfort, offering as it does luxury rooms as well as eight four-posters. Its situation in the centre makes it possible to explore the town on foot. And you can now get married at The Feathers. ♜ CATEGORY 3

Bed & Breakfast per night: single room from £65.00–£80.00; double room from £88.00–£140.00
Half board per person: £64.00–£90.00 daily
Lunch available: 1130–1400
Evening meal 1900 (last orders 2100)

Bedrooms: 11 single, 15 double, 11 twin, 2 triple
Bathrooms: 39 en-suite
Parking for 32
Cards accepted: Access, Visa, Diners, Amex, Switch/Delta

136 NUMBER TWENTY EIGHT

〰〰〰〰 HIGHLY COMMENDED

28 Lower Broad Street, Ludlow, Shropshire SY8 1PQ Tel (01584) 876996 Fax (01584) 876996

This listed town house of charm and character, with its secluded walled garden, is situated close to the river in this 'most lovely of English towns'. We welcome you to our home, where there is generous hospitality and a quiet, relaxed atmosphere. Abounding with pictures, prints and book-lined walls – all adding to your enjoyment. All bedrooms are charmingly individual and en-suite, with every comfort and 'many thoughtful extras'. Lovely woodland and riverside walks, with castles and antique shops galore.

Bed & Breakfast per night: single occupancy from £35.00–£60.00; double room from £45.00–£60.00
Half board per person: £40.00–£47.50 daily; £275.00–£350.00 weekly
Evening meal 1930 (last orders 2030)

Bedrooms: 2 double, 1 twin, 1 triple
Bathrooms: 4 en-suite, 1 public
Cards accepted: Access, Visa, Amex

137 LOWER HOUSE

HIGHLY COMMENDED

Adforton, Leintwardine, Craven Arms, Shropshire SY7 0NF Tel (01568) 770223 Fax (01568) 770592

Lower House originates from the early 17th-century and is situated in North Herefordshire in the Welsh Marches. There is excellent walking in the surrounding hills and the area is quiet and unspoilt. There are many castles, gardens and National Trust properties within an easy drive. We offer first-class, home-cooked food served in our elegant dining room. We are unlicensed, but guests are welcome to bring their own wine.

Bed & Breakfast per night: single occupancy from £22.00–£25.00; double room from £44.00–£50.00
Half board per person: £40.00–£42.00 daily; £260.00 weekly
Evening meal 1900 (last orders 1930)

Bedrooms: 2 double, 2 twin
Bathrooms: 3 en-suite, 1 private
Parking for 10

138 THE HILLS FARM

HIGHLY COMMENDED

Leysters, Leominster, Herefordshire HR6 0HP Tel (01568) 750205

We offer stunning views, scrumptious food and charming bedrooms. The Hills stands on high ground amidst 120 arable acres, complete with a two-mile farm walk. Three of our bedrooms are in lovingly converted barns, each completely self-contained and so offering the ultimate in seclusion and privacy. To round the day off – delicious home-cooked dinners complete with a vegetarian choice if required. No smoking. Brochure available.

Bed & Breakfast per night: double room from £44.00–£48.00
Half board per person: £38.00–£40.00 daily; £266.00–£280.00 weekly
Evening meal 1900 (last bookings 1700)

Bedrooms: 3 double, 2 twin
Bathrooms: 4 en-suite, 1 private
Parking for 5
Open: March–October
Cards accepted: Access, Visa, Switch/Delta

139 HEATH HOUSE

HIGHLY COMMENDED

Stoke Prior, Leominster, Herefordshire HR6 0NF Tel (01568) 760385

Set in peaceful countryside between Hereford and Ludlow and about four miles east of Leominster, this old stone farmhouse is full of character. The bedrooms and the lounge are spacious. Margaret and Peter Neal are both here to help you relax and enjoy your stay. For those who wish to walk and to explore, there is a wealth of history in the unspoilt countryside of the Marches. There are good restaurants and pubs locally.

Bed & Breakfast per night: single occupancy from £22.00–£24.00; double room from £40.00–£44.00
Half board per person: £32.00–£39.00 daily; £203.00–£252.00 weekly
Evening meal 1900 (last orders 2000)

Bedrooms: 1 double, 2 twin
Bathrooms: 2 en-suite, 1 private
Parking for 6
Open: March–November

140 BROXWOOD COURT

HIGHLY COMMENDED

Broxwood, Leominster, Herefordshire HR6 9JJ Tel (01544) 340245 Fax (01544) 340573

This beautiful home, with its sweeping lawns where peacocks roam, magnificent trees and lake, and uninterrupted views of the Black Mountains, offers a unique atmosphere of peace and tranquillity. Relax in the cosy library, enjoy the views from the drawing room, play tennis on the all-weather court, or walk in the lovely thirty-acre garden. Mike and Anne are a relaxed and well-travelled couple who will give you a very warm welcome.

Bed & Breakfast per night: single occupancy £40.00; double room from £60.00–£70.00
Half board per person: £58.00 daily; £336.00 weekly
Evening meal 1900 (last orders 2100)

Bedrooms: 2 double, 1 twin
Bathrooms: 2 en-suite, 1 private
Parking for 15
Cards accepted: Access, Visa

141 THE OLD RECTORY

DE LUXE

Church Street, Willersey, Broadway, Worcestershire WR12 7PN Tel (01386) 853729 Fax (01386) 858061

Built of Cotswold stone, the 17th-century Rectory is quietly tucked away opposite the church. Enclosed by its dry stone wall, the garden with its ancient mulberry tree is truly idyllic. Superb breakfasts served in the elegant dining room (beside a log fire in winter). The Bell Inn, one minute walk away, offers excellent meals. The immaculate bedrooms, including four-posters, are furnished and decorated to a high standard and include all facilities. All rooms have their own bathroom with Crabtree & Evelyn toiletries.

Bed & Breakfast per night: single occupancy from £40.00–£70.00; double room from £60.00–£95.00

Bedrooms: 5 double, 1 twin, 2 triple
Bathrooms: 6 en-suite, 2 private
Parking for 10
Cards accepted: Access, Visa, Switch/Delta

142 THE STEPPES

HIGHLY COMMENDED

Ullingswick, Hereford HR1 3JG Tel (01432) 820424 Fax (01432) 820042

This award-winning country-house hotel with an intimate atmosphere abounds in antique furniture, inglenook fireplaces, oak beams and flag-stoned floors. The old dairy now houses a magnificent cobbled bar with Dickensian atmosphere, and a restored timber-framed barn and converted stable accommodate six large luxury en-suite bedrooms. Outstanding cordon bleu cuisine is served by candle light, and highly praised breakfasts come with an imaginative selection.

Bed & Breakfast per night: single occupancy from £40.00–£50.00; double room from £75.00–£90.00
Half board per person: £50.00–£64.00 daily; £336.00–£350.00 weekly
Evening meal 1930 (last orders 2030)

Bedrooms: 4 double, 2 twin
Bathrooms: 6 en-suite
Parking for 8
Open: February–December
Cards accepted: Access, Visa, Amex, Switch/Delta

143 JONATHANS HOTEL AND RESTAURANT  HIGHLY COMMENDED

16–24 Wolverhampton Road, Oldbury, Warley, Birmingham, West Midlands B68 0LH Tel (0121) 429 3757 Fax (0121) 434 3107

Within the intriguing maze of rooms at Jonathans, one finds an exciting country-house hotel. All the bedrooms and public areas are built for comfort and luxury and are filled with antiques and works of art related to the Victorian era. Well-known for its quality menus, the original Restaurant offers British-based cuisine whilst the Bistro provides distinctly French. Only five miles from Birmingham city centre, this elegant hotel and restaurant provides a haven of tranquillity. Park outside the door.

Bed & Breakfast per night: single room from £69.00–£80.00; double room from £80.00–£120.00
Half board per person: £84.00–£95.00 daily
Lunch available: 1200–1400
Evening meal 1900 (last orders 2230)

Bedrooms: 8 single, 13 double, 2 twin, 9 triple
Bathrooms: 32 en-suite
Parking for 72
Cards accepted: Access, Visa, Diners, Amex, Switch/Delta

144 LEA MARSTON HOTEL AND LEISURE COMPLEX  HIGHLY COMMENDED

Haunch Lane, Lea Marston, Warwickshire B76 0BY Tel (01675) 470468 Fax (01675) 470871

With a host of superb indoor and outdoor activities to choose from, including golf, tennis and swimming, this hotel is a truly first class venue for a relaxing break. Set in its own extensive grounds in rural Warwickshire, with excellent restaurant and bars. For a colour brochure phone 01675 470468. ⚓ CATEGORY 3

Bed & Breakfast per night: single room from £70.00–£92.00; double room from £80.00–£102.00
Half board per person: £86.00–£108.00 daily;
£602.00–£756.00 weekly
Lunch available: 1200–1400

Evening meal 1900 (last orders 2130 Mon–Thurs, 2200 Fri & Sat, 2100 Sun)
Bedrooms: 2 single, 28 double, 19 twin
Bathrooms: 49 en-suite   Parking for 160
Cards accepted: Access, Visa, Amex, Diners, Switch/Delta

145 LORD NELSON'S HOUSE HOTEL  HIGHLY COMMENDED

11 Market Place, Oakham, Leicestershire LE15 6DT Tel (01572) 723199 Fax (01572) 723199

Tourist Board 'Middle England Hotel of the Year' 1995. Come and stay awhile in our charming Grade II listed town house tucked away in the corner of the ancient market town of Oakham. Originally a 16th-century coaching inn, but now tastefully restored and refurbished as a small private hotel, retaining all its character and charm. Log fires, luxury en-suite bedrooms, dinner by candle light in the Trafalgar Room and traditional cuisine all combine to make your stay a memorable one. The chef/owners assure you of their personal attention.

Bed & Breakfast per night: single occupancy from £49.00–£59.00; double room from £69.00–£79.00
Half board per person: £51.00–£61.00 daily
Lunch available: 1200–1430
Evening meal 1900 (last orders 1950)

Bedrooms: 2 double, 2 twin
Bathrooms: 4 en-suite
Parking for 6
Cards accepted: Access, Visa, Amex

146 LAKE ISLE HOTEL

≋≋≋ HIGHLY COMMENDED

16 High Street East, Uppingham, Oakham, Leicestershire LE15 9PZ Tel (01572) 822951 Fax (01572) 822951

The personal touch we provide will make your stay extra special, starting with a decanter of sherry, home-made biscuits and fresh fruit in your room. Our menus, changed weekly, offer fresh produce and a list of over 300 wines, with special 'Wine Dinners' held throughout the year. Whirlpool baths and cottage suites are available. The shops of this sleepy market town surround us, yet we are within a short drive of Rutland Water, Burghley House and many pretty villages.

Bed & Breakfast per night: single room from
£43.00–£59.00; double room from £60.00–£79.00
Half board per person: £49.00–£84.00 daily
Lunch available: 1230–1345
Evening meal 1930 (last orders 2130)

Bedrooms: 1 single, 9 double, 2 twin
Bathrooms: 12 en-suite
Parking for 7
Cards accepted: Access, Visa, Diners, Amex

---

147 HOMESTEAD HOUSE

≋≋ HIGHLY COMMENDED

5 Ashley Road, Medbourne, Market Harborough, Leicestershire LE16 8DL Tel (01858) 565724 Fax (01858) 565324

Homestead House is situated in an elevated position overlooking the Welland Valley on the edge of the picturesque village of Medbourne, which dates back to Roman times. The village has a brook running through the centre and is surrounded by open countryside. There is a wealth of local places of interest to visit. We provide home cooking with local and seasonal produce from our own garden. Our varied menu includes locally-caught trout. A warm welcome awaits you.

Bed & Breakfast per night: single occupancy from
£22.00–£24.00; double room from £38.00–£40.00
Half board per person: £29.00–£34.00 daily
Evening meal 1800 (last orders 2000)

Bedrooms: 3 twin
Bathrooms: 3 en-suite
Parking for 6
Cards accepted: Access, Visa

---

148 FULFORD HOUSE

≋≋ HIGHLY COMMENDED

The Green, Culworth, Banbury, Oxfordshire OX17 2BB Tel (01295) 760355 Fax (01295) 768304

Fulford House is quietly situated with wonderful views over its enchanting gardens and pasturelands. The house, which is 400 years old, is beamed and has an ancient flagged hallway. Its large guest rooms, furnished with soft chintzes and comfortable beds, have colour TVs and sitting areas. A gracious drawing room is available for guests' use and we are licensed. The stableyard and arena are used for the training of competition horses. Superbly situated for Oxford, Stratford, Warwick and the Cotswolds.

Bed & Breakfast per night: double room from
£48.00–£56.00

Bedrooms: 2 double, 1 twin
Bathrooms: 1 en-suite, 2 private
Parking for 6
Open: February–November

149 LANSDOWNE HOTEL

⬦⬦⬦ HIGHLY COMMENDED

87 Clarendon Street, Leamington Spa, Warwickshire CV32 4PF Tel (01926) 450505 Fax (01926) 421313

An elegant Regency hotel, The Lansdowne offers a tranquil atmosphere. The comprehensive menus change daily, providing guests with a choice of freshly prepared dishes. David and Gillian Allen's personal selection of good quality wines underline their policy of excellent value and complements the high standard of cuisine which is recognised by most discerning guides. Licensed bar, ample parking. Discount tickets to Warwick Castle. The Lansdowne is in the town centre, so easy for browsing round the shops.

Bed & Breakfast per night: single room from
£49.95–£54.95; double room from £59.90–£69.90
Half board per person: £42.50–£46.50 daily
Evening meal 1830 (last orders 2130)

Bedrooms: 5 single, 5 double, 5 twin
Bathrooms: 12 en-suite, 1 public
Parking for 12
Cards accepted: Access, Visa, Amex

150 NORTHLEIGH HOUSE

⬦⬦ HIGHLY COMMENDED

Five Ways Road, Hatton, Warwick, Warwickshire CV35 7HZ Tel (01926) 484203 or 0374 101894 Fax (01926) 484006

A personal welcome, the individually-designed rooms with colour co-ordinated furnishings, en-suite bathrooms, television, fridge, kettle and many thoughtful extras make this the perfect hide-away in rural Warwickshire. A full English breakfast is freshly cooked to suit guests' individual tastes. Evening meals can be arranged, although there are excellent country pubs nearby, as well as the historic towns of Stratford-upon-Avon and Warwick, and the exhibition centres. Please call Sylvia Fenwick for brochures. No smoking.

Bed & Breakfast per night: single room from
£30.00–£38.00; double room from £38.00–£55.00

Bedrooms: 1 single, 5 double, 1 twin
Bathrooms: 7 en-suite
Parking for 8
Open: February–November
Cards accepted: Access, Visa

151 PAYTON HOTEL

⬦⬦ HIGHLY COMMENDED

6 John Street, Stratford-upon-Avon, Warwickshire CV37 6UB Tel (01789) 266442 Fax (01789) 266442

Situated in the centre of Stratford-upon-Avon in a quiet exclusive location, yet only three minutes' walk to both the theatre and Shakespeare's birthplace. Experience the delights of a stay in this charming listed Georgian house where the caring proprietors – John and June Rickett – will warmly welcome you. Tasteful, individually-furnished, cosy bedrooms include a Victorian room with an antique brass bed and a four-poster room. An excellent four-course breakfast is served until 0945 at weekends.

Bed & Breakfast per night: single occupancy from
£38.00–£40.00; double room from £56.00–£60.00

Bedrooms: 3 double, 2 twin
Bathrooms: 4 en-suite, 1 private shower
Parking for 3
Cards accepted: Access, Visa

152 STRATFORD COURT HOTEL

〰〰〰 HIGHLY COMMENDED

Avenue Road, Stratford-upon-Avon, Warwickshire CV37 6UX Tel (01789) 297799 Fax (01789) 262449

This beautiful Edwardian residence is situated in one of Stratford's finest locations and is surrounded by an acre of walled gardens, providing a peaceful setting where our guests can relax and be looked after with care and courtesy. All our bedrooms are en-suite, having been refurbished to the highest standard in keeping with the style of the hotel. On the ground floor, antiques, oak and comfy sofas in both the garden bar and lounge ensure a warm and welcoming atmosphere.

Bed & Breakfast per night: single room from
£45.00–£55.00; double room from £80.00–£150.00
Evening meal 1800 (last orders 2030)

Bedrooms: 4 single, 5 double, 2 twin, 2 triple
Bathrooms: 13 en-suite
Parking for 32
Cards accepted: Access, Visa

---

153 BROOK LODGE

〰〰 HIGHLY COMMENDED

192 Alcester Road, Stratford-upon-Avon, Warwickshire CV37 9DR Tel (01789) 295988 Fax (01789) 295988

This immaculately maintained guesthouse is run to the highest standards and has a most warm and friendly atmosphere. The property is only a five-minute walk from Anne Hathaway's cottage and is well situated for all local attractions. The prettily decorated en-suite bedrooms are equipped to ensure that your stay is both happy and comfortable. The knowledgeable local hosts are delighted to assist their guests with information and advice. Ample car parking.

Bed & Breakfast per night: single occupancy from
£25.00–£40.00; double room from £36.00–£50.00

Bedrooms: 4 double, 1 twin, 2 triple
Bathrooms: 6 en-suite, 1 private
Parking for 10
Cards accepted: Access, Visa, Amex, Switch/Delta

---

154 PEARTREE COTTAGE

〰〰 HIGHLY COMMENDED

7 Church Road, Wilmcote, Stratford-upon-Avon, Warwickshire CV37 9UX Tel (01789) 205889 Fax (01789) 262862

Situated in the Shakespearean village of Wilmcote, this Elizabethan Grade II listed building is set in nearly an acre of shady garden, overlooking Mary Arden's House. The cottage, and its later extension, is furnished throughout with country antiques. Breakfast is served in the stone-flagged and beamed dining room. Dinners are available at two good pub/restaurants within walking distance. The cottage provides a convenient centre for Shakespeare country, the Cotswolds and the NEC.

Bed & Breakfast per night: single occupancy £30.00;
double room £45.00

Bedrooms: 4 double, 2 twin, 1 triple
Bathrooms: 7 en-suite
Parking for 8

155 VICTORIA SPA LODGE

HIGHLY COMMENDED

Bishopton Lane, Stratford-upon-Avon, Warwickshire CV37 9QY Tel (01789) 267985 Fax (01789) 204728

An elegant Grade II Listed spa lodge in a country setting close to the town centre, with seven beautifully-appointed en-suite bedrooms. Built in 1837 and the former home of cartoonist Bruce Bairnsfather (Old Bill) and Sir Barry Jackson (Founder, Birmingham Repertory Theatre), this is the first hotel Queen Victoria gave her name to – the Royal Coat of Arms is built into the gables. Full fire certificate. Paul & Dreen Tozer are your hosts and look forward to welcoming you. Totally non-smoking.

Bed & Breakfast per night: single occupancy from £35.00–£40.00; double room from £45.00–£52.00

Bedrooms: 3 double, 1 twin, 3 family rooms
Bathrooms: 7 en-suite, 1 public
Parking for 12
Cards accepted: Access, Visa

156 LOXLEY FARM

HIGHLY COMMENDED

Loxley, Warwick, Warwickshire CV35 9JN Tel (01789) 840265

Picturesque, thatched, half-timbered farmhouse and barn, surrounded by one-and-a-half acres of garden and orchard, in a quiet village on the edge of the Cotswolds. Three-and-a-half miles from Stratford-upon-Avon, seven miles from Warwick. Accommodation is in the recently restored single-storey barn, which has two private suites of rooms, one of which includes a small kitchen. Traditional English breakfasts are served in the farmhouse dining room. Mrs Horton is happy to book theatre tickets at no extra charge.

Bed & Breakfast per night: single occupancy from £32.00–£35.00; double room from £46.00–£50.00

Bedrooms: 2 double
Bathrooms: 2 en-suite
Parking for 10

157 GRAVELSIDE BARN

HIGHLY COMMENDED

Binton, Stratford-upon-Avon, Warwickshire CV37 9TU Tel (01789) 750502 or (01789) 297000 Fax (01789) 298056

Serenely situated on a hilltop in the middle of rolling Warwickshire farmland, with magnificent views of the surrounding countryside and Cotswold Hills, Gravelside Barn offers the discerning traveller all of today's modern conveniences and comforts in a stunning and tranquil setting. A great base for exploring Shakespeare country and the Heart of England, or simply a place to relax. Three-and-a-half miles from Stratford and ten minutes from Junction 15/M40. Please ring for a brochure. Totally non-smoking.

Bed & Breakfast per night: single occupancy from £30.00–£40.00; double room from £50.00–£60.00

Bedrooms: 2 double, 1 twin
Bathrooms: 3 en-suite
Parking for 6
Cards accepted: Access, Visa

158 SALFORD HALL HOTEL

≋≋≋≋ HIGHLY COMMENDED

Abbots Salford, Evesham, Worcestershire WR11 5UT Tel (01386) 871300 Fax (01386) 871301

A romantic Grade I listed Tudor manor situated at the gateway to Shakespeare country and the Cotswolds. With every modern comfort combined with old world charm and quaint black and white passageways, our superb food in the Stanford Room completes the picture for a special memorable visit.

Bed & Breakfast per night: single room from £75.00–£105.00; double room from £105.00–£150.00
Half board per person: £62.50–£85.00 daily
Evening meal 1930 (last orders 2130)

Bedrooms: 2 single, 23 double, 8 twin
Bathrooms: 33 en-suite
Parking for 50
Cards accepted: Access, Visa, Diners, Amex, Switch/Delta

159 THE MILL AT HARVINGTON

≋≋≋≋ HIGHLY COMMENDED

Anchor Lane, Harvington, Evesham, Worcestershire WR11 5NR Tel (01386) 870688 Fax (01386) 870688

Friendly, owner-run hotel, sensitively converted from a beautiful Georgian house and former baking mill. Situated on the banks of the River Avon in acres of private parkland, our hotel offers peace, tranquillity and a view over the garden and river towards the morning sun from every bedroom. Find gentle elegance without formality, good food without fussiness, and friendly staff who will help you relax immediately.

Bed & Breakfast per night: single occupancy from £56.00–£58.00; double room from £89.00–£93.00
Half board per person: £52.00–£72.00 daily;
£364.00–£504.00 weekly
Lunch available: 1145–1345

Evening meal 1900 (last orders 2045)
Bedrooms: 12 double, 3 twin
Bathrooms: 15 en-suite
Parking for 25
Cards accepted: Access, Visa, Diners, Amex, Switch/Delta

160 ORCHARD HILL HOUSE

≋≋ HIGHLY COMMENDED

Broad Campden, Chipping Campden, Gloucestershire GL55 6UU Tel (01386) 841473 Fax (01386) 841030

Situated in one of the most picturesque villages in the Cotswolds, Orchard Hill House dates back to 1646 and has been beautifully restored to provide comfort and style with old original charm. The rooms are beautifully furnished. Two are in the main house and, for something more private, a converted hayloft offers total individuality. Breakfast at our ten-foot elm refectory table in our flagstone-floored dining hall. The friendliest atmosphere you could wish to find. Orchard Hill House is a totally non-smoking establishment.

Bed & Breakfast per night: single occupancy from £40.00–£50.00; double room from £44.00–£55.00

Bedrooms: 2 double, 1 twin, 1 triple
Bathrooms: 3 en-suite, 1 private
Parking for 6

161 DORMY HOUSE

HIGHLY COMMENDED

Willersey Hill, Broadway, Worcestershire WR12 7LF Tel (01386) 852711 Fax (01386) 858636

The 17th-century Dormy House is ideally located for visiting the picturesque villages of the Cotswolds as well as Shakespeare's Stratford-upon-Avon. Enjoy the beautifully appointed rooms, superb restaurant and high standard of cuisine and service. Our croquet lawn, putting green, sauna/steam room, gym, games room and nature trail offer the chance to combine leisure with pleasure. Pamper yourself with a Champagne Weekend or a carefree midweek break in the Heart of England.

Bed & Breakfast per night: single room from £63.00–£84.00; double room from £126.00–£152.00
Half board per person: £77.00–£93.00 daily
Lunch available: Restaurant 1230–1400 Sunday–Friday; or bar meals 1230–1400 daily

Evening meal 1900 (last orders 2130)
Bedrooms: 7 single, 17 double, 24 twin, 1 family room
Bathrooms: 49 en-suite
Parking for 90
Cards accepted: Access, Visa, Diners, Amex, Switch/Delta

162 EVESHAM HOTEL

HIGHLY COMMENDED

Cooper's Lane, Off Waterside, Evesham, Worcestershire WR11 6DA Tel (01386) 765566 or 0800 716969 Fax (01386) 765443

An excellent centre for Stratford, the Cotswolds and the Wye Valley. Fully modernised, the hotel is of Tudor/Georgian origins. The integral indoor pool nestles into the relaxing two-and-a-half acre garden. Consistent guide entries for food guarantee efficiently-served and satisfying meals and the widest range of wines and spirits in the country. National awards for idiosyncrasy suggest that a visit is relaxingly memorable – our style is un-Britishly informal. There is a minimum booking of two nights for half-board accommodation.

Bed & Breakfast per night: single room from £57.00–£65.00; double room from £74.00–£90.00
Half board per person: £47.00–£61.00 daily;
£287.00–£372.00 weekly
Lunch available: 1230–1400

Evening meal 1900 (last orders 2130)
Bedrooms: 6 single, 22 double, 11 twin, 1 triple
Bathrooms: 40 en-suite
Parking for 45
Cards accepted: Access, Visa, Diners, Amex, Switch/Delta

163 WELLAND COURT

HIGHLY COMMENDED

Upton-upon-Severn, Worcestershire WR8 0ST Tel (01684) 594426 or (01684) 594413 Fax (01684) 594426

Welland Court is a gem of a small manor house of great character and charm. Built in about 1450, it was enlarged in the 18th-century when the Georgian façade was added. This gorgeous house has been recently rescued from a dilapidated state and graciously modernised to today's high standard of comfort. Truly beautiful countryside surrounds Welland Court from all angles. There is a two-acre lake, heavily stocked with trout, which is available for use by guests at no extra charge. Cordon bleu cuisine is available at all times and menus are 'tailor-made' to suit all tastes. We do, however, ask that meals are requested in advance.

Bed & Breakfast per night: single occupancy £40.00;
double room £60.00
Half board per person: £55.00–£65.00 daily

Bedrooms: 1 double, 2 twin
Bathrooms: 3 en-suite
Parking for 13
Cards accepted: Access, Visa

164 WYCHE KEEP COUNTRY HOUSE   HIGHLY COMMENDED

22 Wyche Road, Malvern, Worcestershire WR14 4EG Tel (01684) 567018 Fax (01684) 892304

Wyche Keep is a mock castle perched high on the Malvern Hills. Built by the family of Prime Minister Sir Stanley Baldwin, it has a long history of entertaining house guests. All luxury suites enjoy spectacular sixty-mile views, and magical rhododendron gardens lead to hill ridge walks. Guests are treated to personal attention and can savour memorable English four-course candle-lit dinners. We specialise in unique and privileged tour holidays with the resident historian host, through Wales and the Cotswolds. A no smoking establishment. Fully licensed.

Bed & Breakfast per night: double room from
£40.00–£60.00
Half board per person: £38.00–£48.00 daily;
£266.00–£336.00 weekly
Evening meal 1930 (last orders 2000)

Bedrooms: 1 double, 2 twin
Bathrooms: 3 en-suite
Parking for 6

The Malvern Hills

ENGLAND'S OLDEST rocks push their way up through the geological strata to reach fresh air a few miles south-west of Worcester. Looking from the east, the Malverns, rising sheer from the Severn Plain, seem to belie their modest height. The 17th-century traveller Celia Fiennes may have described them as being 'at least 2 or 3 miles up and... in a Pirramidy fashion on the top', but in reality they can claim no more than 1,394 ft at their highest point, Worcestershire Beacon. What they lack in altitude, however, they more than make up for in age, beauty and the panoramas they offer.

Only experienced geologists may recognise the clues which reveal that the Malverns are, in the main, made up of pre-Cambrian rocks created about 600 million years ago. On a clear day, however, all visitors will stare in awe at a view which stretches to a far-distant horizon in all directions. The summit of Worcestershire Beacon has a toposcope – or direction indicator – which confirms that those pimples far to the south are indeed the Mendips of Somerset, that slight bump in the hazy east is Bardon Hill near Leicester, that craggy bulge to the north is the Wrekin, and that peak to the west is Plynlimmon, near the Welsh coast. To look down from the Beacon is also to look into England's history, for the battlefields of Evesham (1265), Shrewsbury (1403), Mortimer's Cross (1461), Tewkesbury (1471), Edge Hill (1642) and Worcester (1651) are all there. Closer to hand, toward the southern end of the Malvern ridge and across the old county boundary are remains of perhaps England's finest hillfort, the 32-acre settlement on Herefordshire Beacon (1,115ft).

The best way to explore these glorious hills – they stretch roughly 8 miles in a north–south direction – is naturally on foot, but several roads cross the Malverns affording magnificent views for the less mobile. If you're not arriving by car, then follow in the footsteps of the Victorian visitors to Great Malvern. In the 19th-century this attractive inland resort was almost as popular a spa as Cheltenham or Bath, with Malvern spring water the main draw. The town's prosperity ensured that an extravagantly ornate station was built – and it serves the town to this day. Great Malvern's architectural highlight is, however, its Priory Church of St Mary and St Michael. Inside the largely 15th-century building can be found a collection of medieval stained glass second only to that in York Minster. The town also makes the most of its considerable musical associations through its highly regarded Elgar festival held in late May and early June.

165 COLWALL PARK HOTEL   ≋≋≋ HIGHLY COMMENDED
Colwall, Malvern, Worcestershire WR13 6QG Tel (01684) 540206 or (01684) 541033 Fax (01684) 540847

Situated on the western slopes of the Malvern Hills, the hotel provides an ideal setting for a relaxing break with the care and comfort required. The award-winning Edwardian Restaurant offers English menus at their most enjoyable, with local fresh produce being used where possible. A wonderful centre from which to appreciate some of England's still unspoilt countryside.

Bed & Breakfast per night: single room from £49.50–£59.50; double room from £75.00–£89.50
Half board per person: £59.50–£65.00 daily; £385.00–£416.50 weekly
Lunch available: 1200–1400

Evening meal 1930 (last orders 2100)
Bedrooms: 3 single, 9 double, 7 twin, 2 triple, 2 suites
Bathrooms: 23 en-suite
Parking for 40
Cards accepted: Access, Visa, Diners, Amex, Switch/Delta

166 THE COTTAGE IN THE WOOD HOTEL   ≋≋≋≋ HIGHLY COMMENDED
Holywell Road, Malvern Wells, Malvern, Worcestershire WR14 4LG Tel (01684) 575859 Fax (01684) 560662

Stunningly set high on the Malvern Hills, looking across thirty miles of the Severn Plain to the horizon formed by the Cotswold Hills. Owned and run by the Pattin family for nine years, the aim is to provide a relaxing and peaceful base from which to tour this area of outstanding natural beauty. The restaurant provides exceptional food backed by an extensive wine list of three hundred and fifty bins. The daily half board price is based on a minimum two-night stay, and the weekly price offers seven nights for the price of six. Special breaks are available all week, all year.

Bed & Breakfast per night: single occupancy from £69.00–£75.00; double room from £89.00–£138.00
Half board per person: £52.00–£66.00 daily; £312.00–£396.00 weekly
Lunch available: 1230–1400

Evening meal 1900 (last orders 2100)
Bedrooms: 16 double, 4 twin
Bathrooms: 20 en-suite
Parking for 40
Cards accepted: Access, Visa, Amex, Switch/Delta

167 HOLDFAST COTTAGE HOTEL   ≋≋≋≋ HIGHLY COMMENDED
Marlbank Road, Little Malvern, Malvern, Worcestershire WR13 6NA Tel (01684) 310288 Fax (01684) 311117

Pretty wisteria-covered country house hotel, set in two acres of gardens and private woodland, tucked into the foot of the Malvern Hills. Highly recommended for its freshly-prepared menu which changes daily and uses the best local and seasonal produce. Delightful dining room and bar. Cosy lounge with log fire. Enchanting en-suite bedrooms are individually furnished. A personal welcome plus care and attention throughout your stay is assured by the resident proprietors, Stephen and Jane Knowles.

Bed & Breakfast per night: single room from £42.00–£44.00; double room from £80.00–£84.00
Half board per person: £53.00–£56.00 daily; £324.00–£336.00 weekly
Evening meal 1900 (last orders 2100)

Bedrooms: 1 single, 5 double, 2 twin
Bathrooms: 8 en-suite, 1 public
Parking for 20
Cards accepted: Access, Visa

168 THE BARN HOUSE

⚡⚡ HIGHLY COMMENDED

New Street, Ledbury, Herefordshire HR8 2DX Tel (01531) 632825

This spacious 17th-century house, of great atmosphere and character, was once the home of Ledbury Mineral Water Company and has a large mature walled garden and secure parking. Situated in the centre of the old market town of Ledbury, close to the foothills of the Malverns and the Wye Valley, it is easily accessible from the cities of Hereford, Worcester and Gloucester. No smoking.

Bed & Breakfast per night: double room from
£42.00–£48.00

Bedrooms: 2 double, 1 twin
Bathrooms: 1 en-suite, 1 public
Parking for 10
Cards accepted: Access, Visa

---

169 THE BURNETT 16TH-CENTURY FARMHOUSE & GRANARY
⚡⚡⚡ HIGHLY COMMENDED

Orcop, Hereford HR2 8SF Tel (01981) 540526

Tucked into the hillside with a view you will remember forever – let the 16th-century charm soothe away the 20th-century strains. Ann and Brian welcome you to share this tranquil haven and enjoy luxury rooms with four-posters, lace, white linen and fresh flowers on the windowsill. Traditional food is always available in our restored granary – also some exciting gourmet dishes you simply must try! Ideal for Hereford, Hay, Ross, Welsh Borders and the Wye Valley.

Bed & Breakfast per night: single occupancy from
£25.00–£35.00; double room from £41.00–£60.00
Half board per person: £39.00–£48.50 daily;
£252.50–£309.50 weekly
Lunch available: 1200–1400

Evening meal 1830–2100
Bedrooms: 3 double
Bathrooms: 2 en-suite, 1 private
Parking for 12

---

170 THE OLD RECTORY
⚡ HIGHLY COMMENDED

Garway, Hereford HR2 8RH Tel (01600) 750363 Fax (01600) 750364

Our home is Victorian, with a wonderfully welcoming atmosphere. Much of the furniture has been in the family for generations – the tick of the grandfather clock, the smell of log fires, arrangements of flowers and Aga cooking all combine to make you feel at home. The Blue Room has a double four-poster and the Pink Room has twin beds; both have beautiful views of the countryside looking towards Wales. The garden is peaceful with many song birds.

Bed & Breakfast per night: single occupancy from
£22.50–£26.00; double room from £35.00–£40.00
Half board per person: £32.50–£35.00 daily;
£194.25–£210.00 weekly
Evening meals by prior arrangement

Bedrooms: 1 double, 1 twin
Bathrooms: 1 public, 1 shower room
Parking for 4
Open: March–December
Cards accepted: Access, Visa

171 GLEWSTONE COURT HOTEL

 **HIGHLY COMMENDED**

Glewstone, Ross-on-Wye, Herefordshire HR9 6AW Tel (01989) 770367 Fax (01989) 770282

Located in the heart of the Wye Valley, an area of outstanding natural beauty, Glewstone Court is a unique hotel where the priority is placed on making guests feel totally welcome. The style is relaxed country-house, with comfortable furnishings, period decor, open log fires and a warm, friendly ambience. Food is always prepared to a high standard using local produce – Hereford beef, Wye salmon and Welsh lamb are constantly on the menu.

Bed & Breakfast per night: single room from £40.00–£65.00; double room from £60.00–£98.00
Half board per person: £65.00–£75.00 daily; £300.00–£475.00 weekly
Lunch available: 1200–1400

Evening meal 1900 (last orders 2130)
Bedrooms: 1 single, 6 double
Bathrooms: 7 en-suite
Parking for 20
Cards accepted: Access, Visa, Amex, Switch/Delta

172 WYNDHAM ARMS

 **HIGHLY COMMENDED**

Clearwell, Coleford, Gloucestershire GL16 8JT Tel (01594) 833666 Fax (01594) 836450

A 14th-century village inn with 20th-century amenities. At the edge of the Royal Forest of Dean, just above the Wye Valley, the Wyndham Arms has been in the Stanford family's competent ownership since 1973. All bedrooms en-suite, award-winning restaurant, traditional beers, lots of different malt whiskies, and very pretty gardens. Just the place for a get-away weekend. Stay free on winter Sundays if you dine in the restaurant.

Bed & Breakfast per night: single room £49.50; double room from £61.00–£65.00
Half board per person: £47.50–£50.00 daily; £280.00 weekly
Lunch available: 1200–1400

Evening meal 1900 (last orders 2130)
Bedrooms: 2 single, 4 double, 9 twin, 2 triple
Bathrooms: 17 en-suite
Parking for 50
Cards accepted: Access, Visa, Diners, Amex, Switch/Delta

173 ORCHARD HOUSE

Listed HIGHLY COMMENDED

Aston Ingham Road, Kilcot, Nr Newent, Gloucestershire GL18 1NP Tel (01989) 720417 Fax (01989) 720770

Orchard House, near Ross-on-Wye, is a delightful Tudor-style country house dated 1710, completely surrounded by peaceful five-acre gardens. A beautifully appointed home with a relaxed and friendly atmosphere, every modern comfort, delicious food and fine wines. Excellent accommodation including a Regency-style dining room, luxurious en-suite and double bedrooms. Original oak beams, television lounge, conservatory, fountain courtyard and croquet lawn. Residential licence. Well located for visiting the Wye Valley, Cotswolds and Malverns.

Bed & Breakfast per night: single occupancy from £30.00–£32.00; double room from £45.00–£65.00
Half board per person: £39.00–£49.00 daily; £231.00–£301.00 weekly
Evening meal 2000

Bedrooms: 2 double, 2 twin
Bathrooms: 2 en-suite, 1 public
Parking for 10
Cards accepted: Access, Visa

174 MILTON HOUSE HOTEL
HIGHLY COMMENDED

12 Royal Parade, Bayshill Road, Cheltenham, Gloucestershire GL50 3AY Tel (01242) 582601 Fax (01242) 222326

Take eight beautiful bedrooms, an impressive Regency lounge and a sun lounge/bar, set them among the elegant terraces of Montpellier, and there you have Milton House – a lovely Grade II listed Regency hotel. Relax in style and comfort only five minutes' walk from the fashionable Promenade and be sure of a warm welcome from your resident hosts, Penny and Alex Gamez.

Bed & Breakfast per night: single room £38.50; double room from £52.00–£68.00

Bedrooms: 2 single, 3 double, 1 twin, 2 triple
Bathrooms: 8 en-suite
Parking for 5
Cards accepted: Access, Visa, Amex

175 BEAUMONT HOUSE HOTEL
HIGHLY COMMENDED

Shurdington Road, Cheltenham, Gloucestershire GL53 0JE Tel (01242) 245986 Fax (01242) 520044

Splendidly positioned where Cheltenham meets the Cotswolds, and only minutes from the town centre or secluded Cotswold walks. Stylishly furnished to offer a gentle blend of past elegance and present comfort. Warm yet fresh bedrooms, some with four-poster beds, and friendly attentive service make for a restful and relaxing stay. Only a short stroll to many of Cheltenham's fine restaurants. Excellently situated for all the Cotswolds, Roman Bath, Shakespeare and centuries of history.

Bed & Breakfast per night: single room from £37.00; double room from £48.00–£58.00
Evening meal 1900 (last orders 2000)

Bedrooms: 2 single, 6 double, 5 twin, 1 triple, 1 family room
Bathrooms: 15 en-suite, 1 public
Parking for 20
Cards accepted: Access, Visa, Amex

176 BEECHWORTH LAWN HOTEL
HIGHLY COMMENDED

133 Hales Road, Cheltenham, Gloucestershire GL52 6ST Tel (01242) 522583 Fax (01242) 522583

Near to the town centre and conveniently located for shopping and leisure activities, Beechworth Lawn offers a period hotel carefully restored. Decorated and furnished with the highest quality beds, linen and soft-furnishings for your complete comfort and pleasure. There is high-quality accommodation and food with discreet friendly service. With our all-year low rates, twenty-four hour access and off-street parking, we will make your stay in Cheltenham a memorable and happy one.

Bed & Breakfast per night: single room from £24.50–£32.00; double room from £42.00–£50.00
Half board per person: £36.50–£44.00 daily
Evening meal 1800 (last orders 1900)

Bedrooms: 2 single, 2 double, 3 twin, 2 triple
Bathrooms: 5 en-suite, 1 public
Parking for 12

177 HOTEL ON THE PARK

〰〰〰〰 DE LUXE

Evesham Road, Cheltenham, Gloucestershire GL52 2AH Tel (01242) 518898 Fax (01242) 511526

This exclusive town house hotel is set within a classic example of a Regency villa and successfully combines the highest standards of traditional hotel-keeping with the charm and character of a period house. The twelve individually-designed bedrooms and suites and the elegant, candle-lit public rooms complement a restaurant serving some of the best modern British cooking on offer today. Situated opposite Pittville Park and five minutes from the race-course and the town centre.

Bed & Breakfast per night: single occupancy £82.75; double room from £106.00–£166.00
Half board per person: £65.78–£92.78 daily
Lunch available: 1200–1430
Evening meal 1900 (last orders 2130)

Bedrooms: 8 double, 4 twin
Bathrooms: 12 en-suite
Parking for 10
Cards accepted: Access, Visa, Diners, Amex

178 DEERHURST HOUSE

〰〰 HIGHLY COMMENDED

Deerhurst, Gloucester, Gloucestershire GL19 4BX Tel (01684) 292135 or 0850 520051

Deerhurst House is a beautiful, classically-proportioned, period country house of mellow brick, adorned by a stone portico, standing in three acres in the ancient riverside village of Deerhurst (containing the oldest dated church in England), three miles south of Tewkesbury. Guest rooms are generous and comfortable with en-suite facilities and glorious views across unspoilt countryside to the Malvern Hills. A perfect centre for walking or touring the Cotswolds, Malverns, or Royal Forest of Dean.

Bed & Breakfast per night: single occupancy £25.00; double room from £40.00–£45.00

Bedrooms: 1 double, 1 twin
Bathrooms: 2 private
Parking for 10

179 CLEEVE HILL HOTEL

〰〰 DE LUXE

Cleeve Hill, Cheltenham, Gloucestershire GL52 3PR Tel (01242) 672052

This award-winning hotel, perched on the slopes of Cleeve Hill, the highest point in the Cotswolds, is a mere ten minute drive from the centre of Cheltenham. The immaculate Edwardian house is elegantly decorated with quality furnishings and fabrics and all of the bedrooms are equipped to a very high standard with all the little extras that make this a very special place to stay. The hotel upholds a strict 'No Smoking' policy.

Bed & Breakfast per night: single room from £45.00–£55.00; double room from £60.00

Bedrooms: 1 single, 5 double, 2 twin, 1 family room
Bathrooms: 9 en-suite
Parking for 12
Cards accepted: Access, Visa, Amex

180 ISBOURNE MANOR HOUSE

≋≋ DE LUXE

Castle Street, Winchcombe, Cheltenham, Gloucestershire GL54 5JA Tel (01242) 602281

Isbourne Manor House is Grade II listed, lovingly restored with beautiful fabrics and family antiques – the accent being on comfort. Guests are invited to drink from our Honour Bar in an elegant drawing room. The dining room has an intimate atmosphere in which to enjoy our extensive breakfast. Three bedrooms (including king four-poster) have television and every conceivable extra. The River Isbourne flows through the garden. Private parking, with Sudeley Castle opposite. The village is but two minutes walk.

Bed & Breakfast per night: single occupancy from £38.00–£50.00; double room from £48.00–£60.00

Bedrooms: 2 double, 1 twin
Bathrooms: 2 en-suite, 1 private
Parking for 4

181 SUDELEY HILL FARM

≋≋ HIGHLY COMMENDED

Winchcombe, Cheltenham, Gloucestershire GL54 5JB Tel (01242) 602344

A friendly welcome awaits you on our eight-hundred-acre sheep and arable farm. The 15th-century listed farmhouse is situated above Sudeley Castle, with a large garden and panoramic views across the valley. A comfortable lounge, log fires, separate dining room, no smoking en-suite bedrooms with television and facilities for hot drinks. Central for exploring the Cotswolds. Good pub food in Winchcombe, half a mile away.

Bed & Breakfast per night: single occupancy from £25.00–£30.00; double room from £42.00–£44.00

Bedrooms: 1 double, 2 triple
Bathrooms: 3 en-suite
Parking for 10

182 WESLEY HOUSE RESTAURANT

≋≋≋ HIGHLY COMMENDED

High Street, Winchcombe, Cheltenham, Gloucestershire GL54 5LJ Tel (01242) 602366 Fax (01242) 602405

A warm welcome from the staff of Wesley House and the friendly small ancient Saxon town of Winchcombe, nestling in the Isbourne Valley only six miles from Cheltenham, with views across the North Cotswold Edge. Our half-timbered building dates from c1435 and every convenience has been introduced that does not affect an historic medieval house. Jonathan Lewis has brought the culinary skills acquired from working around the world to a local restaurant where the emphasis is on freshness of produce and clarity of taste.

Bed & Breakfast per night: single occupancy from £42.00–£55.00; double room from £55.00–£65.00
Half board per person: £49.50–£65.00 daily
Lunch available: 1200–1400
Evening meal 1900 (last orders 2200)

Bedrooms: 3 double, 2 twin
Bathrooms: 5 en-suite
Cards accepted: Access, Visa, Amex, Switch/Delta

183 POSTLIP HALL FARM

 HIGHLY COMMENDED

Winchcombe, Cheltenham, Gloucestershire GL54 5AQ Tel (01242) 603351

Spectacular situation with superb scenery in every direction. Set on the side of Cleeve Hill, off the B4632, one-and-three-quarter miles from Winchcombe. This working farm is a fantastic base for exploring the Cotswolds, Warwick Castle, Blenheim Palace, Bath and the Malverns. Great walking and golf, with horse-riding close by. Cosy, spacious rooms with armchairs, colour TVs and beverages. Lovely, welcoming atmosphere.

Bed & Breakfast per night: single occupancy from £20.00–£30.00; double room from £36.00–£40.00

Bedrooms: 2 double, 1 twin
Bathrooms: 2 en-suite, 1 private
Parking for 6

---

184 WINDRUSH FARM

HIGHLY COMMENDED

Bourton-on-the-Water, Cheltenham, Gloucestershire GL54 3BY Tel (01451) 820419 Fax (01451) 820419

Just one-and-a-half miles from Bourton-on-the-Water, this 150-acre arable farm is situated in the peace and beauty of the glorious Cotswolds. The traditional mullioned farmhouse has a beautiful garden and superb views. The guest rooms are tastefully furnished with many extra touches, and a large visitors' lounge looks out onto the garden. Jenny and David enjoy helping guests to plan their day, suggest good eating places and treat their guests as extended family.

Bed & Breakfast per night: single occupancy from £28.00–£30.00; double room from £38.00–£42.00

Bedrooms: 1 double, 1 twin
Bathrooms: 2 en-suite
Parking for 8
Open: March–December

---

185 CHARLTON KINGS HOTEL

 HIGHLY COMMENDED

London Road, Charlton Kings, Cheltenham, Gloucestershire GL52 6UU Tel (01242) 231061 Fax (01242) 241900

Situated in an area of outstanding natural beauty on the edge of Cheltenham Spa. An ideal touring centre for the walker (the famous Cotswold Way is only a half-mile away) or motorist (ask for your free 'Romantic Road' when booking). The sporting/ activity enthusiast is also well catered for. Whatever you choose, come back and enjoy the creative skills of our talented chef. Although we have high standards, the hotel is informally run by the proprietor and his team of enthusiastic staff.

Bed & Breakfast per night: single room from £42.50–£74.50; double room from £60.00–£92.00
Half board per person: £54.00–£90.00 daily; £294.00–£308.00 weekly
Lunch available: 1200–1400

Evening meal 1900 (last orders 2045)
Bedrooms: 2 single, 8 double, 2 twin, 1 triple, 1 family room
Bathrooms: 14 en-suite
Parking for 26
Cards accepted: Access, Visa, Amex, Switch/Delta

186 GUITING GUESTHOUSE

 HIGHLY COMMENDED

Post Office Lane, Guiting Power, Cheltenham, Gloucestershire GL54 5TZ Tel (01451) 850470 Fax (01451) 850034

The house is a delightful and carefully-restored 16th-century Cotswold stone farmhouse. Everywhere there are exposed beams, inglenook fireplaces, open fires and polished solid pine floors from the Wychwood forest. Most rooms have four-poster beds and are en-suite, with the exception of one room which has totally private facilities. Television and generously-filled hospitality tray in each room. Access to the guesthouse is available at all times. Delicious evening meals, served by candle light, are prepared and presented by the hosts (with the exception of Sunday and Monday).

Bed & Breakfast per night: single occupancy £28.00; double room from £45.00
Half board per person: from £37.00 daily
Evening meal 1845 (last orders 1845)

Bedrooms: 3 double
Bathrooms: 2 en-suite, 1 private
Parking for 2

187 WASHBOURNE COURT HOTEL

 HIGHLY COMMENDED

Lower Slaughter, near Cheltenham, Gloucestershire GL54 2HS Tel (01451) 822143 Fax (01451) 821045

A magnificent 17th-century hotel standing in four acres alongside the river in the centre of Lower Slaughter – one of the most beautiful and unspoilt villages in the Cotswolds. All bedrooms have individual character and private facilities – some with jacuzzi bath and private lounge. The intimate restaurant offers the finest of modern English cuisine using the best of fresh local produce, and there is a lovely riverside terrace for summer lunches. We are an independent hotel. Our aim is to provide the very best of hospitality and culinary excellence in an atmosphere of comfort and tranquillity.

Bed & Breakfast per night: single occupancy £85.00; double room from £95.00–£185.00
Half board per person: £60.00–£105.00 daily; £360.00–£500.00 weekly
Lunch available: 1230–1430

Evening meal 1930 (last orders 2115)
Bedrooms: 12 double, 3 twin, 6 triple
Bathrooms: 21 en-suite
Parking for 69
Cards accepted: Access, Visa, Diners, Amex, Switch/Delta

188 GRAPEVINE HOTEL

 HIGHLY COMMENDED

Sheep Street, Stow-on-the-Wold, Gloucestershire GL54 1AU Tel (01451) 830344 Fax (01451) 832278 Web site http://www.vines.co.uk

An award-winning 17th-century market town hotel in the antiques centre of the Cotswolds. Romantic conservatory restaurant crowned by a magnificent historic vine and finely furnished garden and vine rooms. The outstanding personal service provided by a loyal team of staff is perhaps the secret of the hotel's success. This, along with the exceptionally high standard of overall comfort, hospitality and fine food, has earned the Grapevine its many accolades.

Half board per person: £55.00–£116.00 daily; £350.00–£610.00 weekly
Lunch available: 1200–1430
Evening meal 1900 (last orders 2130)

Bedrooms: 1 single, 10 double, 10 twin, 1 triple, 1 family room
Bathrooms: 22 en-suite, 1 private
Parking for 23
Cards accepted: Access, Visa, Diners, Amex, Switch/Delta

⓭⑧⑨ COLLEGE HOUSE

 ≋≋ DE LUXE

Chapel Street, Broadwell, Moreton-in-Marsh, Gloucestershire GL56 OTW Tel (01451) 832351

College House is a 17th-century residence of great character located in a quiet and enchanting Cotswold village. It has superb bedrooms and luxurious bathrooms, of which two are en-suite, and a sitting-room with a large inglenook fireplace for exclusive guest use. Breakfast and, if desired, three-course dinners are served in the beamed dining-room. Broadwell is just two miles from Stow-on-the-Wold. Oxford, Cheltenham and Stratford-upon-Avon are all easily accessible.

Bed & Breakfast per night: single occupancy from £40.00–£57.00; double room from £45.00–£62.00
Half board per person: £39.00–£47.50 daily; £273.00–£332.00 weekly
Evening meal 1800 (last bookings 1200)

Bedrooms: 3 double
Bathrooms: 2 en-suite, 1 private
Parking for 6

⓭⑨⓪ STOW LODGE HOTEL

≋≋≋≋ HIGHLY COMMENDED

The Square, Stow-on-the-Wold, Gloucestershire GL54 1AB Tel (01451) 830485 Fax (01451) 831671

Privately owned and family-run Cotswold Manor House Hotel set back in its own gardens in a secluded corner of the market square. Bedrooms are comfortably furnished with a private bathroom, and the no smoking restaurant offers excellent home cooking and an interesting extensive wine list. There are warm open fires for those cooler days in both the bar and residents' lounge. The hotel is ideal for those touring the Cotswolds and Shakespeare country and requiring a relaxing holiday.

Bed & Breakfast per night: single room from £40.00–£75.00; double room from £58.00–£95.00
Lunch available: 1200–1400
Evening meal 1900 (last orders 2100)

Bedrooms: 1 single, 9 double, 8 twin, 3 triple
Bathrooms: 21 en-suite
Parking for 30
Open: February–December
Cards accepted: Access, Visa, Diners, Amex, Switch/Delta

⓭⑨① DIAL HOUSE

≋≋≋≋ HIGHLY COMMENDED

The Chestnuts, Bourton-on-the-Water, Gloucestershire GL54 2AN Tel (01451) 822244 Fax (01451) 810126

Built in 1698 of Cotswold stone, the Dial House is set in secluded gardens and reflects the ambience, charm and good manners of times gone by. Tastefully furnished rooms provide bathrooms, satellite television and beverage trays, some have antique four-posters. Dine in style in an intimate restaurant with inglenook fireplace and oak beams. Chef Kevin Chatfield has achieved awards for his excellent cuisine. There is ample parking within the grounds.

Bed & Breakfast per night: single room from £30.00–£44.00; double room from £60.00–£102.00
Half board per person: £53.50–£68.50 daily; £315.00–£400.00 weekly
Lunch available: 1200–1400

Evening meal 1900 (last orders 2100)
Bedrooms: 1 single, 6 double, 3 twin
Bathrooms: 9 en-suite, 1 private
Parking for 18
Cards accepted: Access, Visa, Amex, Switch/Delta

192 COOMBE HOUSE

 HIGHLY COMMENDED

Rissington Road, Bourton-on-the-Water, Gloucestershire GL54 2DT Tel (01451) 821966 Fax (01451) 810477

Quietly located just a river-side walk from the centre of this beautiful Cotswold Village, Coombe House offers a haven of cleanliness, comfort and personal attention from your hosts. Gentle elegance, charming bedrooms and reception rooms, and a delightful garden with unusual plants. Perfect central base for discovering the superb Cotswolds, gardens and castles. London 75 miles. Oxford/Stratford 26 miles. Anticipated assistance with routes, ideas and restaurants. No smoking.

Bed & Breakfast per night: single occupancy from £40.00–£46.00; double room from £56.00–£68.00

Bedrooms: 3 double, 2 twin, 2 triple
Bathrooms: 6 en-suite, 1 private
Parking for 10
Cards accepted: Access, Visa, Amex

---

193 THE SWAN HOTEL

≈≈≈≈ DE LUXE

Bibury, Cirencester, Gloucestershire GL7 5NW Tel (01285) 740695 Fax (01285) 740473

A luxurious hotel with cosy parlours, elegant dining room, sumptuous bedrooms (a few with four-poster beds) and lavish bathrooms (some with large jacuzzi baths). Our head chef presents a regularly changing menu. An ideal base for touring the Cotswolds, visiting Shakespeare's Stratford, Roman Bath, antiques in Burford and the Oxford colleges. Take pleasure in our private garden on the banks of the River Coln – enjoy the ambience or fish for your own trout. Licensed for weddings. Ideal venue for special occasions.

Bed & Breakfast per night: single room from £86.00–£125.00; double room from £115.00–£210.00
Half board per person: £77.50–£120.00 daily
Lunch available: 1200–1430
Evening meal 1930 (last orders 2130)

Bedrooms: 1 single, 12 double, 4 twin, 1 family room
Bathrooms: 18 en-suite
Parking for 20
Cards accepted: Access, Visa, Amex, Switch/Delta

---

194 SHAWSWELL COUNTRY HOUSE

≈≈ DE LUXE

Rendcomb, Cirencester, Gloucestershire GL7 7HD Tel (01285) 831779

'Far from the Madding Crowd'. Centrally located, our 17th-century Cotswold stone house is approached via a no-through road and set in twenty-five acres with spectacular views over the Churn Valley. It has a wealth of beams and inglenooks and has been lovingly restored and furnished with great care. Shawswell offers total peace and tranquillity, the ideal base for touring, walking or cycling. We aim to provide high standards with personal service in a relaxed atmosphere. Your hosts: Muriel and David Gomm.

Bed & Breakfast per night: single room from £30.00–£35.00; double room from £45.00–£55.00

Bedrooms: 1 single, 3 double, 1 twin
Bathrooms: 5 en-suite
Parking for 8
Open: February–November

195 GILBERT'S

Gilbert's Lane, Brookthorpe, Gloucester, Gloucestershire GL4 0UH Tel (01452) 812364 Fax (01452) 812364

This beautiful listed 16th-century house has been tastefully brought up to date with modern comforts and conveniences whilst retaining the dignity and atmosphere of the past. This is also reflected in the surrounding organic grounds. Here goodies are grown for the table amongst a rich tapestry of flora and fauna. Centrally placed beneath the dramatic Cotswold edge, ten minutes from Gloucester and Stroud, this makes an excellent base for exploring Bath, Oxford, Stratford and much more.

Bed & Breakfast per night: single room from
£23.00–£35.00; double room from £46.00–£55.00

Bedrooms: 1 single, 2 double, 1 twin
Bathrooms: 3 en-suite, 1 private
Parking for 6

Slimbridge

ASKED TO NAME THE ONLY PLACE in the whole of Europe where all six species of flamingo can be seen, few would answer Gloucestershire. Surprisingly, however, Slimbridge, on the banks of the River Severn 10 miles south of Gloucester, is the right answer. It was here on 10 November 1946 that the naturalist and painter Peter (later Sir Peter) Scott founded the Wildfowl & Wetlands Trust. Operating from two derelict cottages and using wartime pill-boxes as hides, the charity had distinctly humble beginnings. Today, over 50 years later, Sir Peter's pioneering vision has grown into an organisation employing over 180 staff at a number of sites throughout the country. Slimbridge is now internationally known for the quality of its research into wetland conservation, but above all else it offers a superb opportunity to see a vast range of birds.

Unlike many visitor attractions, this is best visited during the winter (Slimbridge is closed only on Christmas Day). Up to 8,000 birds fly in to the 800-acre reserve to pass the winter here. Early visitors usually include teal, pintail, wigeon and shoveler, which may arrive during September. European white-fronted and dark-bellied Brent geese follow soon afterwards, with Bewick's swans flying in towards the beginning of November. Slimbridge has the world's largest collection of ducks, geese and swans – these have traditionally formed the core of Slimbridge's population – but there are also many waders to be spotted, such as curlews and lapwings,

as well as sandpipers, redshank and greenshank during periods of migration. On a winter visit you may even be lucky enough to spot a peregrine falcon eyeing the waders as potential prey.

But Slimbridge is more than simply a collection of hides: it is an exploration of a habitat which nurtures so many species of bird, insect, plant and animal. At Slimbridge you can walk dryshod through marshland by following a raised boardwalk, discover the fauna and flora of the rainforest in the Tropical House and try your hand at pond-dipping. Thanks to powerful floodlights there's also the option of watching the thousands of avian visitors from the comfort of the heated Peng Observatory on a dark winter's night. If you're feeling more strenuous, join the dawn chorus walk which departs at 4.30 am on a couple of May Sundays. Slimbridge Wildfowl Trust (01453) 890333.

⓲ THE GREY COTTAGE

≋≋ HIGHLY COMMENDED

Bath Road, Leonard Stanley, Stonehouse, Gloucestershire GL10 3LU Tel (01453) 822515 Fax (01453) 822515

Situated in a secluded area of the south Cotswolds, nevertheless with good communications. Andrew and Rosemary Reeves welcome you to their rugged stone-built cottage which permeates warmth and ambience. Fresh flowers abound as we endeavour to maintain our half-acre garden to a high standard throughout the year. Prior reservation is essential as we try to cater for individual preferences and tastes using authentic ingredients.

Bed & Breakfast per night: single room from £25.00–£29.00; double room from £46.00–£49.00 Half board per person: £39.00–£45.50 daily Evening meal by arrangement 1915

Bedrooms: 1 single, 1 double, 1 twin Bathrooms: 1 en-suite, 2 private, 1 public Parking for 6

⓲ HUNTERS LODGE

≋≋ HIGHLY COMMENDED

Dr Brown's Road, Minchinhampton, Stroud, Gloucestershire GL6 9BT Tel (01453) 883588 Fax (01453) 731449

Welcome to a beautifully furnished, large old Cotswold stone house situated six hundred and fifty feet up on the South Cotswold hills. Ideal for walking on six hundred acres of National Trust land – Minchinhampton Common – immediately outside our grounds, with spectacular views into the Stroud valleys. The interesting old wool town centre is only minutes away. Selection of brochures on display for attractions and car and walking tours. Resident Gloucestershire Green Badge tourist guide to help you plan your excursions.

Bed & Breakfast per night: single occupancy from £25.00–£30.00; double room from £38.00–£46.00

Bedrooms: 2 twin, 1 triple Bathrooms: 1 en-suite, 2 private Parking for 8

⓲ TAVERN HOUSE

≋≋ DE LUXE

Willesley, Tetbury, Gloucestershire GL8 8QU Tel (01666) 880444 Fax (01666) 880254

A delightfully situated 17th-century Grade II listed former staging-post, this elegant Cotswold-stone country house is only one mile from Westonbirt Arboretum which has one of Europe's largest collections of trees and shrubs. The four en-suite bedrooms have direct-dial telephone, television, hairdryer and much more. A charming secluded garden offers peace and tranquillity, far from the madding crowd. Convenient for Bath, Gloucester, Cheltenham and Stow. A country house atmosphere with attention to detail being our keynote. ETB 'England for Excellence' Silver Award, 1993.

Bed & Breakfast per night: single occupancy from £45.00–£55.00; double room from £57.00–£67.00

Bedrooms: 3 double, 1 twin Bathrooms: 4 en-suite Parking for 4 Cards accepted: Access, Visa

⟨199⟩ THE OLD RECTORY

 HIGHLY COMMENDED

Didmarton, Gloucestershire GL9 1DS Tel (01454) 238233

This small former rectory is set in the south Cotswolds on the A433. It has a very friendly informal atmosphere and is an ideal base for touring or, since we are close to Bath and the M4/5, is a convenient and comfortable overnight stop. Westonbirt Arboretum is five minutes away and the antiques centre of Tetbury is less than ten. There is ample parking and food is available within walking distance.

Bed & Breakfast per night: single occupancy from £21.00–£25.00; double room from £35.00–£37.00

Bedrooms: 2 double, 1 twin
Bathrooms: 2 en-suite, 1 private
Parking for 4

⟨200⟩ KENWICK PARK HOTEL & LEISURE CLUB

HIGHLY COMMENDED

Kenwick Park, Kenwick, Louth, Lincolnshire LN11 8NR Tel (01507) 608806 Fax (01507) 608027

Country house hotel set in a magnificent 500-acre estate, nationally recognised as an 'area of outstanding natural beauty'. Set adjacent to the 18-hole, par 72 international standard golf course (accessible to residents). The hotel has recently opened an exclusive health complex featuring 2 tennis courts, heated swimming pool, squash, Clarins Salon, and many more activities to ensure a memorable break. Close proximity to several coastal resorts and the tranquil Lincolnshire Wolds.

Bed & Breakfast per night: single occupancy £79.50; double room £115.00
Half board per person: £69.50 daily; £400.00 weekly
Lunch available: 1100–1430
Evening meal 1900 (last orders 2145)

Bedrooms: 18 double, 6 twin
Bathrooms: 24 en-suite
Parking for 120
Cards accepted: Access, Visa, Diners, Amex, Switch/Delta

⟨201⟩ BARNSDALE LODGE HOTEL

 HIGHLY COMMENDED

The Avenue, Exton, Oakham, Leicestershire LE15 8AH Tel (01572) 724678 Fax (01572) 724961

Set in the heart of Rutland's beautiful countryside overlooking Rutland Water, this 17th-century farmhouse welcomes you with luxury and warmth. Traditional English fayre is served in an Edwardian dining room using fresh, locally grown produce. International wines complement the menus. Afternoon tea, elevenses and buttery lunches are always available in the conservatory. Our 29 en-suite bedrooms are filled with antique furniture (with eleven additional bedrooms, a 6-metre spa pool and stress therapy centre available from April 1997). The ideal retreat from everyday life. Come and discover the tranquillity of Rutland.

Bed & Breakfast per night: single room from £55.00; double room from £75.00–£90.00
Lunch available: 1200–1400
Evening meal 1900 (last orders 2145)

Bedrooms: 8 single, 12 double, 7 twin, 2 triple
Bathrooms: 29 en-suite
Parking for 107
Cards accepted: Access, Visa, Switch/Delta

202 THE PRIORY

🌊🌊🌊 HIGHLY COMMENDED

Church Road, Ketton, Stamford, Lincolnshire PE9 3RD   Tel (01780) 720215 Fax (01780) 721881

Historic listed country house in quiet village near Stamford. Award-winning bed and breakfast with spacious en-suite bedrooms offering every comfort and many thoughtful extras. Bedrooms are individually designed with oversize hand-made beds, high ceilings, luxurious fabrics, original panelling and splendid views over the gardens. Each has a resident Teddy. Luxury bathrooms have shower and bath. Resident chef prepares a choice of dishes every day from fresh local produce. Private parking. Close to Rutland Water. Send for our colour brochure.

Bed & Breakfast per night: single occupancy from
£50.00–£55.00; double room from £65.00–£85.00
Half board per person: £50.00–£60.00 daily;
£315.00–£375.00 weekly
Evening meal from 1900 (last bookings 1830)

Bedrooms: 2 double, 1 twin
Bathrooms: 3 en-suite
Parking for 10
Cards accepted: Access, Visa

The Fens

FENLAND HAS A SINGULAR AND, some would say, disturbing atmosphere. Stretching from Boston in the north almost to Cambridge in the south, its vast flatness is relieved only by the occasional church spire. There are few established towns or villages, because until comparatively recently the whole area was nothing but wild and treacherous marsh.

The Romans were the first to build a system of drainage channels, part of which may still be seen at Landbeach, north of Cambridge. When the Romans left, however, the schemes were abandoned and the waters encroached once more. Only where islands rose up from the marsh could settlements be built, often dominated by great monastic institutions, as at Ely. The monasteries drained small areas of land for their own use, but it was not until the 17th-century that any large-scale attempt was made to drain the Fens for agricultural use. In the 1830s one of the most ambitious projects was financed by the Earl of Bedford who employed the Dutch engineer, Cornelius Vermuyden, to construct two great waterways, the Old Bedford River and the New Bedford River, to take excess water to the Wash. The land soon became suitable for growing crops and is now one of the most fertile areas in the country.

Initially, however, draining the Fens was problematic. The peatland dried and shrank so that the ground level fell below that of the drainage ditches, and in some areas even below sea level. Water now had to be pumped out of the fields, at first by means of windpumps, followed in Victorian times by steam-powered engines. Today, if a diesel-driven system were not maintained this area of prime farmland would be submerged once again.

Only a few pockets now remain of the wild wetland which was once the Fens. The National Trust owns Wicken Fen (tel. 01353 720274), near Ely, an area which the Victorians kept wet as a habitat for the prized and collectable swallow-tail butterfly, still found in parts of Norfolk. Around 600 acres of fenland is open to the public here, made accessible by a raised walkway from which the varied plant, insect and birdlife may be viewed. Along the route is a small working windpump, the last survivor of the hundreds of wind-driven machines which once drained the Fens, now used to pump water *into* the reserve. A display in the modern reception building tells the history of 4,000 years of fenland life.

203 CORFIELD HOUSE

 HIGHLY COMMENDED

Sporle, Swaffham, Norfolk PE32 2EA Tel (01760) 723636

Corfield House is an attractive brick-built house standing in half an acre of lawned gardens in the peaceful village of Sporle near Swaffham, an ideal base for touring Norfolk. Some of the comfortable en-suite bedrooms (one ground floor) have fine views across open fields and all have television, clock radio and a fact-file on places to visit. Good home-cooked food using excellent local produce. No smoking throughout.

Bed & Breakfast per night: single room £23.00; double room from £37.00–£43.00
Half board per person: £31.00–£34.00 daily; £205.00–£230.00 weekly
Evening meal 1900 (last bookings 1730)

Bedrooms: 1 single, 2 double, 2 twin
Bathrooms: 5 en-suite
Parking for 5
Open: Easter–December
Cards accepted: Access, Visa

204 WHITE HALL

 HIGHLY COMMENDED

Carbrooke, Near Watton, Thetford, Norfolk IP25 6SG Tel (01953) 885950 Fax (01953) 885950

White Hall is an elegant, listed Georgian house standing in three acres, with a large natural pond, surrounded by fields and providing a haven of peace and tranquillity. Spacious accommodation, full central heating, log fires etc, ensure your stay is enjoyable and relaxing. Situated on the edge of Carbrooke village and in the centre of the interesting and attractive area of Breckland, we are ideally situated for the many attractions of both Norfolk and north Suffolk.

Bed & Breakfast per night: single occupancy from £27.00–£33.00; double room from £34.00–£44.00

Bedrooms: 2 double, 1 twin
Bathrooms: 1 en-suite, 1 public
Parking for 10

205 PEACOCK HOUSE

 HIGHLY COMMENDED

Peacock Lane, Old Beetley, Dereham, Norfolk NR20 4DG Tel (01362) 860371

Allow us to spoil you in our lovely home. We offer bed and breakfast in peaceful, rural surroundings in our beautifully-renovated old farmhouse. All our en-suite guest rooms are traditionally and prettily furnished, offering every comfort. Guests have their own sitting room and may enjoy our lovely garden, good home cooking and our own free-range eggs. Centrally situated, with Norwich, Sandringham, National Trust houses and the coast all within easy reach.

Bed & Breakfast per night: single occupancy from £17.00–£20.00; double room from £34.00–£36.00

Bedrooms: 2 double, 1 twin
Bathrooms: 3 en-suite
Parking for 4

206 **WESTWOOD BARN**

≋≋ HIGHLY COMMENDED

Crabgate Lane South, Wood Dalling, Norwich, Norfolk NR11 6SW Tel (01263) 584108

Westwood Barn is an exclusive 15th-century building converted to provide two double and one twin en-suite ground-floor bedrooms, including a four-poster bedroom. A magnificent sitting room with many original beams and an enormous inglenook fireplace. Idyllic rural location for discovering the charms and tranquillity of north Norfolk: two miles from the picturesque village of Heydon, with National Trust properties, Norwich, the coast and Broads within a twelve mile radius. Illustrated brochure available.

Bed & Breakfast per night: single occupancy £32.00;
double room from £42.00–£48.00
Half board per person: £36.00–£47.00 daily;
£238.00–£257.00 weekly
Evening meal 1900 (last orders 2000)

Bedrooms: 2 double, 1 twin
Bathrooms: 3 en-suite
Parking for 8

Walsingham Pilgrimages

TODAY'S VISITORS to the gentle Norfolk village of Walsingham may be surprised to learn that this was once the second most popular 'tourist' destination in the land. Only the shrine to Saint Thomas à Becket in Canterbury could boast more pilgrims per year than Walsingham. Indeed when Erasmus, the Dutch theologian, came here in 1511, he wrote that its income derived almost entirely from the number of its visitors.

The glorious village of Walsingham ultimately owes its popularity to one Richelde of Fervaques. In a dream the Virgin Mary instructed the widow to erect in Walsingham a replica of the Holy House (where Gabriel announced that Mary would give birth to Jesus). Building began in the early 12th-century (though some claim it was 1061). After initial work was miraculously moved to another nearby site, the Holy House quickly attracted attention. By about 1153 Walsingham Priory had been established to look after the shrine. Henry III was a regular visitor, and royal patronage may have been a major reason for the Augustinian Priory's renown. Fame brought pilgrims, who in turn brought wealth. They gave offerings to the shrine and its guardians and, just as present-day tourists take home souvenirs, so medieval pilgrims would buy a badge as a sign of their piety; the more emblems one had, the more one would command respect from one's fellows as a pious and dedicated pilgrim. One badge in King's Lynn Museum shows what is believed to be a depiction of the wooden Statue of Our Lady of Walsingham. In the 14th-century, thanks to the accretion of funds, work began on a grand, new church and monastic buildings. Today's visitors can see the magnificent East Window and Refectory dating from this time.

Disaster, in the forbidding shape of Henry VIII, eventually struck Walsingham, as it did every monastery in the land. In 1538 the Holy House was demolished, most of the buildings torn down, and the materials sold. Even the venerated statue was burnt. Pilgrims no longer came, and for 350 years Walsingham lived a life much like its neighbouring villages. At the end of the last century, however, the Slipper Chapel at nearby Houghton St Giles was restored as part of the Roman Catholic shrine; the (new) name refers to the enduring tradition of pilgrims walking the last mile or so to Walsingham barefoot. In the 1930s an Anglican shrine was built, and the ecumenical importance of the village is clearly demonstrated by the fact that the old railway station is now a chapel of the Russian Orthodox Church.

---

207 SHRUBLANDS FARM

HIGHLY COMMENDED

Northrepps, Cromer, Norfolk NR27 0AA Tel (01263) 579297 Fax (01263) 579297

We are situated one-and-a-half miles from the sea on the beautiful north Norfolk coast with its sandy beaches and bird sanctuaries. Ideal for those wishing to explore by car, cycle or on foot. The house dates back to the 18th-century and is set in a large garden with lawns and mature trees. We offer a warm welcome and excellent farmhouse cooking. Evening meals are available by arrangement. No smoking.

Bed & Breakfast per night: single occupancy from £23.00–£25.00; double room from £38.00–£42.00
Half board per person: £28.50–£33.00 daily; £167.20–£192.30 weekly
Evening meal 1900 (last orders 2000)

Bedrooms: 1 double, 2 twin
Bathrooms: 1 en-suite, 2 private
Parking for 4

208 GARDEN COTTAGE

HIGHLY COMMENDED

The Limes, 96 Norwich Road, Wroxham, Norwich, Norfolk NR12 8RY Tel (01603) 784376 or (01603) 783192

Situated in the Broads National Park, yet only seven miles from Norwich, this beautifully converted and furnished 18th-century barn is set in a delightful garden with its own private patio. A separate entrance and private dining and sitting rooms provide all the comfort and privacy you would expect of a de luxe hotel plus that little bit extra in personal service to make your stay memorable. Numerous activities can be arranged locally such as sailing, horse-riding, golf, fishing, bird-watching and theatre visits.

Bed & Breakfast per night: single occupancy from £30.00–£40.00; double room from £40.00–£50.00
Half board per person: £30.00–£40.00 daily; £200.00–£260.00 weekly
Evening meal 1900 (last orders 2100)

Bedrooms: 2 double, 1 twin
Bathrooms: 3 en-suite
Parking for 4
Cards accepted: Access, Visa, Amex, Switch/Delta

209 CATTON OLD HALL

HIGHLY COMMENDED

Lodge Lane, Old Catton, Norwich, Norfolk NR6 7HG Tel (01603) 419379 Fax (01603) 400339

Built during the English civil war in 1632 and restored to a high standard, providing luxury bed & breakfast accommodation for business or pleasure. The oak-beamed rooms are tastefully decorated and well-appointed, providing guests with little extras to make a stay memorable, such as romantic candle-light dinners and winter log fires. Ideal for visiting the Cathedral city or exploring the Norfolk countryside. Guests will enjoy the relaxed atmosphere and a chance to be pampered in this impressive family home.

Bed & Breakfast per night: single occupancy from £30.00–£48.00; double room from £60.00–£90.00
Half board per person: £48.00–£66.00 daily; £300.00–£420.00 weekly
Evening meal 1800 (last orders 2000)

Bedrooms: 2 double, 2 twin
Bathrooms: 4 en-suite
Parking for 20
Cards accepted: Access, Visa, Diners, Amex

210 HOTEL NELSON
 HIGHLY COMMENDED

Prince of Wales Road, Norwich, Norfolk NR1 1DX Tel (01603) 760260 Fax (01603) 620008

The Hotel Nelson has a prime city-centre location on the banks of the River Wensum. All bedrooms have an en-suite bathroom, refrigerator with fresh milk, tea and coffee making facilities and remote control Teletext TV. The hotel also has its own leisure club with 40ft indoor pool, spa-pool, sauna, steam room, air-conditioned excercise studio and a gymnasium which is free for residents' use. Other facilities include two riverside restaurants, two bars, a large free car park at the rear of the hotel, its own river quay and riverside gardens.

Bed & Breakfast per night: single room from £79.50–£88.50; double room from £89.50–£101.50
Half board per person: £59.00–£64.00 daily
Evening meal 1845 (last orders 2145)

Bedrooms: 27 single, 67 double, 38 twin
Bathrooms: 132 en-suite
Parking for 180
Cards accepted: Access, Visa, Diners, Amex

211 THE OLD RECTORY
HIGHLY COMMENDED

103 Yarmouth Road, Thorpe St Andrew, Norwich, Norfolk NR7 0HF Tel (01603) 700772 Fax (01603) 700772

Chris and Sally Entwistle invite you to relax and enjoy a friendly atmosphere and traditional hospitality in this charming Georgian house with its extensive gardens and sun terrace, delightful view over the Yare valley and outdoor swimming pool (heated in summer). Our intimate dining room, where a freshly prepared four-course dinner menu is served each evening, is the perfect setting in which to celebrate your special occasion, whilst our spacious, individually furnished bedrooms offer you the highest standards of comfort and amenities.

Bed & Breakfast per night: single occupancy £49.50; double room £65.00
Half board per person: from £45.00 daily
Evening meal 1900 (last orders 2000)

Bedrooms: 7 double, 1 twin
Bathrooms: 8 en-suite
Parking for 16
Cards accepted: Access, Visa, Amex

212 THE LODGE
DE LUXE

Cargate Lane, Saxlingham Thorpe, Norwich, Norfolk NR15 1TU Tel (01508) 471422 Fax (01508) 471682

A listed Regency house, the home of Sally and Roger Dixon, set in three acres of secluded grounds, conveniently located close to the A140 south of Norwich. All the rooms are elegantly furnished in the best country house tradition to provide luxury accommodation in lovely surroundings. Imaginative candle-lit dinners are a speciality, using top quality produce and seasonal contributions from the herb garden. Guests may invite friends to join them for dinner; licensed.

Bed & Breakfast per night: single room £32.00; double room from £54.00–£58.00
Half board per person: £45.50–£50.50 daily; £299.00–£331.50 weekly
Evening meal 1930 (last orders 2000)

Bedrooms: 1 single, 2 double/twin
Bathrooms: 2 en-suite, 1 private
Parking for 12

213 EARSHAM PARK FARM

 HIGHLY COMMENDED

Harleston Road, Earsham, Bungay, Suffolk NR35 2AQ Tel (01986) 892180 or 0374 782449 Fax (01986) 892180

Park Farm has historic links with the 14th-century and the Duke of Norfolk. The beautiful Victorian farmhouse, set on a hill overlooking the Waveney Valley, is secluded with superb views. All the en-suite rooms are spacious, centrally heated, well-fitted and include television and beverage facilities. Enjoy the large gardens, farm walks and superb farmhouse breakfasts using the best local produce. All your comforts will be cared for in this non-smoking home-from-home.

Bed & Breakfast per night: single occupancy from £24.00–£27.00; double room from £37.00–£43.00
Half board per person: £32.50–£41.00 daily
Evening meal 1800 (last orders 2000)

Bedrooms: 2 double, 1 twin
Bathrooms: 3 en-suite
Parking for 10
Cards accepted: Diners

214 IVY HOUSE FARM

 HIGHLY COMMENDED

Ivy Lane, Oulton Broad, Lowestoft, Suffolk NR33 8HY Tel (01502) 501353 or (01502) 588144 Fax (01502) 501539

Relax amid intertwining herbaceous beds or tarry awhile beside the ponds. Take a gentle stroll down a garden path to view Oulton Broad, with its sailing boats, or wander a little further to enjoy a boat trip. Ivy House Farm enjoys a peaceful setting amidst forty acres in the Broads National Park. The accommodation is individually designed with en-suite bathrooms. Lunch and dinner is served in The Crooked Barn — an eighteenth-century thatched barn.

Bed & Breakfast per night: single occupancy from £59.00–£69.00; double room from £79.00–£89.00
Lunch available: 1215–1400
Evening meal 1900 (last orders 2130)

Bedrooms: 7 double, 3 twin, 1 triple, 1 family room
Bathrooms: 12 en-suite
Parking for 50
Cards accepted: Access, Visa, Amex, Diners

215 LOWBROOK FARM

HIGHLY COMMENDED

Semere Green Lane, Dickleburgh, Diss, Norfolk IP21 4NT Tel (01379) 741265 Fax (01379) 741265

Created from the original eighteenth-century timber barn, Lowbrook offers spacious accommodation for guests with a wealth of beams, private lounge with video/TV and music centre, wood fires in winter. Full English/American breakfast, with local and home produce, taken either in the elegant dining room or on the patio. Tastefully appointed double bedrooms overlook the water garden and peaceful fields of the farm. Every comfort of their guests is the first priority of Richard and Beth Hill.

Bed & Breakfast per night: single occupancy from £15.99–£25.00; double room from £35.00–£40.00

Bedrooms: 2 twin
Bathrooms: 1 private, 1 public
Parking for 4
Open: April–October

216 CHIPPENHALL HALL
Fressingfield, Eye, Suffolk IP21 5TD Tel (01379) 586733 or (01379) 588180 Fax (01379) 586272

HIGHLY COMMENDED

A listed Tudor manor of Saxon origin, recorded in Domesday book, enjoying total rural seclusion in seven acres of gardens with ponds, and a heated outdoor pool set in a rose-covered courtyard. The manor is heavily beamed with inglenook log fireplaces. For that special anniversary with friends, arrange for pre-dinner drinks served in the bar and fine food and wines served by candle-light. Located one mile south of Fressingfield, B1116.

Bed & Breakfast per night: single occupancy from
£53.00–£59.00; double room from £59.00–£65.00
Half board per person: £53.00–£56.00 daily;
£354.00–£373.00 weekly
Lunch available: 1230–1400 (by prior request)

Evening meal 1930 (last bookings 1600)
Bedrooms: 3 double
Bathrooms: 3 en-suite
Parking for 12
Cards accepted: Access, Visa

217 LODGE FARMHOUSE BED AND BREAKFAST
The Lodge Farmhouse, Weston Road, Thelnetham, Diss, Norfolk IP22 1JL Tel (01379) 898203 Fax (01379) 898203

HIGHLY COMMENDED

Situated in the heart of East Anglia overlooking its own lake and unspoilt countryside in the beautiful Waveney Valley. Spacious en-suite rooms with tea and coffee making. We specialise in good English cooking, with local produce and vegetables from the kitchen garden, all cooked on the Aga (no microwave). We serve our own English table wine plus a good range of quality wines from around the world. We have our own vineyard, table licence and off licence.

Bed & Breakfast per night: single occupancy from
£20.00–£25.00; double room from £38.00–£42.00
Half board per person: £31.00–£37.00 daily;
£217.00–£259.00 weekly
Evening meal 1900 (last bookings 0900)

Bedrooms: 1 double, 2 twin
Bathrooms: 3 en-suite
Parking for 12
Cards accepted: Diners

218 HILL FARM
Stonham Road, Cotton, Stowmarket, Suffolk IP14 4RQ Tel (01449) 780345 Fax (01449) 780345

HIGHLY COMMENDED

Hill Farm is a 16th-century country house, set in eleven acres, surrounded by open rolling countryside. Our bedrooms are attractively furnished and extremely spacious, with their own sitting areas. When eating with us you will be offered freshly prepared fine food, including seasonal home grown produce from our kitchen garden and fresh free range eggs laid by our own chickens. We are ideally situated for exploring East Anglia's numerous attractions, or for just relaxing in the peace and tranquillity of our beautiful grounds.

Bed & Breakfast per night: double room from
£45.00–£55.00
Half board per person: £35.00–£45.00 daily;
£225.00–£280.00 weekly
Evening meal 1800 (last orders 2100)

Bedrooms: 2 double
Bathrooms: 1 en-suite, 1 private
Parking for 20

㉑㊈ CHERRY TREE FARM   〰〰 HIGHLY COMMENDED

Mendlesham Green, Stowmarket, Suffolk IP14 5RQ Tel (01449) 766376

Martin and Diana Ridsdale invite guests to enjoy their hospitality in this timber-framed farmhouse. Situated in the very heart of rural Suffolk, it makes an ideal base for exploring this and neighbouring counties. Great care is taken in the preparation and cooking of all meals which are served around a refectory table. Bread is home baked and vegetables garden-fresh. The wine list includes an extensive range of East Anglian-produced wines.

Bed & Breakfast per night: single occupancy from £30.00–£35.00; double room from £42.00–£48.00
Half board per person: £36.00–£39.00 daily
Evening meal 1900 (last bookings 1400)

Bedrooms: 3 double
Bathrooms: 3 en-suite
Parking for 3
Open: February–December

The Aldeburgh Festival

THE COMPOSER BENJAMIN BRITTEN (1913–76) was the son of a Lowestoft dentist. Extraordinary musical ability blossomed early and by the age of 16 Britten's eclectic compositional style and brilliant technical virtuosity were apparent. The war years 1939–42 were spent in the USA and it was there that Britten read an article by E M Forster about the Aldeburgh poet, the Reverend George Crabbe. The Suffolk coast was in Britten's blood and he resolved to return there to seek inspiration. Crabbe's best-known poem, *The Borough*, was the source of Britten's first major operatic success, *Peter Grimes*, premiered in 1945 with his lifelong friend, Peter Pears, in the title role.

It was while Britten and a group of fellow artists were touring with the English Opera Group in the Netherlands and Switzerland in summer 1947 that they resolved to do something that would enable British artists to be promoted in sympathetic surroundings at home. Back home in Aldeburgh, Britten and the librettist Eric Crozier negotiated with the mayor and the vicar, and the result was the first Aldeburgh Festival, a nine-day event in June 1948. This modest festival, using local spaces such as the Jubilee Hall and the parish church, successfully demonstrated that there was a willing and appreciative audience for the sort of music that established organisations would not risk promoting.

Britten is perhaps best known for his operas and song settings. Many of his smaller-scale 'stage' works were first produced at the Festival, the three 'church parables' and other semi-religious works being performed in Blythburgh and Orford churches.

The growing success and international artistic importance of the festival created the need for a permanent home and high-quality hall. This was superbly accomplished in 1967 through the conversion of the 19th-century Snape Maltings on the River Alde. The natural appearance of mellow brick and unadorned pine complement one of the finest acoustics in Europe for serious music, and the setting – within a stone's throw of the river and with views of the estuary and marshland – makes the perfect ambience.

From its humble beginnings, the Festival (box office tel. 01728 453543) has now spawned a year-round programme of musical activities. The Festival itself still takes place in June, but is preceded in April by an Early Music Festival and followed in August by the Snape Proms. For most of the rest of the year there are lunchtime Friday concerts and evening events.

220 THE CROWN AT WESTLETON
HIGHLY COMMENDED

Westleton, Saxmundham, Suffolk IP17 3AD Tel (01728) 648777 Fax (01728) 648239

Westleton, halfway between Southwold and Aldeburgh, has a thatched 12th-century church, village green and duck pond. Marvellous coastal heathland leads to the Minsmere bird sanctuary and the coast at Dunwich. Personally managed by its proprietors, the Crown is famous for its fresh fish dishes, traditional menus, cask beers, malts and wines. Four-poster and half-tester beds, jacuzzi bathrooms, log fires, lounge, gardens and friendly service in the best traditions of the English inn. CATEGORY 2

Bed & Breakfast per night: single room from £54.00–£65.00; double room from £73.50–£97.50
Half board per person: from £38.75–£65.00 daily; £240.50–£420.00 weekly
Lunch available: 1200–1415

Evening meal 1900 (last orders 2130)
Bedrooms: 2 single, 14 double, 1 twin, 1 triple, 1 family room
Bathrooms: 19 en-suite
Parking for 36
Cards accepted: Access, Visa, Diners, Amex, Switch/Delta

221 THEBERTON GRANGE
HIGHLY COMMENDED

Theberton, Leiston, Suffolk IP16 4RR Tel (01728) 830625 Fax (01728) 830625

Privately owned country house (mainly Regency and Victorian, but with Tudor origins) set in the heart of the Suffolk heritage coast. There are seven spacious bedrooms, all with period furniture, en-suite or private bathrooms, colour televisions, tea and coffee making facilities and views over open countryside. The house is surrounded by four acres of lovely grounds in a tranquil location close to Minsmere bird reserve. Guests will find a relaxed atmosphere combining informality with a high standard of service. Country cooking using the best local ingredients.

Bed & Breakfast per night: single room £35.00; double room from £60.00–£80.00
Half board per person: from £49.00 daily; from £308.00 weekly
Evening meal 1900 (last orders 1930)

Bedrooms: 1 single, 5 double, 1 twin
Bathrooms: 5 en-suite, 2 private
Parking for 10
Cards accepted: Access, Visa

222 SECKFORD HALL HOTEL
HIGHLY COMMENDED

Woodbridge, Suffolk IP13 6NU Tel (01394) 385678 Fax (01394) 380610

A romantic Elizabethan mansion set in 32 acres of landscaped gardens and woodlands. Personally supervised by the owners, Seckford Hall is a haven of seclusion and tranquillity. Oak panelling, beamed ceilings, antique furniture, four-poster bedrooms, suites, leisure club with indoor pool, gym and spa bath and adjacent 18-hole golf course. Two restaurants featuring fresh lobster and game from local farms, extensive wine cellar. Picturesque Woodbridge with its tide mill, antique shops and yacht harbour is a short walk away. Constable country and Suffolk coast nearby.

Bed & Breakfast per night: single room from £79.00–£110.00; double room from £105.00–£148.00
Lunch available: 1230–1345
Evening meal 1915 (last orders 2130)

Bedrooms: 3 single, 14 double, 10 twin, 1 triple, 4 family rooms
Bathrooms: 32 en-suite
Parking for 102
Cards accepted: Access, Visa, Diners, Amex

223 HIGHFIELD

 HIGHLY COMMENDED

Harkstead Road, Holbrook, Ipswich, Suffolk IP9 2RA Tel (01473) 328250

Relax in the quiet charm of the Suffolk countryside with your hosts Bryan and Sally Morris in their home on the outskirts of Holbrook and Constable Country. All bedrooms and the garden have views over the Stour valley and river. There are many walks in the area, including the River Orwell and Stour estuaries which are havens for bird-watching and sailing. There are many excellent pubs serving food in the area. Sorry, no smoking, children or pets.

Bed & Breakfast per night: single occupancy from £27.00–£33.00; double/twin room from £35.00–£42.00

Bedrooms: 3 double/twin
Bathrooms: 2 en-suite, 1 private
Parking for 6

224 RYEGATE HOUSE

 HIGHLY COMMENDED

Stoke-by-Nayland, Colchester, Suffolk CO6 4RA Tel (01206) 263679

Situated within the Dedham Vale, in a quiet Suffolk village, Ryegate House is a modern property built in the style of a Suffolk farmhouse. It is only a few minutes walk from the local shops, post office, pubs, restaurants and church and an ideal base for exploring 'Constable Country'. A warm welcome, good food and comfortable rooms in a peaceful setting, with easy access to local historic market towns, golf courses and the east coast.

Bed & Breakfast per night: single occupancy from £23.00–£26.00; double room from £34.00–£39.00

Bedrooms: 2 double, 1 twin
Bathrooms: 3 en-suite
Parking for 6

225 HOCKLEY PLACE

 HIGHLY COMMENDED

Hockley Place, Frating, Colchester, Essex CO7 7HG Tel (01206) 251703 Fax (01206) 251578

Peace and tranquillity greet you at this country house built in the 'Lutyens' style. The individually designed bedrooms are en-suite, the standard of cuisine is high and guests eat in the beamed dining room. The outdoor swimming pool and gymnasium are open to guests throughout the day. The coastline of Frinton, Clacton and Brightlingsea, Beth Chatto's gardens, Colchester's Roman castle and the picturesque countryside of Dedham and Constable Country are all within easy reach.

Bed & Breakfast per night: single occupancy £30.00; double room £60.00
Half board per person: £50.00–£50.00 daily; £300.00–£350.00 weekly

Bedrooms: 1 double, 2 twin
Bathrooms: 3 en-suite
Parking for 20
Cards accepted: Access, Visa, Switch/Delta

226 WALLIS FARM

HIGHLY COMMENDED

98 Main Street, Hardwick, Cambridge, Cambridgeshire CB3 7QU Tel (01954) 210347 Fax (01954) 210347

A warm welcome awaits you at our traditional Victorian farmhouse on our working farm in the picturesque village of Hardwick. We are seven miles from the university town of Cambridge and ideally situated for touring Cambridgeshire, Norfolk and Suffolk. All rooms are ground floor, en-suite, twin/ double, furnished to a high standard and look out onto large gardens and farmland which guests are welcome to use. All have colour TVs and tea/coffee making facilities.

Bed & Breakfast per night: single occupancy from £28.00–£32.00; double room from £40.00–£45.00

Bedrooms: 2 double, 1 twin
Bathrooms: 3 en-suite
Parking for 8
Cards accepted: Diners

---

227 MARYGREEN MANOR HOTEL

 **HIGHLY COMMENDED**

London Road, Brentwood, Essex CM14 4NR Tel (01277) 225252 Fax (01277) 262809

16th-century timber-framed building, visited by King Henry VIII. Original Tudor bedrooms with four-poster beds (3). Garden rooms overlook olde-worlde garden. Extensive à la carte or fixed price menus complemented by comprehensive award-winning wine list. Lunch served from 1230–1430, dinner served from 1915–2215. Two minutes from J28 on M25. Motorway links to the Channel Tunnel, Stansted, Gatwick and Heathrow Airports.

Bed & Breakfast per night: single occupancy from £101.50–£110.50; double room from £123.00–£131.50
Lunch available: 1230–1430
Evening meal 1915 (last orders 2215)

Bedrooms: 16 double, 17 twin
Bathrooms: 33 en-suite
Parking for 100
Cards accepted: Access, Visa, Diners, Amex, Switch/Delta

KEY TO SYMBOLS

For ease of use, the key to symbols appears on the back of the cover flap and can be folded out while consulting individual entries. The symbols which appear at the end of each entry are designed to enable you to see at-a-glance what's on offer, and whether any particular requirements you have can be met. Most of the symbols are clear, simple icons and few require any further explanation, but the following points may be useful:

ALCOHOLIC DRINKS: Alcoholic drinks are available at all types of accommodation listed in the guide unless the symbol ⓤ (unlicensed) appears. However, even in licensed premises there may be some restrictions on the serving of drinks, such as being available to diners only.

SMOKING: Many establishments offer facilities for non-smokers, indicated by the symbol ✄. These may include no smoking bedrooms and parts of communal rooms set aside for non-smokers. Some establishments prefer not to accommodate smokers at all, and if this is the case it will be made clear in the establishment description in the guide entry.

PETS: The symbol ✗ is used to show that dogs are not accepted in any circumstances. Some establishments will accept pets, but we advise you to check this at the time of booking and to enquire as to whether any additional charge will be made to accommodate them.

228 SOPWELL HOUSE HOTEL AND COUNTRY CLUB 〰〰〰〰〰 HIGHLY COMMENDED

Cottonmill Lane, Sopwell, St Albans, Hertfordshire AL1 2HQ Tel (01727) 864477 Fax (01727) 844741

Just minutes from four major motorways, half an hour from central London, Sopwell House stands in eleven acres of landscaped gardens and grounds amongst pleasant Hertfordshire countryside. An extensive refurbishment has further enhanced its country-style ambience. The Country Club and Spa, a haven for relaxation and pampering, features an ozone-treated indoor pool, jacuzzi, steam room and sauna, together with beauty and hairdressing salons, full-size snooker table and superbly-equipped fitness studio. Golf available nearby.

Bed & Breakfast per night: single room from
£79.00–£109.25; double room from £113.75–£155.00
Half board per person: £80.38–£132.75 daily
Lunch available: 1230–1500
Evening meal 1930 (last orders 2130)

Bedrooms: 12 single, 54 double, 20 twin, 6 family rooms
Bathrooms: 92 en-suite
Parking for 200
Cards accepted: Access, Visa, Diners, Amex

Hat-making in Luton

LUTON TOWN FOOTBALL CLUB has long been known as 'the Hatters', a name which reveals the town's importance as the centre of the English hat-making industry. The main reason for the Bedfordshire town's pre-eminent position is the quality of the surrounding soil, which allows wheat grown in nearby fields to reach a considerable height. The long stems (or straws), once plaited, were ideal for use in making straw hats. These, together with other straw goods such as corn dollies, were sold in the markets of 17th- and 18th-century Luton and Dunstable.

Special schools known as 'plait schools' appeared in the town as demand for the high-quality products increased. Plaited straws were also imported from the town of Livorno, on Italy's Tuscan coast. Indeed the Italian connection in the history of English hat-making is important, and the word 'millinery' comes from the placename Milan (even preserving the now lost pronunciation, 'Millen'). When the Napoleonic wars meant that Italian imports became scarce, the Luton hat-making industry took off.

Trade continued to grow throughout the 19th-century, although cheaper plait from the Far East was bought in from the 1870s onwards. The area of Luton known as Plaiters' Lea (now a conservation area) was where the hat factories, with their newly installed and adapted sewing machines, congregated. These were usually tall, narrow buildings, with each floor dedicated to a separate process, such as blocking (stretching the materials over

metal moulds), machining, trimming, dyeing and so forth. Good examples of these factories can be seen in Bute and Guildford Streets.

The first half of this century saw continued prosperity in the hat trade, but in the 1960s the hat ceased to be an item of everyday wear and became instead an item of occasional wear. Nevertheless there are still almost 40 manufacturers in the town, and visitors can often view a working factory; check with the Tourist Information Centre (tel. 01582 401579) – itself housed in an old hat factory – for details. They also have leaflets about a millinery trail through Plaiters' Lea, while displays of past Luton-made hats (as well as occasional hat-making demonstrations) can be seen at the Luton Museum and Art Gallery (tel. 01582 36941).

England's West Country

NO OTHER REGION IN ENGLAND feels quite as rural as the West Country. The countryside even seems to spill over into its two large conurbations: Bristol has its Downs and the glorious Avon Gorge, while Plymouth has views up to Dartmoor and across The Sound to Mount Edgecumbe. The West Country may not have the towering fells of the Lake District, but it can boast land over 2,000ft (610m), romantically remote islands and the mildest climes in the land. The combination of scenic beauty and a benevolent climate inevitably makes it a favourite holiday destination.

Cornwall's splendour is at its best where it meets the sea and, thanks to its shape, it has more than its fair share of coastline. It also means that nowhere in the county is more than 20 miles from the sea. With so many drowned river valleys and inlets, estimating the length of the Cornish coast is an imprecise science; however, if you elect to tackle the Cornwall Coast Path, you will have a mere 268 miles in front of you. For those with the time and energy to complete the trek from the 600ft (183m) cliffs of Marsland on the northern Cornwall–Devon border round Land's End to Plymouth Sound, it is one of the most exhilarating walks in England, taking you above seascapes,

▶ Lyme Regis fossils

Impressive dinosaur skeletons are occasionally found in the vicinity of Lyme Regis by professional

fossil hunters, but more exciting for the visitor is that every year huge numbers of beautifully preserved fossils are simply washed down the cliffs on to the beach. The most common of these are ammonites (shell-like spirals, once part of a creature resembling a squid), but other fossils to look out for are belemnites (pencil shaped fossils whose broken ends show fine radiating crystals) and crinoids (feathery fronds attached to a five-sided stalk).

▶ Cidermaking

Somerset is famous for scrumpy, the strong farmhouse cider which has been produced here for at least 700 years. At one time almost every farm had its own cider press, and almost every village its cider house. Today large areas of Somerset are still given over to apple orchards, but the old cottage trees have been replaced by modern, disease-resistant stock. Many cider farms, however, continue to make cider using traditional methods. Perry's cider mills, at Dowlish Wake near Ilminster, and Sheppy's at Bradford-on-Tone, are both open to the public.

landscapes and fishing villages of breath-taking beauty. If this is to your taste, you can always give yourself the stiffer target of walking the 594-mile South West Coast Path (of which the Cornwall Coast Path forms the central section) from Minehead to Poole Harbour. The Camel trail offers less-challenging inland opportunities for both walkers and cyclists. This ends at the western edge of Bodmin Moor, the large, wild upland area at the centre of the county. Visited by few, crossed by fewer roads and peppered with prehistoric remains, the Moor contains Brown Willy, Cornwall's highest point at 1,377ft (420m).

Part of Devon, but 12 miles off the treacherous headland of Hartland Point, is Lundy Island. Sailings leave Ilfracombe, Bideford and, by arrangement, Clovelly, justly renowned for its attractive stone-built cottages tumbling down the steep hillside to the sea. The best approach to the village is to walk from little Buck's Mills (itself an attractive hamlet). The view from the thickly-wooded cliffs is as memorable as the name of the bay below: Bight a Doubleyou! Devon's sublime northern shores reach Exmoor National Park at Combe Martin, and from here to beyond the Somerset border the land plunges hair-raisingly from a thousand feet to sea level in no distance at all. Steep slopes are in fact a Devon hallmark; wherever you venture, be it on a twisting Devonian lane sunk between tall hedges or a busier main road, ensure your car can cope with the rigours of a 1-in-4 incline. As an alternative to the raw beauty of Exmoor and Dartmoor, why not meander along the leafier by-ways west of Tiverton? Villages with the perfect English pub, villages with names such as Mogworthy, Black Dog and Stretch Down, and villages serving the creamiest of cream teas are all to be discovered. Much the same blend is on offer in the South Hams — the farmland south of Totnes — with the added advantage of the mildest weather in the country.

For the traveller leaving north Devon, Somerset seems to be a constant succession of hill ranges: Exmoor, then the Brendon Hills, the Quantocks, the little Polden Hills and finally the Mendips. Coleridge spent many an hour wandering the Quantock Ridge and, for a combination of solitude and scenery, it's hard to beat his choice; the vistas to the county's other ranges, as well as north to Wales, are also inspiring. Equally unvisited are the undulating Black Down Hills south of Taunton, while Windwhistle Hill, east of Chard, boasts views to both English and Bristol Channels.

Cadbury Castle, not far from Yeovil, is one of several putative sites for Camelot. That this massive earthwork, one of the finest hillforts in England, actually was the home of Arthur's court is unlikely to be proved, but it serves as an excellent prelude to the extensive prehistoric remains on and around Salisbury Plain. Not far from Stonehenge is the older Woodhenge, a series of six concentric rings of holes probably designed to hold wooden posts. Like its more illustrious neighbour, its purpose was to indicate where the midsummer sun would rise. On the northern edge of the plain is a knot of other sites of huge significance. The open, treeless landscape now seems a fitting setting for the atmospheric stone circle of Avebury, the vast, conical, man-made mound of Silbury Hill and the burial chamber of West Kennet Long Barrow, but at their construction they would have been surrounded by trees. Some of this woodland remains at nearby Savernake Forest, where countless rides and paths lead past oaks and beeches of great antiquity. Like Savernake, Cranbourne Chase, in the extreme south of Wiltshire, was once a royal hunting ground. Nowadays it is an area of rolling countryside and attractive villages.

South and west lies Dorset, one of the least developed counties in the land. Once again, this makes ideal territory for idle meandering through sleepy lanes and snoozing villages. For the past two thousand or so years the arresting figure of the Cerne Abbas giant has surveyed this pastoral scene from his lofty position, doubtless causing a few eyebrows to be raised. Even older than the chalky giant are the inhabitants of the cliffs around Lyme Regis, for this is England's Mecca for fossil-hunters.

CRANMERE POOL
1.825 FEET
DARTMOOR

► **Dartmoor letterboxes**
In 1854 James Perrott, a guide based in Chagford, left a small waterproof receptacle at Cranmere Pool on Dartmoor. Because it was so remote, those who succeeded in tracking it down were keen to leave some record of their achievement. Walkers would sign a visitors' book and then leave their own visiting cards in the box. From these humble beginnings, the idea has taken off in recent decades and at any one time there may be over 1000 'letterboxes' scattered over Dartmoor. Visitors may also leave self-addressed postcards which can be stamped with a special 'letterbox stamp'. For those interested in signing their name in the visitors' book of the original letterbox, the grid reference is SX603858.

HELEN•CLAIRE
BRIXHAM

Left: Brixham harbour, Devon; inset: Kynance Cove, Cornwall

ISLES OF SCILLY

St Martin's
257
St Mary's
Hugh Town

5 Miles
5 Kilometres

Ilfracombe
230
229
Lynton
231 232
233
234
Barnstaple
235
Bideford
A39
236 237
A361
238
A377
DEVON
Bude
A39
248
Holsworthy
247
246
Okehampton
239 240
241
249
251
250
Launceston
245
A30
A385
242 243
Tavistock
A388
Ashburton
244
A38
A392
A39
A30
273
A385
280
Wadebridge
Bodmin
Liskeard
Totnes
279
Newquay
252
CORNWALL
A38
275
253 254
267
271 272
Plymouth
St Austell
Looe
A38
A30
268 269 270
274
Truro
A390
266
276 278
255
264 265
277
Salcombe
256 A30
Redruth
263
A39
262
258 260 261
Falmouth
Penzance
Helston
259

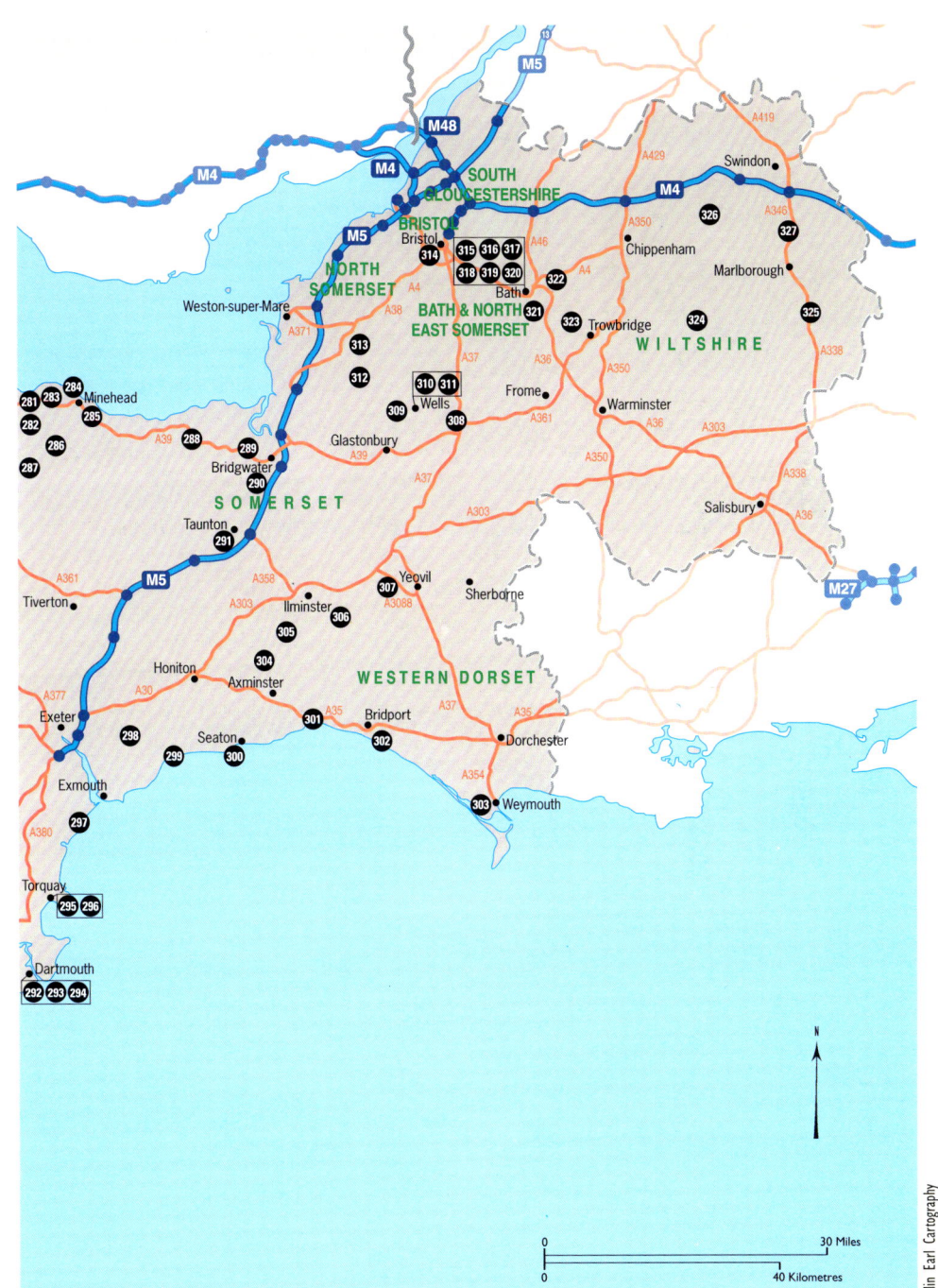

Colin Earl Cartography

229 WOOLACOMBE BAY HOTEL

HIGHLY COMMENDED

Woolacombe, Devon EX34 7BN Tel (01271) 870388 Fax (01271) 870613

Set in six acres of quiet gardens gently leading to three miles of golden sands. Built in the halcyon days of the mid-1800's, the hotel has a relaxed style of comfort and good living. Guests can enjoy unlimited use of superb sporting facilities, or just relax with a good book in spacious lounges overlooking the Atlantic. The 'Hothouse' offers fitness, massage and beauty treatments. Superb cooking of traditional and French dishes. Shooting, fishing, horse-riding and boating available.

Bed & Breakfast per night: single room from
£45.00–£70.00; double room from £90.00–£140.00
Half board per person: £65.00–£85.00 daily;
£350.00–£500.00 weekly
Lunch available: 1215–1330 (Sunday only)

Evening meal 1930 (last orders 2130)
Bedrooms: 1 single, 26 double, 11 twin, 5 triple, 22 family rooms
Bathrooms: 65 en-suite
Parking for 150   Open: February–December
Cards accepted: Access, Visa, Diners, Amex, Switch/Delta

Lundy

THE ISLAND OF LUNDY, 11 miles from *terra firma*, is as remote an island as England has to offer. Nevertheless it makes a magnificent day out from Ilfracombe (summer trips only) and Bideford, both ports some 24 miles distant on the north Devon coast.

The island, 3 miles long and never much more than ½ mile wide, surveys the busy shipping lanes and fishing grounds of the Bristol Channel. There are views north to Pembrokeshire and south to Devon, but there is much to see on Lundy itself. The track from Landing Beach (there is no harbour) was swept away in recent storms. As you climb towards the village, look out for Lundy cabbage, a plant of yellow flowers unique to the island, and for attractive Millcombe House, once home to the aptly named Rev Hudson Heaven. At the top of the 400ft ascent is a collection of picturesque buildings constructed from the ubiquitous Lundy granite. The photogenic Marisco Tavern (named after the Norman owners of the island) is decorated with life belts and other flotsam from the innumerable vessels to founder on the island's rocky shores. The tavern is the centre of island life, acting as information centre and meeting place as well as brewery, restaurant and hostelry.

The Marisco family, who turned to the traditional Lundy pursuit of piracy before being dispossessed in the mid-13th-century, also gave their name to the small castle near the southern tip. Other relics of antiquity include several inscribed crosses dating from the first millennium. These are in the cemetery beside the old lighthouse.

Lundy's true glories, however, are the scenery and the wildlife, and there can be no better way of passing time here than strolling its gentle paths. Wherever you

venture there is always something to admire: in the south are a spectacular 300ft pit called the Devil's Limekiln and excellent vantage points for gazing at seabirds (though puffins have sadly declined of late); on the east are steep slopes plunging into the waters of the Bristol Channel, some clad with rhododendrons that shelter the secretive sika deer; on the north, beside the 1896 North Light, grey seals can be spied throughout the year, as can curlews and a host of different gulls. The west coast is the highlight of the island; here Soay sheep and feral goats pick their way over countless beautiful stacks of granite tumbling hundreds of feet to the Atlantic waves while ravens wheel above. The influence of mankind seems distant indeed.

230 HEDDONS GATE HOTEL

HIGHLY COMMENDED

Heddons Mouth, Parracombe, Barnstaple, Devon EX31 4PZ Tel (01598) 763313 Fax (01598) 763363

Six miles west of Lynton and beneath the winding lanes of Martinhoe is a private drive leading to Heddons Gate Hotel. This Victorian house overlooks the spectacular wooded hills of coastal Exmoor and terraced gardens lead down to the famous South West peninsular footpath with the river and sea beyond. Finest English cooking by chef/proprietor Robert Deville. Log fires, all en-suite rooms, elegant public rooms and ample private parking complete this haven of peace.

Half board per person: £47.50–£67.70 daily;
£330.00–£402.00 weekly
Evening meal 2000

Bedrooms: 1 single, 8 double, 5 twin
Bathrooms: 14 en-suite
Parking for 14
Open: April–October
Cards accepted: Access, Visa, Amex

231 HIGHCLIFFE HOUSE

HIGHLY COMMENDED

Sinai Hill, Lynton, Devon EX35 6AR Tel (01598) 752235 Fax (01598) 752235

Small luxury Victorian gentleman's summer residence, 800ft above picturesque bay, commanding panoramic views of Exmoor and its fine coastline. Antiques, fine furnishings, beautifully decorated spacious en-suite rooms with all the modern comforts one could wish for. Roaring log fires throughout the cooler months. Our cuisine embodies the best of Victorian values, assembled with love and presented with panache. Come and share our unique house – we'd like to pamper you. Totally non-smoking.

Bed & Breakfast per night: single occupancy £45.00;
double room from £70.00–£76.00
Half board per person: £53.50–£56.50 daily;
£346.50–£367.50 weekly
Evening meal 1930–2000

Bedrooms: 4 double, 2 twin
Bathrooms: 6 en-suite
Parking for 8
Cards accepted: Access, Visa, Switch/Delta

232 SEAWOOD HOTEL

HIGHLY COMMENDED

North Walk Drive, Lynton, Devon EX35 6HJ Tel (01598) 752272

Seawood is situated at one of the loveliest spots on the North Devon coast, right in the heart of Lorna Doone country. Nestling on wooded cliffs 400ft above the sea, the hotel has some magnificent views. It looks right out across Lynmouth Bay and the Grand Headland of Countisbury where Exmoor meets the sea. On a clear night you can easily see the twinkling lights of Wales.

Bed & Breakfast per night: single room from
£27.00–£29.00; double room from £54.00–£58.00
Half board per person: £39.00–£40.00 daily;
£255.00–£265.00 weekly
Evening meal 1900 (last orders 1930)

Bedrooms: 1 single, 9 double, 2 twin
Bathrooms: 12 en-suite, 2 public
Parking for 10
Open: April–October

233 RISING SUN HOTEL

 HIGHLY COMMENDED

Harbourside, Lynmouth, Devon EX35 6EQ Tel (01598) 753223 Fax (01598) 753480

An award-winning 14th-century thatched smugglers' inn overlooking a tiny picturesque harbour and Lynmouth Bay with its stunning backdrop of the highest hogback cliffs in England. The Rising Sun Hotel is steeped in history, with oak panelling, crooked ceilings and creaky, uneven floorboards. Lynmouth Bay lobster, local game and salmon served in the romantic candle-lit, oak-panelled dining room, all add to the atmosphere of quintessential British innkeeping at its best.

welcome datacomp Bed & Breakfast per night: single room £47.00; double room from £83.50–£103.00 Half board per person: £59.00–£72.50 daily; £385.00–£445.00 weekly Evening meal 1900 (last orders 2100)

Bedrooms: 1 single, 11 double, 2 twin, 2 triple
Bathrooms: 16 en-suite
Cards accepted: Access, Visa, Diners, Amex, Switch/Delta

The Tarka Trail

THE WRITER HENRY WILLIAMSON (1895–1977) was born and bred in London, but in 1921 he decided to leave the city, mounted his motorcycle and headed south-west. His eventual destination was the Devonshire village of Georgeham, near Barnstaple, where he rented a small cottage and stayed for many years. Here he was given an orphaned otter cub which he reared and cared for. It gave him the inspiration for his famous book, *Tarka the Otter*, in which he displayed not only his fascination for these shy and beautiful creatures, but also his deep knowledge and love of the wildlife and landscapes of this most beautiful part of Devon.

An area roughly corresponding to that featured in the book is now being promoted as Tarka Country, a region which extends along Devon's north coast from Bideford to Lynton and southwards to the northern fringes of Dartmoor. As part of a major eco tourism initiative, the Tarka Country Tourism Association has set up a long-distance route – the Tarka Trail – designed to encourage the visitor to explore the countryside without the use of the car. Describing an irregular figure of eight, the trail loops between Exmoor and Dartmoor, with Barnstaple at its centre, covering 180 miles of varied and often stunning scenery.

It is of course possible to walk the entire length of the Tarka Trail (except the section between Eggesford and Barnstaple which is a train journey), but shorter walks and cycle routes with starting points on or near the trail have also been devised. Some are circular, some involve a return by bus. Full details of

all the different options are available from the Tarka Country Tourism Association (tel: 01837 83399).

The Tarka Trail passes many places mentioned in Williamson's famous book. Tarka's fictional birthplace, for example, is on the Torridge, just upstream from Bideford, while remote Cranmere Pool on Dartmoor was visited by Tarka after the death of his mate, Greymuzzle. But don't expect to see any otters on your travels. Due to river pollution and loss of habitat, otters are one of Europe's most endangered mammals. The best place to see them is at the Tamar Otter Sanctuary, near Launceston, Cornwall (about 25 miles from Barnstaple) where otters are bred and re-introduced to the wild in a bid to save them from extinction (tel: 01566 785646).

234 SIMONSBATH HOUSE HOTEL

HIGHLY COMMENDED

Simonsbath, Minehead, Somerset TA24 7SH Tel (01643) 831259

The first house to be built within the Royal Forest of Exmoor in 1654, Simonsbath House is now a small and friendly family-run country house hotel situated in an ideal position for exploring the Exmoor National Park and the north Devon coastline, on foot or by car. Receive peace and quiet, unstinting comfort, generous and deliciously interesting home-cooked food, rooms with log fires and panelling and some four-poster beds.

Bed & Breakfast per night: single occupancy from £54.00–£64.00; double room £92.00
Half board per person: £66.00–£84.00 daily; £420.00–£546.00 weekly
Evening meal 1900 (last orders 2030)

Bedrooms: 4 double, 3 twin
Bathrooms: 7 en-suite
Parking for 30
Open: February–November
Cards accepted: Access, Visa, Diners, Amex

235 YEOLDON COUNTRY HOUSE HOTEL AND RESTAURANT
HIGHLY COMMENDED

Durrant Lane, Northam, Bideford, Devon EX39 2RL Tel (01237) 474400 Fax (01237) 476618

Set in two acres of gardens overlooking the River Torridge, Yeoldon House offers real hospitality and a refreshingly casual atmosphere in this uniquely unspoilt part of Devon. Individually decorated rooms with an air of elegance and charm – all en-suite with tea and coffee making facilities. Imaginative à la carte cuisine using fresh local produce and an extensive wine list.

Bed & Breakfast per night: single occupancy from £29.50–£44.00; double room from £59.00–£75.00
Evening meal 1900 (last orders 2100)

Bedrooms: 7 double, 3 twin
Bathrooms: 10 en-suite
Parking for 22
Cards accepted: Access, Visa, Diners, Amex, Switch/Delta

236 WHITECHAPEL MANOR
HIGHLY COMMENDED

South Molton, Devon EX36 3EG Tel (01769) 573377 Fax (01769) 573797

Whitechapel Manor is a Grade I listed Elizabethan manor house set within fifteen acres of terraced gardens, woodlands and pastures. It is the ideal base for exploring Exmoor with its ancient woodlands, dramatic coastline, hidden valleys, high moors and thatched villages. The National Trust has many attractions nearby and The Royal Horticultural Society's gardens at Rosemoor are also close by. The restaurant is recognised as one of the West Country's best and has won many accolades over the years.

Bed & Breakfast per night: single room from £70.00–£85.00; double room from £110.00–£170.00
Half board per person: £80.00–£119.00 daily; £560.00–£770.00 weekly
Lunch available: 1200–1345 (reservations essential)

Evening meal 1900 (last orders 2045)
Bedrooms: 1 single, 3 double, 5 twin, 1 family room
Bathrooms: 10 en-suite
Parking for 40
Cards accepted: Access, Visa, Diners, Amex, Switch/Delta

237 MARSH HALL COUNTRY HOUSE HOTEL   HIGHLY COMMENDED

Marsh Hall, South Molton, Devon EX36 3HQ Tel (01769) 572666 Fax (01769) 574230

Marsh Hall is a lovely Victorian country house with stained-glass windows, chandeliers and log fires in winter, set in three acres of gardens and woodland. With its spacious lounges, gallery and bedrooms, it is the ideal place in which to relax and enjoy the comforts of life. The delightful award-winning restaurant serves a four-course dinner with mouth-watering dishes devised from local fare and fresh produce grown in the hotel's herb, vegetable and fruit gardens.

Bed & Breakfast per night: single room from £43.00–£48.00; double room from £70.00–£88.00
Half board per person: £54.00–£67.00 daily; £308.00–£364.00 weekly

Evening meal 1900 (last orders 2030)
Bedrooms: 1 single, 4 double, 2 twin
Bathrooms: 7 en-suite
Parking for 20
Cards accepted: Access, Visa, Diners, Amex

238 NORTHCOTE MANOR HOTEL   HIGHLY COMMENDED

Burrington (directly off A3777), Umberleigh, Devon EX37 9LZ Tel (01769) 560501 Fax (01769) 560770

A beautifully situated country house hotel, midway between Exmoor and Dartmoor, set in the seclusion of twenty acres of sweeping lawns, landscaped gardens and lush woodland. This Grade II listed building, home to the local squire for 300 years, is equipped with every modern amenity and the public rooms are both spacious and elegant. Outstanding continental cuisine and excellent service. Many leisure facilities on site or nearby, including golf, fishing and horseback riding. The Manor is ideally placed for touring the whole of Devon, the Cornish coasts, Somerset and beyond. Licensed for civil marriages.

Bed & Breakfast per night: single occupancy from £79.00–£89.00; double room from £109.00–£129.00
Half board per person: £70.00–£80.00 daily
Evening meal 1900 (last orders 2130)

Bedrooms: 10 double, 2 twin
Bathrooms: 12 en-suite
Parking for 20
Open: January and March–December
Cards accepted: Access, Visa, Diners, Amex, Switch/Delta

239 THE MEWS   Listed HIGHLY COMMENDED

Meldon Hall, Chagford, Devon TQ13 8EJ Tel (01647) 433466

A former coach house and stables set in the private grounds of Meldon Hall. Large natural gardens and walled courtyard. Unusual and comfortable lounge with woodburner. Wonderful views over the village and across to the high moor. Home cooking using fresh produce. Ideal base for walking or just being lazy with a good book. A warm Devonshire welcome assured.

Bed & Breakfast per night: single occupancy from £16.50–£19.00; double room from £33.00–£38.00
Half board per person: £26.50–£29.00 daily; £185.50–£203.00 weekly
Evening meal 1800 (last orders 1930)

Bedrooms: 3 double
Bathrooms: 2 en-suite, 1 private
Parking for 3

240 MILL END HOTEL

HIGHLY COMMENDED

Sandypark, Chagford, Newton Abbot, Devon TQ13 8JN Tel (01647) 432282 Fax (01647) 433106

Converted from a working mill, Mill End has retained all its rural charm. The mill wheel still turns in the courtyard and the Teign, which runs by the door, is one of the ten best sea-trout rivers in the country, with fishing available to guests. The gardens and walks are delightful and the hotel is ideal as a touring centre for the West. Then again, you could just sleep!

Bed & Breakfast per night: single room from £50.00–£65.00; double room from £80.00–£95.00
Half board per person: £55.00–£75.00 daily
Lunch available: 1230–1345
Evening meal 1930 (last orders 2100)

Bedrooms: 2 single, 5 double, 8 twin, 2 triple
Bathrooms: 15 en-suite, 2 private
Parking for 21
Cards accepted: Access, Visa, Diners, Amex, Switch/Delta

241 WOOSTON FARM

HIGHLY COMMENDED

Moretonhampstead, Newton Abbot, Devon TQ13 8QA Tel (01647) 440367 Fax (01647) 440367

Wooston Farm is situated above the Teign Valley in the Dartmoor National Park, with views over open moorland. The farmhouse is surrounded by a delightful garden. There are plenty of walks to take on the moor and in the wooded Teign Valley. Good home cooking and cosy log fires await you at Wooston with two double (one four-poster) and one twin room. Mountain bikes available. Open all year except Christmas.

Bed & Breakfast per night: double room from £36.00–£40.00
Half board per person: £29.00–£31.00 daily
Evening meal by arrangement

Bedrooms: 2 double, 1 twin
Bathrooms: 2 en-suite, 1 private
Parking for 3

242 BEL ALP HOUSE COUNTRY HOTEL

HIGHLY COMMENDED

Haytor, Bovey Tracey, Newton Abbot, Devon TQ13 9XX Tel (01364) 661217 Fax (01364) 661292

The views from Bel Alp's spectacular setting on the edge of Dartmoor are simply breathtaking. Other great attractions are superb award-winning set dinners, beautiful furnishings, large comfortable bedrooms and the English country house atmosphere. Dartmoor, one of southern England's last great wildernesses, has its own magical beauty and is wonderful to explore. Bel Alp is ideally situated for discovering the heritage, beautiful countryside and coastline of Devon and into Cornwall. Excellent local golf, walking and riding.

Bed & Breakfast per night: single occupancy from £78.00–£87.00; double room from £120.00–£156.00
Half board per person: £87.00–£117.00 daily; £588.00–£777.00 weekly
Evening meal 1930 (last orders 2030)

Bedrooms: 4 double, 5 twin
Bathrooms: 9 en-suite
Parking for 20
Open: March–November
Cards accepted: Access, Visa, Switch/Delta

243 EDGEMOOR HOTEL

⟐⟐⟐⟐ HIGHLY COMMENDED

Haytor Road, Bovey Tracey, Devon TQ13 9LE Tel (01626) 832466 Fax (01626) 834760

'Loaded with charm', this wisteria-clad country house hotel is personally run by resident proprietors Rod and Pat Day. With its beautiful gardens and lovely en-suite bedrooms (including some four-posters) the Edgemoor provides the ideal setting in which to unwind from the cares of modern life. Friendly attentive staff, good food, fine wines and beautiful countryside combine to help make your stay memorable and enjoyable.

Bed & Breakfast per night: single room from £42.50–£49.50; double room from £75.00–£89.00
Half board per person: £47.50–£60.00 daily; £332.50–£385.00 weekly
Lunch available: 1200–1400

Evening meal 1930 (last orders 2100)
Bedrooms: 3 single, 9 double, 3 twin, 2 triple
Bathrooms: 17 en-suite
Parking for 50
Cards accepted: Access, Visa, Diners, Amex, Switch/Delta

244 HOLNE CHASE HOTEL AND RESTAURANT

⟐⟐⟐⟐ HIGHLY COMMENDED

Tavistock Road, Ashburton, Newton Abbott, Devon TQ13 7NS Tel (01364) 631471 Fax (01364) 631453

Holne Chase has been "Somewhere Special" for more years than any reader of this guide can remember. White's Directory of Devon mentioned "the singularly secluded and romantic situation" in 1849. The hotel and restaurant are open all year to offer hospitality to guests. Open grounds, fly fishing, well-stocked library, log fires, good kitchen and well-stocked cellar combine to make Holne Chase the hotel for all seasons.

Bed & Breakfast per night: single room £55.00; double room from £110.00–£140.00
Half board per person: £80.00–£95.00 daily
Lunch available: 1200–1400
Evening meal 1915 (last orders 2100)

Bedrooms: 1 single, 7 double, 10 twin
Bathrooms: 18 en-suite
Parking for 30
Cards accepted: Access, Visa, Diners, Amex, Switch/Delta

245 LYDFORD HOUSE HOTEL

⟐⟐⟐⟐ HIGHLY COMMENDED

Lydford, Okehampton, Devon EX20 4AU Tel (01822) 820347 Fax (01822) 820442

A country house hotel of considerable charm in a beautiful garden setting just on the edge of Dartmoor. There are delightful bedrooms with every facility, comfortable lounges and a well-stocked bar. The restaurant offers the finest traditional English fare and an interesting wine list. Service is by friendly, efficient staff and the resident proprietors are always on hand to ensure that guests receive personal attention. Riding stables in the grounds provide superb hacking over Dartmoor.

Bed & Breakfast per night: single room £35.00; double room £70.00
Half board per person: £49.00 daily; £280.00–£297.00 weekly
Evening meal 1900 (last orders 2030)

Bedrooms: 3 single, 3 double, 3 twin, 2 triple, 2 family rooms
Bathrooms: 11 en-suite, 2 private
Parking for 30
Cards accepted: Access, Visa

246 BLAGDON MANOR COUNTRY HOTEL

HIGHLY COMMENDED

Ashwater, Beaworthy, Devon EX21 5DF Tel (01409) 211224 Fax (01409) 211634

Welcome to Blagdon Manor. A truly wonderful 17th-century manor nestling in eight acres with superb views of the rolling countryside. Beautifully appointed en-suite guest rooms. Log fires during the cooler months, and a profusion of fresh flowers throughout the spring and summer, provide a relaxing and welcoming atmosphere. Guests dine together in a country houseparty atmosphere and enjoy the best of English cuisine, the ingredients of which will be the finest available. Smoking restricted.

Bed & Breakfast per night: single occupancy from £60.00; double room from £95.00–£110.00
Half board per person: £66.00–£73.50 daily (2 people sharing)
Evening meal 2000 (last orders 2000)

Bedrooms: 5 double, 2 twin
Bathrooms: 7 en-suite
Parking for 8
Cards accepted: Access, Visa, Amex, Switch/Delta

247 COURT BARN COUNTRY HOUSE HOTEL

HIGHLY COMMENDED

Clawton, Holsworthy, Devon EX22 6PS Tel (01409) 271219 Fax (01409) 271309

Situated in quiet Devon countryside, this is one of the South West's great small touring hotels in five acres of gardens. Quiet country roads and clean safe beaches just a few miles away on the Heritage coast with nature walks, cycle trails, National Trust houses and gardens close by. Enjoy the best of hospitality and award-winning food and wines in a peaceful setting with an outdoor croquet lawn, badminton and lawn tennis court. Court Barn is a place to remember.

Bed & Breakfast per night: single room from £35.00–£45.00; double room from £60.00–£80.00
Half board per person: £56.00–£60.00 daily; £300.00–£375.00 weekly
Lunch available: 1200–1430

Evening meal 1900 (last orders 2130)
Bedrooms: 1 single, 3 double, 2 twin, 2 triple
Bathrooms: 8 en-suite, 1 public
Parking for 17
Cards accepted: Access, Visa, Diners, Amex, Switch/Delta

248 THE OLD RECTORY

HIGHLY COMMENDED

Marhamchurch, Bude, Cornwall EX23 0ER Tel (01288) 361379

Situated just five minutes from Bude and Widemouth Bay in the lovely village of Marhamchurch, which gives you peace and tranquillity. You will experience a very warm welcome, enabling you to feel at home, where you can relax and unwind in comfort. Spacious en-suite accommodation with colour TV and tea/coffee making facilities. There is a varied menu of plentiful good English cooking. No smoking.

Bed & Breakfast per night: single occupancy from £18.00–£20.00; double room from £32.00–£40.00
Half board per person: £26.00–£30.00 daily; £182.00–£210.00 weekly
Evening meal 1830 (last orders 1830)

Bedrooms: 2 double, 1 twin
Bathrooms: 3 en-suite
Parking for 4

249 TREWORGIE BARTON

HIGHLY COMMENDED

Crackington Haven, Bude, Cornwall EX23 0NL Tel (01840) 230233 Fax (01840) 230233

Beautifully situated close to Crackington Haven and the spectacular north Cornwall coast, Treworgie Barton is an ideal place to unwind in peace, tranquillity and seclusion. We have fresh flowers in the bedrooms, a log fire for chilly evenings and personal attention at all times. Our specialities are winter weekend breaks, with cosy candle-lit dinners and our excellent carefully prepared food, which bring guests back time and again.

Bed & Breakfast per night: double room from
£36.00–£46.00
Half board per person: £32.00–£37.00 daily;
£214.00–£249.00 weekly
Evening meal 1900 (last orders 1900)

Bedrooms: 2 double, 1 twin, 1 family suite
Bathrooms: 3 en-suite, 1 private
Parking for 4
Open: April–September (November, February and March:
advance bookings only)

Cornish Tin

TIN HAS BEEN MINED in Cornwall since prehistoric times, but the county's rich industrial archaeology dates mainly from the last 200 years. The Industrial Revolution created an unprecedented demand for tin, which Cornwall, almost alone in the land, could supply. It soon became the foremost producer in the world, helped by the achievements of the Cornish inventor, Richard Trevithick, who developed the steam engine (two impressive beam engines owned by the National Trust may be seen at Pool, near Redruth, tel: 01209 216657). The distinctive chimneys dotting the landscape are the remains of engine houses, once containing the steam machinery which operated the mines.

The industrial boom transformed Cornwall; its ports bustled with activity, and a network of inland routes developed to transport the minerals across country. Walkers can now follow the Tinners' Way, a 13-mile route from St Just to St Ives on the Land's End peninsula. But in the late 19th-century the already volatile industry was dealt a mortal blow when cheaper deposits of tin were discovered in Bolivia and Malaya. The effect was dramatic, and by 1896 only a handful of mines were left. One of very few to be sunk subsequently was Geevor (tel: 01736 788662), near St Just, which was operating until 1991. The site was later developed as a 'mining heritage centre'; a museum covers the history of mining in the St Just area and guided tours take visitors to the surface workings of the mine.

The Poldark Mine Heritage Centre (tel: 01326 573173), north of Helston, re-creates the mining practices

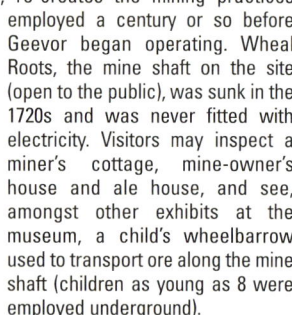

employed a century or so before Geevor began operating. Wheal Roots, the mine shaft on the site (open to the public), was sunk in the 1720s and was never fitted with electricity. Visitors may inspect a miner's cottage, mine-owner's house and ale house, and see, amongst other exhibits at the museum, a child's wheelbarrow used to transport ore along the mine shaft (children as young as 8 were employed underground).

The complex was named after the Poldark novels by Winston Graham, based on the partly real, partly fictitious lives of a late 18th-century mining community. Graham was living at Perranporth when he wrote the first novel of the series, and to experience the atmosphere of the books, explore nearby St Agnes (Poldark's St Annes), surrounded by the chimneys of old engine houses. Of these, Wheal Coates, to the north, is perched on the cliffs of a particularly breathtaking stretch of Cornish coastal scenery.

---

250 THE OLD VICARAGE

 HIGHLY COMMENDED

Treneglos, Launceston, Cornwall PL15 8UQ Tel (01566) 781351

An elegant Grade II listed Georgian vicarage set within its own grounds amidst beautiful countryside, close to the spectacular north Cornwall coast. Peaceful and tranquil, yet ideally located as a touring base. Renowned for our hospitality and personal service which, together with the highest standards throughout, assure your absolute comfort. The en-suite bedrooms are individually-furnished, together with fresh flowers and personal touches. Superb food, using produce from our own organic kitchen gardens. Non-smoking.

Bed & Breakfast per night: double room from
£44.00–£48.00
Half board per person: £36.00–£39.00 daily;
£252.00–£259.00 weekly
Evening meal 1900–2000

Bedrooms: 2 double
Bathrooms: 2 en-suite
Parking for 10
Open: April–October

---

251 POLKERR GUEST HOUSE

 HIGHLY COMMENDED

Molesworth Street, Tintagel, Cornwall PL34 0BY Tel (01840) 770382 or (01840) 770132

Somewhere special was what we envisaged when we planned the decor of our bedrooms, dining room and the recently constructed large and restful sun lounge that overlooks the garden: guests visiting Polkerr Guest House enjoy accommodation of the highest standard. Situated within a few minutes' walk of Tintagel village, the historic castle and cliffs that offer superb views of the coast, we are also ideally located for exploring the beauty of the countryside.

Bed & Breakfast per night: single room from
£17.00–£21.00; double room from £34.00–£42.00
Half board per person: £25.50–£29.50 daily
Evening meal 1830 (last bookings 1200)

Bedrooms: 1 single, 3 double, 2 twin, 1 family room
Bathrooms: 6 en-suite
Parking for 9

---

252 TRENANCE LODGE HOTEL

 HIGHLY COMMENDED

83 Trenance Road, Newquay, Cornwall TR7 2HW Tel (01637) 876702 Fax (01637) 872034

An attractive house standing in its own grounds overlooking the lakes and gardens of Trenance Valley, which leads to the Gannel Estuary. The restaurant has a reputation for serving superior food in elegant surroundings, with local fish a speciality. Adjoining the restaurant is a spacious, relaxing bar lounge. Five comfortable en-suite bedrooms with colour TVs, radios and tea/coffee facilities. An excellent base for touring this beautiful and historic region, with a warm welcome assured.

Bed & Breakfast per night: single occupancy from
£25.00–£32.00; double room from £46.00–£56.00
Half board per person: £37.00–£46.00 daily;
£259.00–£275.00 weekly
Evening meal 1900 (last orders 2230)

Bedrooms: 4 double, 1 twin
Bathrooms: 5 en-suite
Parking for 32
Cards accepted: Access, Visa

253 ROSE COTTAGE

 HIGHLY COMMENDED

Shepherds Farm, St Newlyn East, Newquay, Cornwall TR8 5NW Tel (01872) 540502

A warm welcome awaits you on our 700-acre mixed working farm. Come and share our warm and friendly atmosphere with first class service. All rooms are en-suite, with colour TVs and tea making facilities – all beautifully furnished and decorated. Delightful enclosed garden with a play area for children. Free horse and pony riding (seasonal). Central location, ideal for touring. Set in the small hamlet of Fiddlers Green, three miles from the beautiful Cornish coast, five miles from Newquay and twenty minutes from the south coast. Beautiful, breathtaking views along the clifftops. Good pub food close by. Come and join us!

Bed & Breakfast per night: single occupancy from £15.00–£17.00; double room from £30.00–£34.00

Bedrooms: 2 double, 1 twin
Bathrooms: 3 en-suite
Parking for 3

254 DEGEMBRIS FARMHOUSE

 HIGHLY COMMENDED

St Newlyn East, Newquay, Cornwall TR8 5HY Tel (01872) 510555 Fax (01872) 510230

If you are searching for a tranquil, undisturbed holiday in a picturesque corner of Cornwall, make your way to Degembris where a warm welcome awaits you. Overlooking a beautiful wooded valley, our farmhouse offers you comfortable accommodation, seasonal log fires and delicious home cooking. Our own country trail allows you to explore the natural surroundings. We will provide you with comfort and a taste of country life.

Bed & Breakfast per night: single room £18.00; double room from £36.00–£40.00
Half board per person: £28.00–£30.00 daily
Evening meal 1830

Bedrooms: 1 single, 1 double, 1 twin, 1 triple, 1 family room
Bathrooms: 3 en-suite, 1 public
Parking for 8

255 AVIARY COURT HOTEL

 HIGHLY COMMENDED

Marys Well, Illogan, Redruth, Cornwall TR16 4QZ Tel (01209) 842256 Fax (01209) 843744

A charming three-hundred-year-old Cornish country house set in its own grounds on the edge of Illogan Woods, ideal for touring the South West peninsular and its many local attractions. Six well-equipped individual bedrooms with tea/coffee making facilities, biscuits, mineral water, fresh fruit, direct dial telephone, remote control television and a view of the gardens. The resident family proprietors ensure personal service, offering well-cooked varied food that uses as much Cornish produce as possible.

Bed & Breakfast per night: single occupancy from £40.00; double room from £56.00
Half board per person: from £52.00 daily; £480.00 weekly
Lunch available: 1230–1330 (Sunday only)
Evening meal 1900 (last orders 2030)

Bedrooms: 4 double, 1 twin, 1 triple
Bathrooms: 6 en-suite
Parking for 25
Cards accepted: Access, Visa, Diners, Amex

256 TREGLISSON
 HIGHLY COMMENDED

11 Wheal Alfred Road, Hayle, Cornwall TR27 5JT   Tel (01736) 753141

Situated in the quiet Cornish countryside, Treglisson is a listed 18th-century farmhouse which offers pretty bedrooms with comfortable beds, antique furniture and fresh flowers. Start the day with a swim in the heated indoor pool before tucking into a hearty breakfast served in the elegant dining room or conservatory. St Michael's Mount, St Ives and Land's End are all within easy reach of Treglisson.

Bed & Breakfast per night: single occupancy £24.00; double room £38.00

Bedrooms: 2 double, 1 twin, 2 family rooms
Bathrooms: 5 en-suite
Parking for 20
Open: all year, except Christmas and New Year
Cards accepted: Access, Visa, Switch/Delta

257 ST MARTIN'S ON THE ISLE
 HIGHLY COMMENDED

The Island of St. Martin's, Isles of Scilly TR25 0QW   Tel (01720) 422092   Fax (01720) 422298

'Somewhere Special' perfectly describes this tranquil choice of island holiday break with a difference. Glorious uncrowded beaches and crystal-clear waters for safe swimming, fascinating diving and even snorkelling with Atlantic grey seals. 'Genesis', our 45ft Bermudan cutter, is exclusively available to our guests for island-hopping, sailing and picnics on remote islands, and then there are fishing and stunning scenic walks with birdlife and flora galore. The hotel, which is at the water's edge, has fabulous panoramic views over uninhabited islands, a heated swimming pool and an award-winning restaurant specialising in local seafood.

Half board per person: £95.00–£135.00 daily; £665.00–£945.00 weekly
Lunch available: 1000–1700
Evening meal 1915 (last orders 2045)

Bedrooms: 4 double, 16 twin, 2 triple, 2 family rooms
Bathrooms: 24 en-suite, 2 public
Open: March–October
Cards accepted: Access, Visa, Diners, Amex, Switch/Delta

258 NANSLOE MANOR
 HIGHLY COMMENDED

Meneage Road, Helston, Cornwall TR13 0SB   Tel (01326) 574691   Fax (01326) 564680

Nansloe, a Georgian manor, is set in the lovely wooded Loe Valley near Helston and is well placed for exploring Cornwall. It is owned and managed by John and Wendy Pyatt who take every care for your comfort and well-being. The food is delicious and imaginatively prepared, using as much local produce as possible. Log fires in the winter and lovely fresh flowers in the summer add to the welcoming atmosphere of the house. The dining room is no smoking.

Bed & Breakfast per night: single room from £44.00–£60.00; double room from £90.00–£115.00
Half board per person: £60.00–£72.00 daily
Lunch available: 1200–1345
Evening meal 1900 (last orders 2045)

Bedrooms: 1 single, 2 double, 4 twin
Bathrooms: 6 en-suite, 1 private
Parking for 30
Cards accepted: Access, Visa

259 HOUSEL BAY HOTEL

HIGHLY COMMENDED

Housel Cove, The Lizard, Helston, Cornwall TR12 7PG Tel (01326) 290417 or (01326) 290917 Fax (01326) 290359

An elegant Victorian hotel at Britain's most southerly coast. The views across the ocean are spectacular and a secluded and sandy beach nestles below the hotel. The Cornish coastal path, which runs through the hotel gardens, leads east towards Cadgwith and Coverack and west towards Kynance Cove. Fully licensed with a stylish restaurant and a bar with panoramic views. All bedrooms are en-suite with satellite television and there is a passenger lift.

Bed & Breakfast per night: single room from
£28.00–£43.00; double room from £56.00–£84.00
Half board per person: £43.00–£58.00 daily;
£249.00–£360.00 weekly
Lunch available: 1200–1400

Evening meal 1900 (last orders 2130)
Bedrooms: 4 single, 10 double, 6 twin, 1 family room
Bathrooms: 21 en-suite
Parking for 32
Cards accepted: Access, Visa, Amex, Switch/Delta

260 THE BAY HOTEL

HIGHLY COMMENDED

Coverack, Helston, Cornwall TR12 6TF Tel (01326) 280464

This very comfortable family-run hotel, which is exclusively for adults, combines good food and wines, fresh air, exhilarating walks and good company to provide a tonic for all. We take great pleasure in preparing fine food for you, from local lobster and Helford oysters to traditional dishes such as roast lamb in the hay and grilled local fish. Our wine list boasts over eighty wines from which to choose. There is nowhere quite like it!

Bed & Breakfast per night: single room from
£26.40–£43.00; double room from £68.80–£84.00
Half board per person: £34.40–£47.50 daily;
£244.00–£345.00 weekly
Evening meal 1830 (last orders 2030)

Bedrooms: 1 single, 7 double, 6 twin
Bathrooms: 13 en-suite, 1 private
Parking for 14
Open: January and March–December
Cards accepted: Access, Visa, Switch/Delta

261 PENMORVAH MANOR HOTEL

HIGHLY COMMENDED

Budock, Falmouth, Cornwall TR11 5ED Tel (01326) 250277 Fax (01326) 250509

Here is your opportunity to find peace and tranquillity at this recently-extended, elegant Victorian manor house set in six acres of private woodland and mature gardens. We offer twenty seven beautifully-appointed bedrooms. Dine by candle light and enjoy superb food in a friendly, relaxed atmosphere. A 'Cornish hideaway' situated close to the picturesque Helford River, yet just two miles from Falmouth.

Bed & Breakfast per night: single room from
£35.00–£43.00; double room from £70.00–£80.00
Half board per person: £51.50–£59.50 daily;
£267.00–£302.00 weekly
Lunch available: 1200–1330

Evening meal 1900 (last orders 2030)
Bedrooms: 1 single, 15 double, 10 twin, 1 triple
Bathrooms: 27 en-suite
Parking for 100
Cards accepted: Access, Visa, Amex

262 GREEN LAWNS HOTEL

☆☆☆☆ HIGHLY COMMENDED

Western Terrace, Falmouth, Cornwall TR11 4QJ Tel (01326) 312734 Fax (01326) 211427 E-mail green.lawns@dial.pipex.com

Where can you relax in an elegant, centrally positioned, chateau-style hotel with views across the beautiful bay? The Green Lawns Hotel and the famous Garras restaurant! If you are looking for a holiday where high standards and personal attention are paramount, you will enjoy an excellent choice of imaginative cuisine from a table d' hôte or à la carte menu. All our guests enjoy free membership to the Garras Leisure Club with its magnificent indoor swimming pool. 'Britain in Bloom' winners 1994, 1995 and 1996.

Bed & Breakfast per night: single room from £45.00–£80.00; double room from £80.00–£116.00
Half board per person: £56.00–£96.00 daily; £350.00–£605.00 weekly
Lunch available: 1200–1400

Evening meal 1845 (last orders 2200)
Bedrooms: 6 single, 17 double, 9 twin, 2 triple, 6 family rooms
Bathrooms: 40 en-suite
Parking for 60
Cards accepted: Access, Visa, Diners, Amex, Switch/Delta

263 ROSEVINE HOTEL

☆☆☆☆ HIGHLY COMMENDED

Porthcurnick Beach, Portscatho, Truro, Cornwall TR2 5EW Tel (01872) 580230 or (01872) 580206 Fax (01872) 580230

Located immediately above an attractive sandy beach, this quiet country house hotel is set in large pleasant gardens and enjoys superb sea views across Gerrans Bay and the unspoilt fishing village of Portscatho. Family-run with friendly staff, its top-class chefs provide excellent international cuisine in its spacious dining room with sea views. The hotel is situated within easy reach of many National Trust properties and gardens and numerous delightful coastal walks.

Bed & Breakfast per night: single room from £28.00–£40.00; double room from £56.00–£80.00
Half board per person: £44.00–£74.00 daily; £295.00–£490.00 weekly
Lunch available: 1200–1400

Evening meal 1915 (last orders 2030)
Bedrooms: 1 single, 4 double, 8 twin, 2 triple
Bathrooms: 15 en-suite
Parking for 40   Open: March–October
Cards accepted: Access, Visa

264 THE HUNDRED HOUSE HOTEL

☆☆☆ HIGHLY COMMENDED

Ruan Highlanes, near Truro, Cornwall TR2 5JR Tel (01872) 501336 Fax (01872) 501151

Delightful 19th-century Cornish country house set in three acres. Near St Mawes on the Fal estuary and surrounded by superb countryside and unspoilt sandy coves. It is now a charming small hotel, beautifully decorated and furnished like an elegant English home. Delicious candle-lit dinners, Cornish cream teas, log fires and croquet on the lawn make a relaxing short break or a longer stay a memorable delight. Ideal for exploring Cornwall, its sub-tropical gardens or walking the coastal path.

Bed & Breakfast per night: single room from £36.00–£38.50; double room from £72.00–£77.00
Half board per person: £50.00–£59.00 daily; £301.00–£364.00 weekly
Evening meal 1930 (last bookings 1900)

Bedrooms: 2 single, 4 double, 4 twin
Bathrooms: 10 en-suite
Parking for 15
Open: March–October
Cards accepted: Access, Visa, Amex

265 LUGGER HOTEL

 HIGHLY COMMENDED

Portloe, Truro, Cornwall TR2 5RD Tel (01872) 501322 Fax (01872) 501691

Dating from the 17th-century and originally an inn frequented by smugglers, The Lugger is situated at the very waters-edge of a picturesque cove on the beautiful and unspoilt Cornish Roseland Peninsula. Internationally renowned for its first-class accommodation, superb food and wide selection of wines, the hotel has been in the ownership of the welcoming Powell family for three generations. It is the perfect place for lovers of nature and those in search of peace and seclusion.

Half board per person: £60.00–£75.00 daily;
£400.00–£460.00 weekly
Lunch available: 1200–1400
Evening meal 1900 (last orders 2130)

Bedrooms: 3 single, 8 double, 8 twin
Bathrooms: 19 en-suite
Parking for 25
Open: March–November
Cards accepted: Access, Visa, Diners, Amex, Switch/Delta

266 KERRY ANNA COUNTRY HOUSE

HIGHLY COMMENDED

Treleaven Farm, Mevagissey, St Austell, Cornwall PL26 6RZ Tel (01726) 843558 Fax (01726) 843558

Kerry Anna Country House is set amidst beautiful gardens with an outdoor heated summer pool. Overlooking the village, which is just a few minutes' walk away, with outstanding views of the countryside and with sea glimpses. Romantic en-suite bedrooms, all with their own personal touches. Three lounges, two of which are non-smoking. The dining room serves the best of farmhouse cooking using fresh local produce. Car parking close to the house. Sorry, no pets. Children over five most welcome during school holidays.

Bed & Breakfast per night: double room from
£40.00–£50.00
Half board per person: £30.50–£35.50 daily
Evening meal 1900 (last orders 1200)

Bedrooms: 4 double, 1 twin, 1 family room
Bathrooms: 6 en-suite
Parking for 6
Open: April–October

267 BOSCUNDLE MANOR

HIGHLY COMMENDED

Tregrehan, St Austell, Cornwall PL25 3RL Tel (01726) 813557 Fax (01726) 814997

A lovely house in over ten acres of secluded grounds with a practice golf area. The rooms are very attractively furnished with antiques, pictures and family possessions. The bedrooms are extremely comfortable and most have spa baths and power showers. There is an outstanding wine list and beautifully prepared fresh food is served. Andrew and Mary Flint have been here for over eighteen years and their personal involvement and enthusiasm create a relaxed and happy atmosphere.

Bed & Breakfast per night: single room from
£60.00–£80.00; double room from £110.00–£130.00
Half board per person: £75.00–£100.00 daily;
£455.00–£560.00 weekly
Evening meal 1930 (last orders 2030)

Bedrooms: 2 single, 3 double, 5 twin
Bathrooms: 10 en-suite
Parking for 15
Open: April–October
Cards accepted: Access, Visa, Amex

268 MARINA HOTEL

〰〰〰〰 HIGHLY COMMENDED

Esplanade, Fowey, Cornwall PL23 1HY Tel (01726) 833315 Fax (01726) 832779

This Georgian hotel, originally built as the summer residence of the Bishop of Truro, is situated on the waterside with its own moorings. The hotel faces south and most rooms (four have balconies) overlook the estuary. The walled garden provides an ideal spot for observing the waterside traffic. The restaurant overlooking the water provides a feast of local fish, shell fish and meat. Early and late season offers of two nights for the price of one.

Bed & Breakfast per night: single occupancy from £39.00–£51.00; double room from £52.00–£88.00
Half board per person: £42.00–£60.00 daily;
£266.00–£392.00 weekly
Evening meal 1900 (last orders 2030)

Bedrooms: 5 double, 5 twin
Bathrooms: 10 en-suite
Open: March–December
Cards accepted: Access, Visa, Amex, Switch/Delta

269 LANHAEL HOUSE

〰〰 HIGHLY COMMENDED

Langreek Road, Polperro, Looe, Cornwall PL13 2PW Tel (01503) 272428 Fax (01503) 273077

Lovely 17th-century house set in one-and-a-half acres of gardens, with sun terrace and heated swimming pool. All rooms are tastefully decorated, with hospitality trays and colour televisions with satellite channels. Guest lounge with local information. Four-course breakfasts included. Car parking available. Lanhael is a short walk away from local restaurants, the harbour and the coastal path.

Bed & Breakfast per night: double room from £38.00–£42.00

Bedrooms: 4 double, 1 twin
Bathrooms: 3 private, 1 private shower, 2 public
Parking for 5
Open: April–October

270 TALLAND BAY HOTEL

〰〰〰〰 HIGHLY COMMENDED

Talland Bay, Looe, Cornwall PL13 2JB Tel (01503) 272667 Fax (01503) 272940

A delightful old Cornish manor house set in two acres of gardens overlooking the sea. All bedrooms are furnished to a high standard and many have sea views. Dinners feature fresh regional produce – local seafood, Cornish lamb, West Country cheeses. Talland Bay is a magically peaceful spot from which to explore this part of Cornwall. Breathtaking cliff paths lead to Looe and Polperro, and there are fascinating sub-tropical gardens and National Trust properties within easy reach.

Bed & Breakfast per night: single room from £39.00–£79.00; double room from £78.00–£158.00
Half board per person: £54.00–£94.00 daily;
£340.20–£592.20 weekly
Lunch available: 1230–1400

Evening meal 1930 (last orders 2100)
Bedrooms: 3 single, 5 double, 9 twin, 2 family rooms
Bathrooms: 19 en-suite
Parking for 20   Open: February–December
Cards accepted: Access, Visa, Diners, Amex

271 COMMONWOOD MANOR HOTEL

HIGHLY COMMENDED

St Martins Road, Looe, Cornwall PL13 1LP Tel (01503) 262929 Fax (01503) 262632

Formerly a spacious and elegant Victorian family villa, Commonwood is set in six acres of landscaped gardens and woodland, enjoying spectacular views over the Looe river valley and countryside. Here you can relax in one of the lounges, around the swimming pool – which is a real suntrap – or in the garden. Our friendly unhurried service, with the best of local food and fresh fish, makes the Commonwood an ideal base. Only a few minutes walk to Looe town, harbour and beaches.

Bed & Breakfast per night: single room from
£30.00–£37.50; double room from £60.00–£75.00
Half board per person: £44.00–£54.00 daily;
£300.00–£330.00 weekly
Evening meal 1900 (last orders 2000)

Bedrooms: 1 single, 7 double, 2 twin, 1 family room
Bathrooms: 11 en-suite
Parking for 20
Cards accepted: Access, Visa, Amex, Switch/Delta

272 COOMBE FARM

HIGHLY COMMENDED

Widegates, near Looe, Cornwall PL13 1QN Tel (01503) 240223 Fax (01503) 240895

Come and enjoy peace, comfort and good food in the warm, friendly atmosphere of our small country house hotel. Relax in a wonderfully tranquil setting of lawns, meadows, woods and streams with superb views down a woooded valley to the sea. Log fires, candle-lit dining, outdoor pool, nearby National Trust houses and gardens, golf, fishing, tennis, horse-riding and glorious walks and beaches. We offer short break terms and seasonal bargain breaks.

Bed & Breakfast per night: single occupancy from
£20.00–£30.00; double room from £40.00–£60.00
Half board per person: £34.00–£44.00 daily;
£224.00–£296.00 weekly
Evening meal 1900 (last orders 1900)

Bedrooms: 3 double, 3 twin, 2 triple, 2 family rooms
Bathrooms: 10 en-suite
Parking for 12
Open: March–October
Cards accepted: Access, Visa, Diners, Amex, Switch/Delta

273 EAST CORNWALL FARMHOUSE

HIGHLY COMMENDED

Fullaford Road, Callington, Cornwall PL17 8AN Tel (01579) 350018

Beautifully situated, former silver-mine Captain's home. Sympathetically restored in the style of a farmhouse. Close to National Trust's Cotehele House, the Rivers Tamar and Lynher and St. Mellion Golf Club. Ideal for exploring Dartmoor and Bodmin Moor, and within easy reach of both the north and south coasts. A warm friendly welcome with service above and beyond expectations. Evening meals of home grown and local produce by arrangement.

Bed & Breakfast per night: single occupancy from
£15.00–£17.00; double room from £30.00–£40.00
Half board per person: £25.00–£35.00 daily;
£168.00–£238.00 weekly
Evening meal 1830 (last orders 2030)

Bedrooms: 2 double, 1 twin
Bathrooms: 2 en-suite, 1 private, 1 public
Parking for 6
Open: March–November

274 HALFWAY HOUSE INN

〰️〰️〰️ HIGHLY COMMENDED

Fore Street, Kingsand, Torpoint, Cornwall PL10 1NA Tel (01752) 822279 Fax (01752) 823146

Situated on the Cornwall coastal path, just thirty yards from the beach. At the heart of the historical colour-washed villages of Kingsand and Cawsand, adjacent to Mount Edgcumbe Park and a ferry ride away from the great naval city of Plymouth. The intimate restaurant specialises in locally-caught sea food, complemented by a selection of fine wines and real ales. A haven of peace and tranquillity, your stay here will be a truly unforgettable experience.

Bed & Breakfast per night: single room from
£22.00–£32.00; double room £44.00
Half board per person: £35.00–£40.00 daily;
£200.00–£280.00 weekly
Lunch available: 1200–1430

Evening meal 1900 (last orders 2130)
Bedrooms: 1 single, 3 double, 1 family room
Bathrooms: 5 en-suite
Cards accepted: Access, Visa, Diners, Amex,
Switch/Delta

275 BOWLING GREEN HOTEL

〰️〰️ HIGHLY COMMENDED

9-10 Osborne Place, Lockyer Street, Plymouth, Devon PL1 2PU Tel (01752) 209090 Fax (01752) 209092

Situated in the historic naval city of Plymouth opposite the world famous 'Drakes Bowling Green', this elegant Georgian hotel has superbly appointed bedrooms offering all the modern facilities the traveller requires. With a full breakfast menu and friendly and efficient family staff, you can be sure of a memorable visit to Plymouth. The Bowling Green Hotel is centrally situated for the Barbican, Theatre Royal, leisure/conference centre and ferry port, with Dartmoor only a few miles away.

Bed & Breakfast per night: single room from £34.00;
double room from £46.00

Bedrooms: 1 single, 7 double, 2 twin, 2 triple
Bathrooms: 11 private, 1 private shower
Cards accepted: Access, Visa, Diners, Amex,
Switch/Delta

276 THURLESTONE HOTEL

〰️〰️〰️〰️〰️ HIGHLY COMMENDED

Thurlestone, Kingsbridge, Devon TQ7 3NN Tel (01548) 560382 Fax (01548) 561069

An intimate atmosphere, characteristic of grand establishments, distinguishes us from others due to our location on the Devon coast, in an area of outstanding natural beauty. Sixty five en-suite bedrooms (includes three suites), well furnished with every facility, including video in some rooms. A restaurant with a reputation for fine food, superb wine and long-serving staff. Leisure activities include indoor swimming pool, spa bath, sauna, solarium, 9-hole championship golf course and tennis, squash and badminton courts as well as opportunities for walks and fishing. Please telephone for brochure.

Bed & Breakfast per night: single room from
£40.00–£75.00; double room from £80.00–£150.00
Half board per person: £45.00–£93.00 daily;
£315.00–£651.00 weekly
Lunch available: 1230–1400

Evening meal 1930 (last orders 2100)
Bedrooms: 7 single, 16 double, 32 twin, 13 triple
Bathrooms: 65 en-suite
Parking for 119
Cards accepted: Access, Visa, Amex

277 TIDES REACH HOTEL
HIGHLY COMMENDED

South Sands, Salcombe, Devon TQ8 8LJ Tel (01548) 843466 Fax (01548) 843954

Located in a tree-fringed sandy cove where country meets the sea, with a glorious view across the Salcombe Estuary, you can relax in style in this beautifully furnished and decorated hotel. Pamper yourself in the superb leisure complex, extensively-equipped and with a sunny tropical atmosphere. Award-winning creative cuisine served with courtesy and care in our garden-room restaurant.

Half board per person: £60.00–£95.00 daily;
£380.00–£595.00 weekly
Evening meal 1900 (last orders 2130)

Bedrooms: 18 double, 17 twin, 3 family rooms
Bathrooms: 38 en-suite, 2 public
Parking for 100
Open: February–December
Cards accepted: Access, Visa, Diners, Amex, Switch/Delta

278 WHITE HOUSE HOTEL
HIGHLY COMMENDED

Chillington, Kingsbridge, Devon TQ7 2JX Tel (01548) 580580 Fax (01548) 581124

The White House is a lovely Grade II listed building of great aesthetic and architectural appeal. Set in an acre of lawned and terraced gardens in one of the most beautiful corners of coastal England, the house has a unique atmosphere reminiscent of a quieter and less hurried age. An elegant restaurant and cosy bar, comfortable lounges with log fires, interesting wines and home cooking from the kitchen range are all here for your delight.

Bed & Breakfast per night: single occupancy from
£42.00–£56.00; double room from £66.00–£92.00
Half board per person: £46.00–£59.00 daily;
£273.00–£350.00 weekly
Evening meal 1900 (last orders 2005)

Bedrooms: 3 double, 5 twin
Bathrooms: 7 en-suite, 1 private, 1 public
Parking for 12
Open: April–December
Cards accepted: Access, Visa, Amex

279 THE WATERMANS ARMS
HIGHLY COMMENDED

Bow Bridge, Ashprington, Totnes, Devon TQ9 7EG Tel (01803) 732214 Fax (01803) 732214

This ancient hostelry has the most enviable riverside setting imaginable, nestling in a sheltered valley at the head of Bow Creek on the River Dart. Riverside tables, 15 award-winning en-suite bedrooms, sumptuous food to satisfy all tastes, real ales and cider, log fires, candle-lit restaurant, caring staff and a world of character in this famous historic inn, only two-and-a-half miles from Totnes. An ideal place to relax, central for exploring the South Hams. Children and pets welcome. Nominated by the West Country Tourist Board for 'England for Excellence' B&B Award 1994. Winner 'South Hams for All Seasons' 1995 for providing excellent service, quality and value in all seasons.

Bed & Breakfast per night: single occupancy £36.00;
double room from £54.00–£70.00
Lunch available: 1200–1430
Evening meal 1830 (last orders 2130)

Bedrooms: 10 double, 3 twin, 2 triple
Bathrooms: 15 en-suite
Parking for 60
Cards accepted: Access, Visa, Switch/Delta

280 THE OLD FORGE AT TOTNES

Seymour Place, Totnes, Devon TQ9 5AY Tel (01803) 862174

This beautiful 600-year-old building, now a licensed hotel, is a haven of comfort and relaxation not far from the town centre. Rooms are en-suite and delightfully co-ordinated, offering hair dryer, radio alarm, central heating, colour television, beverage tray and continental bedding. We also have ground-floor family rooms and a cottage suite. Leisure lounge with whirlpool spa. Enjoy breakfast in the Tudor-style dining room which offers a wide choice of menu including vegetarian and special diets. Golf Breaks are a speciality as we are ideally located near to fifteen courses. No smoking indoors.

Bed & Breakfast per night: single room from
£35.00–£46.00; double room from £50.00–£66.00

Bedrooms: 2 single, 4 double, 2 twin, 2 family rooms
Bathrooms: 9 en-suite, 1 private, 1 public
Parking for 10
Cards accepted: Access, Visa, Switch/Delta

281 SEAPOINT

Upway, Porlock, Minehead, Somerset TA24 8QE Tel (01643) 862289

A warm welcome awaits you at Seapoint – a comfortable Edwardian guesthouse with panoramic sea views. We ensure that your stay is a memorable one and pay particular attention to individual requirements. We prepare delicious traditional and vegetarian meals and have a good range of fine wines. The luxurious bedrooms are all en-suite and our tastefully furnished Edwardian house makes the perfect setting for dining by candle light, with a blazing log fire on chilly evenings.

Bed & Breakfast per night: single occupancy £20.00;
double room £40.00
Half board per person: £32.50 daily; £204.00 weekly
Evening meal 1830

Bedrooms: 2 double, 1 twin
Bathrooms: 3 en-suite
Parking for 3

282 PORLOCK VALE HOUSE

Porlock Weir, Minehead, Somerset TA24 8NY Tel (01643) 862338 Fax (01643) 862338

Formerly a hunting lodge, now a magnificent Edwardian country house hotel in a wonderful situation. Set in twenty five acres of grounds which sweep down to the sea, Porlock Vale House nestles at the foot of the ancient wooded fringe where Exmoor meets the coast. A friendly, unpretentious hotel where you can enjoy good food and fine wines served in a relaxed, informal atmosphere, with beautiful, uninterrupted views across Porlock Bay. Whether you enjoy the great outdoors, or sitting by a log fire, Porlock Vale is the perfect place for a short break at any time of the year.

Bed & Breakfast per night: single occupancy from
£41.00–£43.00; double room from £62.00–£66.00
Half board per person: £48.50–£50.50 daily;
£275.00–£289.00 weekly
Lunch available: 1200–1400

Evening meal 1900 (last orders 1930)
Bedrooms: 9 double, 5 twin
Bathrooms: 13 en-suite, 1 private, 2 public
Parking for 20
Cards accepted: Access, Visa, Diners, Amex, Switch/Delta

283 HILLSIDE

HIGHLY COMMENDED

Higher Allerford, Minehead, Somerset TA24 8HS Tel (01643) 862831

Delightful thatched West Country cottage with superb views overlooking the picturesque National Trust village of Allerford. Ideally situated for exploring Exmoor – walks start from our front door – or just sit in the garden and relax. On cold winter evenings enjoy the warmth of a real wood fire. Peaceful, warm and comfortable accommodation. Our own free-range eggs, home-made organic bread, preserves, etc – real West Country living! Well behaved pets welcome.

Bed & Breakfast per night: single occupancy from £18.00–£19.00; double room from £36.00–£38.00

Bedrooms: 1 double, 1 twin
Bathrooms: 1 public
Parking for 4

284 CHANNEL HOUSE HOTEL

HIGHLY COMMENDED

Church Path, Off Northfield Road, Minehead, Somerset TA24 5QG Tel (01643) 703229

An elegant Edwardian country house perfectly located for exploring the beauty of Exmoor and situated on the lower slopes of Minehead's picturesque North Hill where it nestles in two acres of award-winning gardens. The high standards of cuisine and accommodation will best suit those seeking superior quality and comfort. If you would like to experience smiling service in the tranquil elegance of this lovely hotel, we will be delighted to send you our brochure and sample menu.

Bed & Breakfast per night: double room from £74.00–£96.00
Half board per person: £49.00–£58.00 daily; £329.00–£347.00 weekly
Evening meal 1900 (last orders 2030)

Bedrooms: 2 double, 5 twin, 1 triple
Bathrooms: 8 en-suite
Parking for 10
Open: March–November and Christmas
Cards accepted: Access, Visa, Diners, Switch/Delta

285 EXMOOR HOUSE HOTEL

HIGHLY COMMENDED

12 West Street, Dunster, Somerset TA24 6SN Tel (01643) 821268 Fax (01643) 821268

Situated in this delightful Medieval village close to Dunster Castle and two miles from the coast, we can accommodate just fourteen guests, thus enabling us to provide a friendly, personal but professional service in exclusive premises. Quality farm-fresh food, incorporated into varied menus (including vegetarian), is served in our licensed and candle-lit dining room. You can relax in our south-facing rear garden or enjoy walks on Exmoor, horse-riding, shooting, golf and more. No smoking.

Bed & Breakfast per night: single occupancy from £27.50–£38.50; double room from £55.00–£61.00
Half board per person: £38.00–£47.00 daily; £266.00–£287.00 weekly
Evening meal 1930 (last bookings 1900)

Bedrooms: 4 double, 3 twin
Bathrooms: 7 en-suite, 1 public
Open: February–November
Cards accepted: Access, Visa, Diners, Amex

286 CUTTHORNE
☰☰☰ HIGHLY COMMENDED

Luckwell Bridge, Wheddon Cross, Minehead, Somerset TA24 7EW Tel (01643) 831255 Fax (01643) 831255

Situated in the heart of Exmoor National Park, Cutthorne is a traditional Yeoman farmhouse offering a peaceful haven all year round. Totally secluded in one of the last truly unspoilt areas of the country. All our bedrooms are en-suite and the master bedroom boasts a four-poster bed. Dinner is served by candle light and a big fire warms the chillier evenings. There is an excellent choice of continental or English breakfasts.

Bed & Breakfast per night: double room from £42.00–£54.00
Half board per person: £33.50–£39.50 daily; £217.00–£231.00 weekly
Evening meal 1930 (last bookings 1800)

Bedrooms: 2 double, 1 twin
Bathrooms: 3 en-suite
Parking for 6

287 WESTERCLOSE COUNTRY HOUSE
☰☰☰ HIGHLY COMMENDED

Withypool, Minehead, Somerset TA24 7QR Tel (01643) 831302 Fax (01643) 831307

This hotel, situated just above the quiet Exmoor village of Withypool, is a peaceful retreat for those who have come to walk, ride or simply enjoy the beauty of the moor. Its ten en-suite bedrooms are all comfortably and individually furnished and benefit from wonderful views over Withypool Hill. Downstairs there are rooms filled with books and plants where you can relax, have a cream tea or a drink, and a candle-lit restaurant in which you can enjoy the carefully prepared and excellent food.

Bed & Breakfast per night: single room from £30.00–£35.00; double room from £65.00–£80.00
Half board per person: £48.00–£62.50 daily
Lunch available: 1200–1430
Evening meal 1930 (last orders 2115)

Bedrooms: 2 single, 3 double, 4 twin, 1 triple
Bathrooms: 10 en-suite
Parking for 15
Open: March–December
Cards accepted: Access, Visa, Amex

288 COMBE HOUSE HOTEL
☰☰☰ HIGHLY COMMENDED

Holford, Bridgwater, Somerset TA5 1RZ Tel (01278) 741382 Fax (01278) 741382

In the heart of the Quantock Hills (renowned as an area of outstanding natural beauty) lies this 17th-century house of great character. Once a tannery, this cottage-style hotel offers absolute peace and quiet in beautiful surroundings. Inside the beamed building, with its charming collection of pictures, porcelain and period furniture, the visitor will find the relaxed atmosphere and friendly service ideal to enjoy Combe House, the Quantocks and the many attractions in the area.

Bed & Breakfast per night: single room from £33.50–£45.00; double room from £67.00–£95.00
Half board per person: £38.50–£57.00 daily; £145.00–£360.00 weekly
Lunch available: Light bar lunches 1130–1430

Evening meal 1930 (last orders 2030)
Bedrooms: 4 single, 6 double, 8 twin
Bathrooms: 16 en-suite, 1 private, 2 public
Parking for 20   Open: March–October
Cards accepted: Access, Visa, Amex, Switch/Delta

289 BLACKMORE FARM

 HIGHLY COMMENDED

Cannington, Bridgwater, Somerset TA5 2NE Tel (01278) 653442 Fax (01278) 653442

A unique Grade I listed 14th-century manor house retaining many period features including oak beams, stone archways, log fires and its own private chapel. A traditional farmhouse breakfast is served in the Great Hall. All the bedrooms are en-suite, one with a four-poster bed. You can be assured of a warm welcome to this family home situated in a quiet, rural location, with views of the Quantock Hills. An ideal base for touring Bath, Somerset and Exmoor. A prize winner in the 1995 West Country Farm Holiday Awards. Facilities for disabled people.

Bed & Breakfast per night: single occupancy from £20.00–£25.00; double room from £36.00–£50.00

Bedrooms: 2 double, 1 triple
Bathrooms: 3 en-suite
Parking for 6

---

290 WALNUT TREE HOTEL

HIGHLY COMMENDED

North Petherton, Bridgwater, Somerset TA6 6QA Tel (01278) 662255 Fax (01278) 663946

It is rare to find a delightful hotel with such easy access to the M5 as the Walnut Tree. This former 18th-century coaching inn has been tastefully designed with the accent on comfort. All bedrooms are individually designed with every facility for today's travellers. Good food is served in the pleasing surroundings of the Sedgemoor Restaurant, whilst with its three meeting rooms, cosy bar and friendly staff, the Walnut Tree is a popular venue for honeymooners, travellers and those seeking a relaxing break.

Bed & Breakfast per night: single room from £35.00–£75.00; double room from £50.00–£90.00
Half board per person: £48.00 daily
Lunch available: 1200–1400
Evening meal 1900 (last orders 2200)

Bedrooms: 2 single, 23 double, 8 twin
Bathrooms: 33 en-suite
Parking for 74
Cards accepted: Access, Visa, Diners, Amex, Switch/Delta

---

291 ORCHARD HOUSE

 HIGHLY COMMENDED

Fons George, Middleway, Taunton, Somerset TA1 3JS Tel (01823) 351783 Fax (01823) 351785

A lovely Georgian Grade II listed house situated in a superior residential area of Taunton, yet only five minutes' walk into the town centre through beautifully-kept Vivary Park. Orchard House, elegantly furnished and decorated, was once lived in by Elizabeth Barrett Browning and her husband Robert. The house, easily accessible from the M5, is conveniently placed to explore Somerset, including the Blackdowns, the Quantocks and Exmoor. Short breaks at reduced rates available. No smoking in the house.

Bed & Breakfast per night: single occupancy from £30.00–£35.00; double room from £50.00–£55.00
Evening meal 1900 (last orders 2130)

Bedrooms: 1 double, 5 twin
Bathrooms: 6 en-suite
Parking for 8
Cards accepted: Access, Visa, Switch/Delta

292 ROYAL CASTLE HOTEL
 HIGHLY COMMENDED

11 The Quay, Dartmouth, Devon TQ6 9PS Tel (01803) 833033 Fax (01803) 835445

A unique 17th-century coaching hostelry in the heart of the historic port of Dartmouth – an unrivalled location ideal for short breaks at any time of year. Twenty five luxuriously appointed en-suite bedrooms are individually decorated and furnished, some with four-poster or brass beds and jacuzzis. The elegant restaurant on the first floor overlooks the estuary and specialises in select regional produce and locally-caught sea food. Two bars serve delicious food, traditional ales and a good choice of wines. We look forward to welcoming you.

Bed & Breakfast per night: single room from £47.50–£57.50; double room from £85.00–£127.00
Half board per person: £52.50–£93.50 daily; £315.00–£441.00 weekly
Lunch available: Bar meals 1100–1430

Evening meal 1845 (last orders 2200)
Bedrooms: 4 single, 10 double, 7 twin, 4 triple
Bathrooms: 25 en-suite
Parking for 4
Cards accepted: Access, Visa, Switch/Delta

293 FORD HOUSE
 HIGHLY COMMENDED

44 Victoria Road, Dartmouth, Devon TQ6 9DX Tel (01803) 834047 or 0378 771971 Fax (01803) 834047

Situated within walking distance from Dartmouth's historic quay and town centre. Ford House has a friendly, lived-in atmosphere with three attractively decorated and fully equipped en-suite rooms. Breakfast is served until noon around a large mahogany dining table, with smoked haddock, kippers, scrambled egg with smoked salmon, freshly squeezed orange juice, bacon and eggs. Special mid-week dinner, bed & breakfast packages have been arranged with the famous Carved Angel restaurant.

Bed & Breakfast per night: single occupancy from £35.00–£75.00; double room from £50.00–£75.00
Half board per person: £50.00–£62.50 daily; £350.00 weekly
Evening meal 1900 (last bookings 1200)

Bedrooms: 3 double
Bathrooms: 3 en-suite
Parking for 4
Open: March–October
Cards accepted: Access, Visa, Amex

294 THE CAPTAINS HOUSE
 HIGHLY COMMENDED

18 Clarence Street, Dartmouth, Devon TQ6 9NW Tel (01803) 832133

A charming small Grade II listed house built c1730 and containing the original staircase and Adam-style fire surroundings. It is conveniently situated in a quiet street just off the River Dart, and a three-minute walk from the harbour and historic town centre. Each bedroom is individually furnished and decorated but with every modern facility. Full English breakfast with a choice, served with home-made breads and preserves, can be taken either downstairs or upstairs.

Bed & Breakfast per night: single room from £25.00–£30.00; double room from £40.00–£50.00

Bedrooms: 1 single, 3 double, 1 twin
Bathrooms: 4 en-suite, 1 private
Cards accepted: Amex

295 BLUE HAZE HOTEL

⌇⌇⌇ HIGHLY COMMENDED

Seaway Lane, Torquay, Devon TQ2 6PS Tel (01803) 607186 or (01803) 606205 Fax (01803) 607186

Set in lovely grounds in a quiet country lane by the sea – a small, friendly hotel where we have been welcoming guests since 1979. Delicious home cooking served straight from the oven – Devon cider pork, home-baked rolls, gooseberry pie. Desserts all lovingly home-made shortly before they are served. Spacious quality en-suite rooms, all sparkling clean and well-appointed, with the extra luxury of a small fridge plus fresh milk for your hot drinks.

Bed & Breakfast per night: single occupancy from £35.00–£37.00; double room from £54.00–£58.00
Half board per person: £39.00–£41.00 daily; £225.00–£240.00 weekly
Evening meal 1900 (last orders 1900)

Bedrooms: 4 double, 2 twin, 2 triple, 1 family room
Bathrooms: 9 en-suite
Parking for 15
Open: April–October
Cards accepted: Access, Visa, Amex

296 FAIRMOUNT HOUSE HOTEL

⌇⌇⌇ HIGHLY COMMENDED

Herbert Road, Chelston, Torquay, Devon TQ2 6RW Tel (01803) 605446 Fax (01803) 605446

Enjoy the best of both worlds – coast and country. In lovely gardens overlooking a quiet, residential valley close to Cockington and a few minutes from the sea, Fairmount is a lovingly restored Victorian family house with high ceilings, polished brass, beautifully appointed bedrooms, a cosy conservatory bar and log fires. Fairmount has won its reputation over the years for mouth-watering menu choices and delicious home cooking, complemented by fine international wines and friendly, personal service. Dogs welcome too.

Bed & Breakfast per night: single room from £23.00–£30.00; double room from £46.00–£60.00
Half board per person: £34.50–£41.50 daily; £221.50–£270.50 weekly
Lunch available: 1200–1330 Bar Snack Lunches

Evening meal 1830 (last orders 1930)
Bedrooms: 2 single, 4 double, 2 triple/twin
Bathrooms: 8 en-suite, 2 public
Parking for 8   Open: March–October
Cards accepted: Access, Visa, Amex

297 OAK COTTAGE

⌇⌇ HIGHLY COMMENDED

Luscombe Hill, Dawlish, Devon EX7 0PX Tel (01626) 863120

Set in a peaceful woodland location with terrace views of the sea and close to Dartmoor, this 19th-century Tudor revival house is described as having a National Trust atmosphere and was used in the 'Miss Marple' TV series. Stone mullions, leaded lights, classically styled gardens with pools and woodland birdsong. Paintings, old prints, antiques, log fires and warm hospitality. Dinner is freshly prepared to a high standard using local produce. Ample private parking.

Bed & Breakfast per night: double room from £50.00
Half board per person: from £37.00 daily
Evening meal 1930

Bedrooms: 1 double, 1 twin
Bathrooms: 2 en-suite
Parking for 3

❷❾❽ GREAT HOUNDBEARE FARMHOUSE

〰〰 HIGHLY COMMENDED

Aylesbeare, Exeter, Devon EX5 2DB Tel (01404) 822771 Fax (01404) 822877

Spoil yourself in tranquil surroundings where you can relax and unwind. 16th-century farmhouse set in front of acres of lawn and woodland, with a lake to fish on and lots of country walks to enjoy. All rooms are en-suite with colour televisions, hospitality trays, radio alarms etc. Guests have a separate dining room and sitting room with log fire and colour television. Cottage also available. Telephone for colour brochure and further details.

Bed & Breakfast per night: single occupancy from £18.00–£22.00; double room from £36.00–£44.00

Bedrooms: 2 double, 1 twin, 1 family room
Bathrooms: 4 en-suite
Parking for 20

❷❾❾ HOTEL RIVIERA

〰〰〰〰 DE LUXE

The Esplanade, Sidmouth, Devon EX10 8AY Tel (01395) 515201 Fax (01395) 577775

Splendidly positioned at the centre of Sidmouth's Esplanade overlooking Lyme Bay. With its mild climate and the beach just on the doorstep, the setting echoes the south of France and is the choice for the discerning visitor in search of relaxation and quieter pleasures. Behind the fine Regency façade lies an alluring blend of old-fashioned service and present-day comforts. Glorious sea views can be enjoyed from the recently re-designed and refurbished en-suite bedrooms, all of which are fully appointed. In the elegant bay-view dining rooom, guests are offered a fine choice of dishes from the extensive menus prepared by French and Swiss-trained chefs.

Bed & Breakfast per night: single room from £62.00–£85.00; double room from £108.00–£154.00
Half board per person: £63.00–£86.00 daily; £441.00–£539.00 weekly
Lunch available: 1230–1400

Evening meal 1900 (last orders 2100)
Bedrooms: 7 single, 6 double, 14 twin
Bathrooms: 27 en-suite
Parking for 21
Cards accepted: Access, Visa, Diners, Amex

❸⓪⓪ BEACH END GUEST HOUSE

〰〰 HIGHLY COMMENDED

8 Trevelyan Road, Seaton, Devon EX12 2NL Tel (01297) 23388

We are situated at the mouth of the River Axe in unspoilt Seaton, from where you can enjoy unrivalled views over Axmouth Harbour and Seaton Bay. We offer you fine food and friendly, attentive service in our lovely Edwardian guesthouse. You can be sure that we will try our best to make your holiday really special.

Bed & Breakfast per night: double room max £42.00
Half board per person: max £30.95 daily; max £206.50 weekly
Evening meal 1900 (last bookings 1500)

Bedrooms: 4 double, 1 twin
Bathrooms: 3 en-suite, 1 public
Parking for 5
Open: February–October

301 HENSLEIGH HOTEL

Lower Sea Lane, Charmouth, Bridport, Dorset DT6 6LW Tel (01297) 560830

〰〰〰 HIGHLY COMMENDED

A family-run hotel with a reputation for friendly service, comfort, hospitality and delicious food, complemented by a relaxing atmosphere which has made it a favourite with visitors to Charmouth. Situated just three hundred metres from the beach, in an area of outstanding beauty, with spectacular cliff walks and fossil hunting, we have ample car parking within the grounds.

Bed & Breakfast per night: single room from £24.00–£26.00; double room from £48.00–£52.00
Half board per person: £37.00–£39.00 daily; £234.00–£250.00 weekly
Evening meal 1830 (last orders 1930)

Bedrooms: 2 single, 4 double, 4 twin, 1 triple
Bathrooms: 11 en-suite
Parking for 15
Open: March–October
Cards accepted: Access, Visa, Amex

Cerne Abbas Giant

EVEN WITHOUT ITS MOST FAMOUS landmark, Cerne Abbas in Dorset has many attractions. The town grew up around a Benedictine abbey founded in 987, and although only a few ancient remains of the abbey still stand, many of the prettiest houses date from the abbey's 500-year domination of the community. Later, the town flourished as a small market centre, but its decline in the 19th-century meant that it never grew large or industrialised, and today it ranks as one of the prettiest villages in Dorset, complete with duckpond, village stocks, a holy well in the churchyard and a superb 14th-century tithe barn.

But what makes Cerne Abbas uniquely memorable is the enormous and extraordinary figure cut into the chalky hillside near by. Brandishing a knobbly club, the Cerne giant strides across the turf, arms outstretched, his naked form leaving little to the imagination. His origins and identity are obscure. Strangely, given that the abbey was a centre of literacy, there is no written record of the figure before 1754, but the current opinion is that the giant is most likely to be a representation of the Roman god Hercules, carved during the first few centuries AD.

Only two other similarly ancient hill-carvings exist in Britain – the White Horse of Uffington, Oxfordshire, and the Long Man of Wilmington, East Sussex. These were probably not the only ones; perhaps a whole panoply of colossal figures and beasts once marched across the English downland, only to be slowly smothered in vegetation and lost forever. The giant has survived through regular and rigorous 'scourings', usually at seven-year intervals, a practice which was presumably,

and rather surprisingly, condoned by the Benedictines despite the giant's obviously pagan nature and indecent nakedness. Today the National Trust is responsible for maintenance.

For obvious reasons the Cerne giant has always been regarded as something of a fertility symbol. It is thought that the village's annual spring revelries were held on a site near by, and to this day it is claimed that merely sitting on the giant's impressive 30ft member is a certain cure for infertility. This is not to be encouraged, however, because of the risk of eroding the carving's most prominent feature! Perhaps the best view of the Cerne giant is to be had from a viewpoint at the junction where Duck Street meets the A352 Sherborne–Dorchester road.

302 BRITMEAD HOUSE
〰〰〰 HIGHLY COMMENDED

West Bay Road, Bridport, Dorset DT6 4EG Tel (01308) 422941 Fax (01308) 422516

An elegant and spacious, recently refurbished detached house. Situated between Bridport and West Bay harbour with its beaches, Chesil Beach and the Dorset Coastal Path. An ideal base from which to discover Dorset. The spacious, south-west facing dining room and lounge overlook an attractive garden and open countryside beyond. Well appointed bedrooms all with many thoughtful extras. Delicious meals, table d'hôte dinner. Quite simply everything, where possible, is tailored to suit your needs.

Bed & Breakfast per night: single occupancy from £25.00–£35.00; double room from £40.00–£56.00
Half board per person: £33.00–£41.00 daily;
£203.00–£238.00 weekly
Evening meal 1900 (last bookings 1700)

Bedrooms: 4 double, 3 twin
Bathrooms: 6 en-suite, 1 private
Parking for 8
Cards accepted: Access, Visa, Diners, Amex

---

303 BAY LODGE
〰〰〰 HIGHLY COMMENDED

27 Greenhill, Weymouth, Dorset DT4 7SW Tel (01305) 782419 Fax (01305) 782828

Bay Lodge is set in a tranquil position in its own grounds at the centre of Weymouth Bay and enjoys extensive sea views towards the harbour and surrounding cliffs. The luxurious bedrooms, some of which are on the ground floor, are furnished to accentuate their own unique features with king-size beds, jacuzzi bathrooms and open log fires. We have an elegant dining room where our chef prides himself on serving fresh local produce. The lounges have deep, comfortable armchairs and, together with the dining room, have open log/coal fires. Private car park. Three-day bargain breaks from £95 per person.

Bed & Breakfast per night: single room from £29.50–£55.00; double room from £44.00–£86.00
Half board per person: from £35.00 daily; £210.00–£350.00 weekly
Evening meal 1830

Bedrooms: 1 single, 7 double, 4 twin
Bathrooms: 12 en-suite
Parking for 18
Cards accepted: Access, Visa, Diners, Amex, Switch/Delta

---

304 LEA HILL HOTEL
〰〰〰〰 HIGHLY COMMENDED

Membury, Axminster, Devon EX13 7AQ Tel (01404) 881881 or (01404) 881388

14th-century hotel set in eight acres of grounds overlooking a secluded valley in peaceful Devon countryside, only ten miles from the coast. Mellow stone, oak beams and inglenook fireplaces enhance the relaxed, informal and friendly atmosphere. The beamed restaurant offers superb cuisine which is freshly prepared using local produce such as Lyme Bay seafood and Devonshire lamb and game. Lea Hill is ideally situated for touring the West Country, walking, bird-watching, golfing or simply relaxing away from it all.

Bed & Breakfast per night: single occupancy from £49.00–£52.00; double room from £78.00–£84.00
Half board per person: £53.00–£57.00 daily;
£308.00–£320.00 weekly
Lunch available: 1200–1430

Evening meal 1900 (last orders 2030)
Bedrooms: 3 double, 3 twin, 1 triple, 2 family rooms
Bathrooms: 9 en-suite
Parking for 50
Cards accepted: Access, Visa, Amex, Switch/Delta

305 HORNSBURY MILL

 HIGHLY COMMENDED

Eleighwater, Chard, Somerset TA20 3AQ Tel (01460) 63317 Fax (01460) 63317

A working watermill set in a five-acre beauty spot with character en-suite bedrooms and a locally renowned restaurant and bar open to non-residents. Attractions include the lake with many breeds of duck, the curious and bygones museum and speciality cream teas. Hornsbury Mill is open all year and is conveniently situated on the borders of Dorset, Devon and Somerset between Chard and Ilminster. Please contact the owners, Keith and Sarah Jane Lewin, for brochure and further details.

Bed & Breakfast per night: single occupancy max £49.50;
double room max £65.00
Half board per person: max £67.00 daily; £295.00–£380.00
weekly
Lunch available: 1200–1400

Evening meal 1900 (last orders 2100)
Bedrooms: 3 double, 1 twin, 1 triple
Bathrooms: 5 en-suite
Parking for 80
Cards accepted: Access, Visa, Amex, Switch/Delta

306 BROADVIEW GARDENS

 DE LUXE

East Crewkerne, Somerset TA18 7AG Tel (01460) 73424 Fax (01460) 73424

Unusual Colonial-style bungalow with en-suite rooms overlooking our acre of beautiful secluded 'National Garden Scheme' gardens with lawns and hundreds of unusual plants. Furnished in keeping in the Edwardian style. Relax and enjoy the very best quality English home cooking in a friendly, informal atmosphere. Stay awhile and visit this wonderful area for garden visits, antique shops, the Dorset coast and quaint old villages – our list provides fifty varied places. A completely no smoking house.

Bed & Breakfast per night: single occupancy from
£25.00–£35.00; double room from £46.00–£54.00
Half board per person: £35.50–£39.50 daily;
£248.50–£276.50 weekly
Evening meal 1830 (last bookings 1200)

Bedrooms: 1 double, 2 twin
Bathrooms: 2 en-suite, 1 private
Parking for 6
Cards accepted: Access, Visa

307 KINGS ARMS INN

HIGHLY COMMENDED

Montacute, Somerset TA15 6UU Tel (01935) 822513 Fax (01935) 826549

The historic village of Montacute boasts a real gem: a traditional English inn offering first-class cuisine and comfort – the ideal venue for the discerning guest. The Kings Arms is a handsome 16th-century building of local Ham stone, offering thirteen charming well-appointed en-suite bedrooms. Chef Mark Lysandrou's cuisine is establishing a reputation in the West Country – try a tasty snack by a roaring log fire in the Pickwick Bar or enjoy a more formal meal in the Abbey Restaurant. A central location for numerous National Trust properties and gardens.

Bed & Breakfast per night: single occupancy from
£53.00–£59.00; double room from £69.00–£85.00
Half board per person: £73.00–£79.00 daily
Lunch available: 1200–1400
Evening meal 1900 (last orders 2100)

Bedrooms: 9 double, 4 twin
Bathrooms: 13 en-suite
Parking for 20
Cards accepted: Access, Visa, Amex

308 BOWLISH HOUSE

≋≋≋ HIGHLY COMMENDED

Coombe Lane, Shepton Mallet, Somerset BA4 5JD Tel (01749) 342022 Fax (01749) 342022

An elegant Georgian restaurant with rooms, wonderfully counterbalanced by the relaxed atmosphere. The award-winning restaurant and wine list are famous for their range and eclectic mix of modern classics and local produce. Shepton Mallet is a market town on the south-west slopes of the Mendip Hills, just ten minutes from the cathedral city of Wells. It is an ideal centre for exploring nearby Bath, Stourhead, Longleat, Glastonbury and Cheddar.

Bed & Breakfast per night: single occupancy £48.00; double room £48.00
Half board per person: £46.50 daily
Lunch available: by appointment
Evening meal 1900 (last orders 2130)

Bedrooms: 2 double, 1 twin
Bathrooms: 3 en-suite
Parking for 10
Cards accepted: Access, Visa

309 GLENCOT HOUSE

≋≋≋≋ HIGHLY COMMENDED

Glencot Lane, Wookey Hole, Somerset BA5 1BH Tel (01749) 677160 Fax (01749) 670210

Idyllically set in eighteen acres of gardens and parkland with river frontage, this elegantly furnished Victorian mansion offers high-class accommodation and excellent cuisine. Glencot has a homely atmosphere and friendly service. Facilities abound, with a small indoor pool, sauna, snooker, table-tennis, private fishing and more.

Bed & Breakfast per night: single room £55.00; double room from £78.00–£90.00
Half board per person: £110.00–£125.00 daily
Evening meal 1830 (last orders 2030)

Bedrooms: 2 single, 8 double, 2 twin
Bathrooms: 12 en-suite
Parking for 21
Cards accepted: Access, Visa, Amex

310 SWAN HOTEL

≋≋≋≋ HIGHLY COMMENDED

Sadler Street, Wells, Somerset BA5 2RX Tel (01749) 678877 Fax (01749) 677647

The Swan Hotel is a 15th-century coaching hotel, with original four-poster beds and log fires, facing the magnificent west front of Wells Cathedral. Providing traditional English cuisine in our oak-panelled restaurant. Ideal for touring Avon and Somerset, with Cheddar Gorge and Wookey Hole caves close by. Merit awards for restaurant and hospitality.

Bed & Breakfast per night: single room from £67.50–£72.50; double room from £87.50–£95.00
Half board per person: £53.00–£55.00 daily
Lunch available: 1230–1400
Evening meal 1900 (last orders 2130)

Bedrooms: 9 single, 19 double, 10 twin
Bathrooms: 38 en-suite
Parking for 35
Cards accepted: Access, Visa, Diners, Amex, Switch/Delta

311 BERYL

Beryl, Wells, Somerset BA5 3JP Tel (01749) 678738 Fax (01749) 670508

'Beryl' – a precious gem in a perfect setting. Small 19th-century Gothic mansion, set in peaceful gardens, one mile from the centre of Wells. Well placed for touring the area. Offers comfortable, well-equipped bedrooms and relaxed use of the beautifully furnished reception rooms. Dinner is served with elegant style using fresh produce from the vegetable garden and local supplies. Children and pets are welcome. Outdoor heated pool, June-September. Open all year, except Christmas.

Bed & Breakfast per night: single occupancy £50.00;
double room from £65.00–£75.00
Half board per person: £70.00 daily; £490.00 weekly
Evening meal 2000

Bedrooms: 2 double, 4 twin
Bathrooms: 6 en-suite
Parking for 14
Cards accepted: Access, Visa

Bristol Glass

THROUGHOUT THE 18TH- and early 19th-centuries Bristol's skyline was punctuated by the distinctive bottle-shaped chimneys of its many glass-making workshops, and for much of this time the city had the largest concentration of glass factories outside London. All have now gone and, not surprisingly, remaining examples of the fragile commodities produced in them are extremely scarce.

Bristol had all the requirements for the creation of a major glass-making centre. The raw materials – sand, limestone and red lead – were readily available, while other necessary products could easily be imported by sea. Furthermore, the city was already a centre for the wine trade and for liquor distilling; a strong and regular demand for glass bottles was assured.

By the 1720s there were at least 12 glass factories in Bristol. While bottles and window glass formed the backbone of the industry, the most prestigious products were expensive items of high quality tableware. In the late 18th-century these were often made from coloured glass, and the most famous of Bristol's products was a beautiful and vibrant blue glass created by the addition of a deep-hued cobalt from Saxony. So strongly did this colour come to be associated with Bristol glass that it became known as 'Bristol Blue'. By the early 19th-century though, in response to popular taste, Bristol's factories were increasingly turning out clear cut-glass tableware, at that time considered highly desirable.

Despite the profitability of such prestigious commissions the glass trade in mid-19th-century Bristol went into serious decline, caused in part by high taxes and cheap foreign competition and in part by the increasing limitations of Bristol as a port. The last glass factory closed in 1851.

It is always difficult to establish with any certainty that an individual bottle or wine glass was created in Bristol (except in a very few cases where products are signed or stamped with the maker's mark). Two of the city's museums, however, contain substantial collections of glassware, some items of which are known to have been manufactured locally. Bristol's Museum and Art Gallery (tel: 0117 922 3571) has a permanent display of many types of Bristol glass from bottles and window glass to exquisite items of expensive tableware. The wine company, Harvey's, based in Bristol since 1796, has its own wine museum (tel: 0117 927 5036) which boasts a splendid collection of early glass, including Bristol-made items.

312 TOR FARM

 HIGHLY COMMENDED

Nyland, Cheddar, Somerset BS27 3UD Tel (01934) 743710

Our working farm is situated on the beautiful Somerset levels, with open views from every window. The farmhouse is fully central-heated and has log fires on cold evenings in the guests' own lounge. En-suite and four-poster bedrooms available, some with private patios. Ideal base for visiting Bath, Wells, Glastonbury, Cheddar Gorge and the coast.

Bed & Breakfast per night: single room from £19.00–£25.00; double room from £33.00–£44.00
Half board per person: £30.00–£36.00 daily
Evening meal 1800

Bedrooms: 1 single, 5 double, 1 twin, 1 family room
Bathrooms: 5 en-suite, 2 public
Parking for 10
Cards accepted: Access, Visa

313 DANESWOOD HOUSE HOTEL

HIGHLY COMMENDED

Cuck Hill, Shipham, Winscombe, North Somerset BS25 1RD Tel (01934) 843145 Fax (01934) 843824

Standing in the heart of the Mendip Hills, Daneswood has been transformed into a charming country hotel. Each bedroom is well furnished and individually decorated with striking fabrics. The restaurant, where the emphasis is placed on presentation and taste, has received many accolades – each dish is freshly prepared in a style that combines traditional English and French cuisine. Within easy reach of Cheddar Gorge, Bath, Bristol, Wells and Glastonbury. Nearest motorway – junction 21, M5 south. Shipham is just inland from A38 Bristol–Bridgwater road.

Bed & Breakfast per night: single occupancy from £59.50–£72.50; double room from £65.00–£112.50
Half board per person: £50.00–£60.00 daily
Evening meal 1900 (last orders 2130)

Bedrooms: 9 double, 3 twin
Bathrooms: 12 en-suite
Parking for 30
Cards accepted: Access, Visa, Diners, Amex, Switch/Delta

314 SWALLOW ROYAL HOTEL

HIGHLY COMMENDED

College Green, Bristol BS1 5TA Tel (0117) 9255100 or (0117) 9255200 Fax (0117) 9251515

On College Green, next to the Cathedral, this elegant Victorian hotel has been fully restored and has reclaimed its rightful place as one of Bristol's finest hotels. 242 bedrooms equipped with private bathroom, individually-controlled air conditioning, satellite television, direct dial telephone with three extensions, tea and coffee making facilities, mini-bar, hairdryer and trouser press. Full valet service is available. Roman-styled Swallow Leisure Club with heated indoor swimming pool, spa bath, sauna, steam room, fitness room, solarium.

Bed & Breakfast per night: single room from £70.00–£125.00; double room from £105.00–£135.00
Half board per person: £90.00–£145.00 daily
Evening meal 1900 (last orders 2230)

Bedrooms: 16 single, 104 double, 108 twin, 14 triple
Bathrooms: 242 en-suite
Parking for 200
Cards accepted: Access, Visa, Diners, Amex, Switch/Delta

315 LEIGHTON HOUSE

 HIGHLY COMMENDED

139 Wells Road, Bath BA2 3AL Tel (01225) 314769 Fax (01225) 443079

You are assured of a warm welcome at Leighton House, a Victorian house set in an attractive garden with views over the city. Ample private parking and a ten-minute walk to Bath's centre. The rooms are spacious, tastefully decorated and furnished to high standards with bedrooms offering every comfort and en-suite bathrooms. An excellent and wide choice of breakfasts including fresh fruit salad and scrambled eggs with smoked salmon – the hospitality is a delight to experience. Special breaks available.

Bed & Breakfast per night: single occupancy from £47.00–£53.00; double room from £62.00–£68.00

Bedrooms: 3 double, 4 twin, 1 family room
Bathrooms: 8 en-suite
Parking for 8
Cards accepted: Access, Visa

316 SIENA HOTEL

 HIGHLY COMMENDED

24/25 Pulteney Road, Bath BA2 4EZ Tel (01225) 425495 Fax (01225) 469029

A fine example of early Victorian architecture, carefully renovated to reflect the splendour of the period. Set in landscaped gardens, Siena Hotel offers today's business and leisure traveller excellent accommodation and car parking close to the city centre. The bedrooms are spacious, well appointed, comfortable and en-suite. A high standard of service is maintained throughout, particularly in the presentation of an interesting and varied menu, served in the elegant dining room with panoramic city views.

Bed & Breakfast per night: single room from £42.50–£59.50; double room from £62.50–£80.00
Half board per person: £57.50–£70.00 daily;
£375.00–£440.00 weekly
Evening meal 1900 (last orders 2030)

Bedrooms: 2 single, 6 double, 2 twin, 3 triple, 1 family room
Bathrooms: 14 en-suite
Parking for 14
Cards accepted: Access, Visa, Diners, Amex, Switch/Delta

317 THE BATH TASBURGH HOTEL

 HIGHLY COMMENDED

Warminster Road, Bath BA2 6SH Tel (01225) 425096 Fax (01225) 463842

This beautiful Victorian mansion stands in five acres of lovely gardens and grounds with canal frontage and breathtaking views, creating a calm and peaceful setting conveniently near the centre of the magnificent Georgian city of Bath. There are tastefully furnished en-suite rooms (three four-posters) with imaginative and pleasant colour schemes, combining Victorian elegance with all the comforts of a good hotel, and a fine sitting room and conservatory. Ample parking and delightful hospitality.

Bed & Breakfast per night: single occupancy from £45.00–£55.00; double room from £64.00–£74.00

Bedrooms: 7 double, 2 twin, 3 triple/family rooms
Bathrooms: 12 en-suite, 1 public
Parking for 15
Cards accepted: Access, Visa, Diners, Amex

318 SARNIA

19 Combe Park, Weston, Bath BA1 3NR Tel (01225) 424159

Superb bed and breakfast in our large Victorian home. Spacious bedrooms, individually decorated, with television, tea/coffee, central heating and private facilities. Comfortable lounge and secluded garden. Enjoy a four-course breakfast in the sunny dining room with English, continental and vegetarian menus and home-made jams. Off-road parking, frequent bus service into Bath centre (1.5 miles) and special provision for children (under 3s free). Our aim is to make you welcome and help you enjoy Bath and its surroundings.

Bed & Breakfast per night: single occupancy from £25.00–£35.00; double room from £40.00–£52.00

Bedrooms: 2 double, 1 twin
Bathrooms: 2 en-suite, 1 private
Parking for 5

319 THE BATH SPA HOTEL

 DE LUXE

Sydney Road, Bath BA2 6JF Tel (01225) 444424 Fax (01225) 444006

The Bath Spa Hotel, a former Georgian mansion, is set in seven acres of lovingly restored gardens just ten minutes walk from the centre of Bath. The elegance of the city is recreated here in a sumptuous and traditionally English style. Exceptional comfort is combined with attentive personal service and friendly informality. With a choice of restaurants – the distinctive Alfresco or the more formal Vellore – and for relaxation, the Laurels Health and Leisure Spa.

Bed & Breakfast per night: single room from £143.95–£163.95; double room from £188.90–£368.90
Half board per person: from £133.45–£203.45 daily; £747.32–£1251.32 weekly
Lunch available: 1200–1400

Evening meal 1830 (last orders 2200)
Bedrooms: 7 single, 45 double, 46 twin
Bathrooms: 98 en-suite
Parking for 156
Cards accepted: Access, Visa, Diners, Amex, Switch/Delta

320 BROMPTON HOUSE

Saint Johns Road, Bath BA2 6PT Tel (01225) 420972 Fax (01225) 420505 E-mail BromptonHouse@msn.com

A charming former Georgian rectory (1777) set in beautiful secluded gardens, Brompton House has been converted and extended with exquisite care and attractive furnishings and is only a few minutes' level walk from the city centre. All en-suite rooms are equipped with colour television, direct dial telephone, radio, hairdryer and tea/coffee making facilities. A very friendly welcome is assured from the Selby family in a relaxing and informal atmosphere. Car park. Short breaks available. Strictly no smoking.

Bed & Breakfast per night: single room from £32.00–£50.00; double room from £55.00–£78.00

Bedrooms: 2 single, 9 double, 5 twin, 2 family rooms
Bathrooms: 18 en-suite
Parking for 18
Cards accepted: Access, Visa, Amex, Switch/Delta

⓷²¹ MONKSHILL

 HIGHLY COMMENDED

Shaft Road, Monkton Combe, Bath BA2 7HL Tel (01225) 833028 Fax (01225) 833028

Five minutes from the centre of Bath lies this secluded and very comfortable country residence, surrounded by its own peaceful gardens and enjoying far-reaching views over one of the most spectacularly beautiful parts of the Avon Valley. You can be assured of a warm welcome at Monkshill, where the emphasis is on luxurious comfort and complete relaxation. The drawing room, with its fine antiques and open log fire, is for the exclusive use of the guests and the spacious bedrooms enjoy fine views over the gardens and valley below. Monkshill is situated within a designated Area of Outstanding Natural Beauty. Totally non-smoking.

Bed & Breakfast per night: single occupancy from
£35.00–£45.00; double room from £55.00–£70.00

Bedrooms: 2 double, 1 twin
Bathrooms: 2 en-suite, 1 private, 1 public
Parking for 8
Cards accepted: Access, Visa

⓷²² THE OLD SCHOOL HOUSE

 HIGHLY COMMENDED

Church Street, Bathford, Bath BA1 7RR Tel (01225) 859593 Fax (01225) 859590

Rodney and Sonia Stone are delighted to welcome guests to their picturesque Victorian schoolhouse in the peaceful conservation village of Bathford, overlooking the Avon Valley. A tranquil tow-path walk along the Kennet & Avon Canal leads into the city centre. Our four bedrooms are individually furnished and decorated - two ground-floor and suitable for the less mobile. The pretty walled garden, antique furniture and winter log fires contribute to a charming country-house ambience. No smoking.

Bed & Breakfast per night: single occupancy from
£50.00–£60.00; double room from £65.00–£70.00

Bedrooms: 3 double, 1 twin
Bathrooms: 4 en-suite
Parking for 6
Cards accepted: Access, Visa

⓷²³ WIDBROOK GRANGE

 HIGHLY COMMENDED

Trowbridge Road, Widbrook, Bradford-on-Avon, Wiltshire BA15 1UH Tel (01225) 864750 or (01225) 863173 Fax (01225) 862890

An elegant Georgian house with courtyard rooms, exquisitely decorated and furnished with antiques, and all rooms having baths and showers en-suite. Set in its own grounds of eleven acres, the emphasis is on peaceful comfort and relaxation. Widbrook Grange has its own magnificent heated indoor swimming pool with a small gymnasium area, and superb conference facilities in the Manvers Suite. Evening dinner is served Monday to Thursday and all is home-prepared, with an interesting wine list.

Bed & Breakfast per night: single occupancy from
£52.00–£79.00; double room from £79.00–£89.00
Half board per person: £72.00–£99.00 daily
Evening meal 1830 (last orders 2000)

Bedrooms: 12 double, 5 twin, 1 triple, 1 family room
Bathrooms: 19 en-suite, 1 public
Parking for 55
Cards accepted: Access, Visa, Diners, Amex,
Switch/Delta

324 SPOUT COTTAGE

 HIGHLY COMMENDED

Stert, Devizes, Wiltshire SN10 3JD Tel (01380) 724336

In an idyllic, peaceful retreat, Spout Cottage is located in the secluded and attractive valley of Stert and is well away from the road. This picturesque and unspoilt part of Wiltshire is a few minutes from Devizes, an historic and bustling market town, and an easy driving distance from places like Bath, Stonehenge and Avebury. The cottage is spacious, comfortable and tastefully furnished. Delicious and imaginative meals are served in the south-facing conservatory, overlooking the beautiful garden.

Bed & Breakfast per night: single room £20.00; double room £36.00
Half board per person: £35.50 daily
Evening meal 2000

Bedrooms: 1 single, 1 twin
Bathrooms: 2 public
Parking for 4

---

325 THE OLD VICARAGE

 HIGHLY COMMENDED

Burbage, Marlborough, Wiltshire SN8 3AG Tel (01672) 810495 Fax (01672) 810663

The Old Vicarage is a lovely brick and flint Victorian gothic house, between Hungerford and Marlborough. Beautifully decorated, furnished and centrally heated throughout, with log fires on cold days and many special extras in the three en-suite bedrooms. Come and share the comfort and welcome of our no smoking home, relax in the peaceful gardens, explore the Kennet & Avon Canal, Savernake Forest, the Vale of Pewsey and the many other wonderful places to visit, such as Bath, Oxford and Salisbury.

Bed & Breakfast per night: single room from £30.00–£40.00; double room from £60.00–£80.00

Bedrooms: 1 single, 1 double, 1 twin
Bathrooms: 3 en-suite
Parking for 10
Cards accepted: Access, Visa

---

326 FENWICKS

HIGHLY COMMENDED

Buccabank, Lower Goatacre, Lyneham, Calne, Wiltshire SN11 9HY Tel (01249) 760645 Fax (01249) 821329

A delightful, secluded country home, idyllically set in two-and-a-half acres of beautiful gardens and meadowland on the outskirts of a hamlet. A haven from which to explore the many local places of interest. The bedrooms are comfortably and charmingly furnished. Relax and take tea in the peaceful garden in summer. Quoting a much-travelled guest – "a gem". We are central for Bath, Salisbury, the Cotswolds, Oxford and the Wye valley. A no smoking house.

Bed & Breakfast per night: single room from £25.00–£28.00; double room from £36.00–£40.00
Half board per person: £30.00–£43.00 daily; £214.00–£280.00 weekly
Evening meal 1900 (last orders 2030)

Bedrooms: 1 single, 1 twin, 1 triple
Bathrooms: 2 en-suite, 1 private
Parking for 4
Cards accepted: Amex

327 LAUREL COTTAGE GUEST HOUSE

HIGHLY COMMENDED

Southend, Ogbourne St Geaorge, Marlborough, Wiltshire SN8 1SG Tel (01672) 841288

Situated in a fold of the Marlborough Downs, this picturesque 16th-century thatched cottage offers you a unique opportunity to savour a traditional English home. Lovingly and tastefully restored with modern facilities, including two en-suite bedrooms, this is an experience that will live long in the memory. Full English breakfast is taken in the low-beamed dining room around the family table. Guests are invited to enjoy the half acre of attractive gardens. We are a non-smoking establishment.

Bed & Breakfast per night: single occupancy £35.00;
double room from £42.00–£50.00

Bedrooms: 2 double, 1 twin
Bathrooms: 2 en-suite, 1 private
Parking for 5
Open: April–October

Maud Heath's Causeway

IF YOU CLIMB to the modest summit of Wick Hill, 3 miles north-east of Calne, a pleasing view – typical of large tracts of lowland England – will be your reward. In good weather the panorama extends beyond the valley of the Avon to the Bristol Channel and the distant Welsh hills. On cloudier days you may struggle to discern the old Wiltshire market town of Chippenham some 4 or 5 miles due west. Whatever the weather, you will not be alone. For the past 150 years the dumpy, bonneted figure of Maud Heath, sitting comfortably atop an octagonal stone pillar, has stared down the hill towards Kellaways, the village that was probably her home in the 15th-century. A few years ago, during the fearsome winter gales of 1990, she suffered the ignominy of having her head blown from her torso, but fortunately injury was slight and she was soon restored to her original state.

So why is she thus commemorated and why does a straw basket rest beside her generous hips? As a regular trader, Maud Heath was well aware of the perils of the journey from her home to the Chippenham market. In particular she was concerned that the heavy clay of the Avon valley meant that she and her fellow travellers rarely arrived in town dryshod. So in 1474, the widow had a 4½ mile causeway built from Wick Hill through East Tytherton, Kellaways and Langley Burrell into Chippenham. She also appointed a body of trustees to ensure the causeway's maintenance; the lands which Maud Heath consigned to their care yielded an annual income of £8 (Wiltshire

County Council is now largely responsible for maintaining the causeway).

The best-preserved section, starting at the Kellaways Weir, carries those bound for market over 64 arches, a stretch long enough to ensure all had dry feet even during the worst of floods. Monuments to Maud Heath on the route include another pillar at Kellaways, a modern (1974) pyramid of stone blocks at East Tytherton and an inscription at the causeway's terminus in Chippenham: 'Hither extendeth Maud Heath's gift/For where I stand is Chippenham Clift'. The Kellaways pillar bears verse by the 19th-century eccentric local vicar of nearby Bremhill parish: 'Haste traveller, the sun is sinking now/He shall return again – but never thou'.

South & South East England

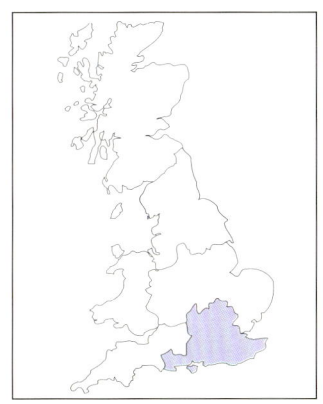

ENGLAND'S WARMEST and sunniest region is also its leafiest corner. It is perhaps surprising that a high concentration of human inhabitants is often matched by a similar density of trees. Hampshire, for example, is particularly rich in woodland, and the yew is locally known as the 'Hampshire weed'. On the eastern side of the county, the pretty village of Selborne is one of several that sit beneath hangers of beechwoods. These are at their best in May when the improbably bright green leaves burst forth from the grey winter branches. In the south-west of the county lies the New Forest, former hunting ground of kings. This attractive mix of forest, heathland and pasture offers endless recreational opportunities. Though visitors flock to the area on sunny weekends, a short stroll from the car soon leads the walker to quiet glades where company may be a rare butterfly such as the elusive white or purple emperor, or a New Forest pony.

Just across the water from Southampton is the region's only island of any size. The short ferry journey to the Isle of Wight seems to take visitors – or 'overners' as they are sometimes known here – to a world far remote from the pressures of mainland life. Cars dawdle on small, empty roads; orchids grow on downland; life moves at a slow pace in picturesque villages;

and birds wheel above spectacular chalk cliffs. The benign climate also encourages viticulturists to produce some of the best wines in the land. Clearly visible from the island's western tip is the Isle of Purbeck. This is firmly part of Dorset, and an island in name only. Nevertheless it has glorious beaches – as at Studland – and majestic cliffs along its southern coast.

Moving north and east to the meeting of Hampshire, Berkshire and Wiltshire takes you to the highest chalk down in England. Inkpen Hill was once thought to nose above 1,000ft (305m), but current estimates put it at 976ft (297m). Whatever its precise altitude, it offers one of the finest views in the South East. If you visit on a breezy day, you will probably have hang-gliders as colourful companions. Those admiring the panorama a few centuries ago might rather have seen the sombre sight of a hanged felon on Coombe Gibbet. Striking north into Berkshire you encounter four separate east–west routes, each devoted to a different form of transport. In turn are the Kennet and Avon Canal, the M4, the Great Western Railway and the Ridgeway. For those with time to spare, the first and last are the most appealing. Keeping to the downland ridge wherever possible, the Ridgeway, one of England's most ancient tracks, leads walkers past White Horse Hill and on towards the Chilterns.

Oxfordshire can claim some of the country's most glorious towns and villages in its northern reaches – who can resist the charms of Burford and Great Tew, or the medieval wealth of Oxford? – but it can also boast the sumptuous Thames-side town of Henley. Not far away, and just over into Buckinghamshire, is a magnificent trio of small settlements at the heart of the Chiltern Hills: Fingest, Turville and Skirmett, all within a mile of one another, lie in a maze of beautiful, wooded valleys. These trees form the raw material for the county's furniture industry, still thriving in the Chiltern town of High Wycombe.

Skirting London to its west, the chalk of the Chilterns gives way to the heathlands of Surrey. It is ironic that this infertile area, for centuries as wild and unpopulated as the northern Pennines, is now England's wealthiest county. Early residents often decided that the sandy soil was too poor to make enclosure worthwhile, ensuring that, once again, this is a leafy corner of the land. Wherever you venture, however, you are never far from chalk, and towards the Sussex border the North Downs rise up, offering more spectacular views. Despite the Downs' proximity to London, it is not difficult to escape the crowds, though the top of Box Hill, named after the box trees that grow on its flanks, can be reached by car. For a quieter – and higher – experience, clamber up Leith Hill. Its summit lies at 965ft (294m), but an 18th-century tower takes visitors well over 1,000ft (305m).

The North Downs then march eastwards into Kent. The fruit trees, bushes and hops of the 'Garden of England' are watered by the Medway. This river has long played an

important role in the history of the county, traditionally dividing the Men of Kent (to the east) from the Kentish Men (to the west). It also carried the oak trees from the Wealden forests down to Chatham, where they were turned into ships for Henry VIII's navy. Remnants of the vast woodlands that once filled the Weald (the land between the North and South Downs) can still be seen in St Leonard's and Ashdown Forests.

The coast of both Kent and Sussex is steeped in history; Dover's lighthouse is almost 2,000 years old, while the alliance of the Cinque Ports dates back over a thousand years. Today's visitor in search of a quiet beach may need either to rise early in the morning or walk some distance from the car, but journey inland to the South Downs and you can have acres of open downland to yourself. The South Downs Way follows the ridge for about 80 miles, where fine views, Southdown sheep and skylarks will never desert you for long. Descend from the high ground and you will also find some of the finest of gardens and stately homes.

▶ **Chairmaking at High Wycombe**
High Wycombe's reputation as the 'chair capital of England' stems from a tradition going back over 300 years. From the 17th-century, agricultural workers eked out a winter living making chairs in the Chilterns' beechwoods. Later, factories were set up in High Wycombe for their larger-scale manufacture. Many of the chairlegs, however, continued to be made by lone woodturners (known as 'bodgers'), living in huts deep in the forest. By the mid-19th century the town boasted over 100 factories, producing 1½ million chairs a year, and continues to produce furniture to this day. The Wycombe Local History and Chair Museum contains a fascinating record of this highly successful industry.

▶ **Wight Wine**
The Isle of Wight's first vineyard was established as recently as 1967 but the island now produces some of the best English wines on the market. The wines are (naturally!) white, making use of German grape varieties specially developed to sweeten in cool northerly latitudes. These grapes, which in Germany can become too sweet, never over-ripen in England and can consequently impart subtle aromatic flavours to the bouquet.

Left: Hertford College, Oxford; inset: Rye, East Sussex

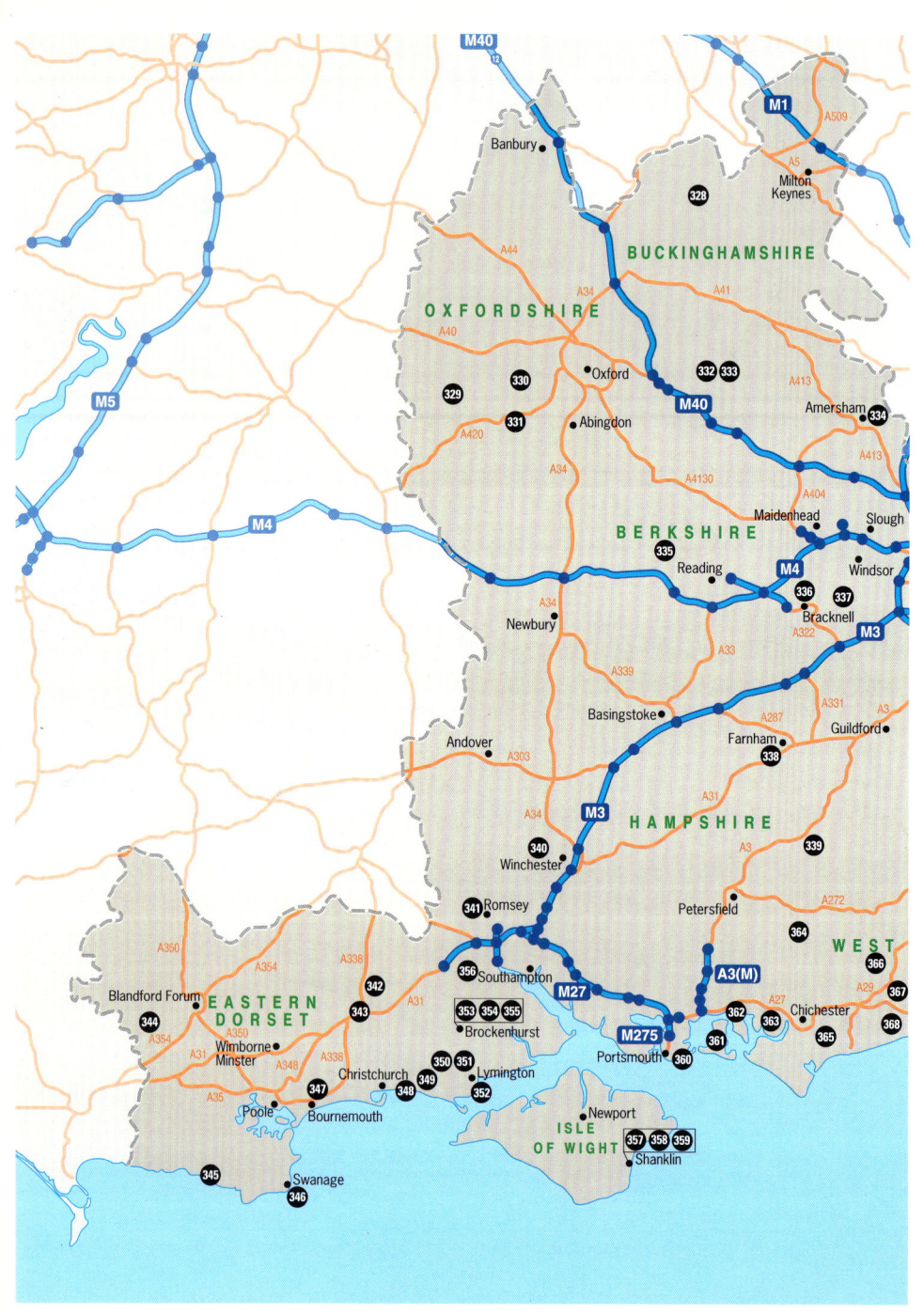

Colin Earl Cartography

328 VILLIERS HOTEL

🦢🦢🦢🦢🦢 HIGHLY COMMENDED

3 Castle Street, Buckingham, Buckinghamshire MK18 1BS Tel (01280) 822444 Fax (01280) 822113

When we created Villiers Hotel from the old Swan and Castle Inn, we set out to build a very special and individual hotel. Drawing upon the character of the 400-year-old hostelry we included the highest quality facilities and services, with comfort a priority for you, our guest – a home away from home.

Bed & Breakfast per night: single room from
£59.00–£75.00; double room from £79.00–£89.00
Half board per person: £50.00–£62.00 daily;
£300.00–£372.00 weekly
Lunch available: 1200–1400

Evening meal 1900 (last orders 2230)
Bedrooms: 3 single, 17 double, 14 twin, 4 suites
Bathrooms: 38 en-suite
Parking for 38
Cards accepted: Access, Visa, Diners, Amex, Switch/Delta

The gardens of Stowe

THE HOUSE AT STOWE in Buckinghamshire is of great architectural significance, and its south front, designed in part by Robert Adam, is considered one of the finest classical façades in England. Yet Stowe is not so much known for its great house (now a public school) as for the gardens that surround it, possibly the supreme example of their kind in England.

Three successive owners, members of the Temple and Grenville families, were responsible for the transformation of Stowe into the great 18th-century showpiece it became. All were ambitious, strong-minded individuals who required that their home should reflect their public image. They employed some of the leading architects of the day, amongst them John Vanbrugh, William Kent and James Gibbs. 'Capability' Brown, the country's most influential exponent of informal garden design, was appointed head gardener in 1741 and supervised all the garden alterations for the following 10 years.

Behind all the grand plans was the example of ancient Rome. In redesigning the gardens the intention was to mimic an idealised classical landscape. The result was a completely artificial creation, a landscape remodelled and replanted to look as natural as possible, while at the same time matching a particular aesthetic blueprint. Existing features were beautified, lakes were created, and vistas and avenues were constructed to allow glimpses of columns, temples and grottos.

The monuments – there are some 30 of them dotted about the grounds – are Stowe's most memorable feature. While many structures were purely decorative, others were designed to be more functional; the Temple

of Friendship, for example, was used as a banqueting hall and political meeting place. Throughout the 18th-century, the owners of Stowe were staunch supporters of the Whig cause, and a number of monuments were erected as tributes to political allies; the Temple of British Worthies numbers amongst the likes of Shakespeare and Elizabeth I an obscure MP, Sir John Barnard, who happened to support Sir Richard Temple in parliament!

The gardens at Stowe (tel: 01280 822850) were acquired by the National Trust comparatively recently and are still undergoing an extensive programme of restoration. A visit there offers a revealing insight both into the political and philosophical beliefs of the gardens' creators and the broader tastes of Augustan England. They are the product of the supreme confidence of the age and its belief that English culture, in particular its political institutions, could emulate and surpass those of the great civilisation of Rome.

329 PLOUGH HOTEL & RESTAURANT

 HIGHLY COMMENDED

Clanfield, Oxford, Oxfordshire OX18 2RB Tel (01367) 810222 Fax (01367) 810596

The Plough at Clanfield is a 16th-century country manor house set in the delightful village of Clanfield in the picturesque Oxfordshire countryside. All six bedrooms have en-suite facilities, colour television, hairdryer, trouser press, direct-dial telephone and tea-making facilities. The hotel is in an ideal location for visiting the surrounding Cotswolds and then returning to a relaxing atmosphere to enjoy the culinary delights of our award-winning restaurant.

Bed & Breakfast per night: single occupancy from £75.00–£95.00; double room from £90.00–£115.00
Half board per person: £75.00–£85.00 daily
Lunch available: 1200–1400
Evening meal 1900 (last orders 2100)

Bedrooms: 6 double
Bathrooms: 6 en-suite
Parking for 40
Cards accepted: Access, Visa, Diners, Amex, Switch/Delta

330 PINKHILL COTTAGE

 HIGHLY COMMENDED

45 Rack End, Standlake, Witney, Oxfordshire OX8 7SA Tel (01865) 300544

A charming 17th-century thatched cottage in half-acre gardens fronting the River Windrush in a quiet Oxfordshire village, offering exclusive, private bed & breakfast accommodation for two. The old stable has been transformed into a sitting room with its own external door and staircase to the hayloft – now an airy double bedroom with en-suite shower room. Many original beams are a feature of our cottage. Standlake is ideal for touring Oxford and the Cotswolds.

Bed & Breakfast per night: single occupancy from £29.00–£30.00; double room from £38.00–£40.00

Bedrooms: 1 double
Bathrooms: 1 en-suite
Parking for 1
Open: February–December

331 FALLOWFIELDS COUNTRY HOUSE HOTEL HIGHLY COMMENDED

Kingston Bagpuize with Southmoor, Oxford, Oxfordshire OX13 5BH Tel (01865) 820416 Fax (01865) 821275

The Fallowfields' recipe – take near-organic garden produce, add meticulously chosen meat and fish, mix in a three hundred year old (in parts) manor farmhouse, add interesting company, personal care of the owners, and serve in a candle-lit dining room, preferably by a log fire – leave with your bank manager still talking to you and you have the perfect recipe for a stay on business or pleasure. 'The next step is heaven' said one guest.

Bed & Breakfast per night: double room from £79.00–£95.00
Half board per person: £66.00–£74.00 daily
Evening meal 2000 (last orders 2100)

Bedrooms: 2 double, 1 twin
Bathrooms: 3 en-suite, 1 public
Parking for 17
Cards accepted: Access, Visa, Amex, Switch/Delta

332 BELFRY HOTEL

HIGHLY COMMENDED

Milton Common, Thame, Oxfordshire OX9 2JW Tel (01844) 279381 Fax (01844) 279624

A privately-owned and extended mock-Tudor hotel. Situated on the A40 near Junction 7 and 8/M40, this hotel is an ideal location for touring the Thames, the Chilterns, Oxford and the Cotswolds. One hour from London and Birmingham, with Heathrow a 45 minute drive away.

Bed & Breakfast per night: single room from £79.50–£90.00; double room from £95.00–£120.00
Lunch available: 1230–1400
Evening meal 1930 (last orders 2130)

Bedrooms: 11 single, 34 double, 30 twin
Bathrooms: 75 en-suite
Parking for 200
Cards accepted: Access, Visa, Diners, Amex, Switch/Delta

333 THE SPREAD EAGLE HOTEL

HIGHLY COMMENDED

Cornmarket, Thame, Oxfordshire OX9 2BW Tel (01844) 213661 Fax (01844) 261380

A caringly-converted former coaching inn, dating back to the 16th-century, set in the centre of Thame — an interesting market town and a good centre for visiting Oxford and the villages of the Vale of Aylesbury and the Thames Valley. The hotel provides comfortable accommodation, a large car park and a high standard of cuisine in Fothergills Restaurant. Vegetarians and special diets catered for.

Bed & Breakfast per night: single room from £89.75–£99.95; double room from £107.10–£122.95
Half board per person: £66.00 daily; £625.00–£685.00 weekly
Lunch available: 1230–1400

Evening meal 1900 (last orders 2200)
Bedrooms: 5 single, 22 double, 5 twin, 1 triple
Bathrooms: 33 en-suite
Parking for 80
Cards accepted: Access, Visa, Diners, Amex

334 DRAKES BARN

HIGHLY COMMENDED

Cherry Lane, Woodrow, Amersham, Buckinghamshire HP7 0QG Tel (01494) 722366 Fax (01494) 432462

A peaceful courtyard in the countryside, two miles from Old Amersham, surrounded by listed barns and other farm buildings dating from the 17th-century which have been converted into a family home, provides the setting for two centrally-heated, ground floor guest rooms. One has a vaulted ceiling over a four-poster double bed, the other has twin beds, and each has its own bathroom. The guest sitting room offers spectacular views over the Chilterns.

Bed & Breakfast per night: single occupancy from £38.00–£48.00; double room from £55.00–£75.00

Bedrooms: 1 double, 1 twin
Bathrooms: 2 en-suite
Parking for 12
Cards accepted: Access, Visa

335 THE COPPER INN HOTEL & RESTAURANT 〰〰〰 HIGHLY COMMENDED

Church Road, Pangbourne, Reading, Berkshire RG8 7AR Tel (0118) 984 2244 Fax (0118) 984 5542

Georgian coaching inn, carefully restored in 1995, next to the old parish church and with secluded gardens. This is a good centre for touring the valley of the River Thames and visiting Oxford, Henley and Windsor. The hotel takes pride in its friendly service, comfortable lounges and bedrooms, and its cuisine. Michel Rosso, the new proprietor, comes from the Alpes Maritimes and the cooking, whilst based on the best local produce, owes much to the recipes and flavours of his native Provence.

Bed & Breakfast per night: single room £89.50; double room £107.00
Half board per person: £102.50 daily
Lunch available: 1200–1430
Evening meal 1900 (last orders 2130; 2200 Fri & Sat)

Bedrooms: 2 single, 14 double, 5 twin, 1 triple
Bathrooms: 22 en-suite
Parking for 20
Cards accepted: Access, Visa, Diners, Amex, Switch/Delta

336 COPPID BEECH HOTEL 〰〰〰〰 HIGHLY COMMENDED

John Nike Way, Bracknell, Berkshire RG12 8TF Tel (01344) 303333 Fax (01344) 301200

A luxury alpine-style hotel with 205 bedrooms, including 19 suites, five minutes from Junction 10/M4 and close to Ascot, Windsor, Henley and Legoland. A fine dining restaurant, a brasserie at the Keller, night club and health and fitness club. Dry-skiing and ice skating are also available on site. Golf, hot air ballooning, Thames boat trips, horse-riding and fly-fishing can also be arranged. 24-hour room service and ample free car parking. Baby-listening facilities.
 ♿ CATEGORY 1

Bed & Breakfast per night: single room from £64.50–£195.00; double room from £74.50–£195.00
Half board per person: £57.50–£195.00 daily
Lunch available: 1200–1430, Sunday–Friday
Evening meal 1800 (last orders 2230)

Bedrooms: 44 single, 50 double, 111 twin
Bathrooms: 205 en-suite
Parking for 350
Cards accepted: Access, Visa, Diners, Amex, Switch/Delta

337 BIRCHCROFT HOUSE 〰〰 HIGHLY COMMENDED

Birchcroft, Brockenhurst Road, South Ascot, Ascot, Berkshire SL5 9HA Tel (01344) 20574

This charming Edwardian house, built in 1910, is set amidst mature trees in spacious grounds which afford ample parking. Guests appreciate the warm welcome and friendly atmosphere, combined with the very highest standards of service and superb quality en-suite accommodation. A perfect location for golf at Sunningdale, Wentworth or Berkshire and an ideal touring base. London is only forty minutes by train from Ascot, and Heathrow is twenty five minutes away. There is an excellent choice of local restaurants for evening meals.

Bed & Breakfast per night: single occupancy from £36.00–£38.00; double room from £48.00–£50.00

Bedrooms: 1 double, 2 twin
Bathrooms: 3 en-suite
Parking for 6

338 THE BISHOP'S TABLE HOTEL & RESTAURANT ≈≈≈≈ HIGHLY COMMENDED

27 West Street, Farnham, Surrey GU9 7DR Tel (01252) 710222 Fax (01252) 733494

An elegant, award-winning hotel where hospitality is at its best. All bedrooms are individually decorated. The walled garden is a walk into another world. The restaurant is well known and offers an excellent cuisine to include a full vegetarian menu.

Bed & Breakfast per night: single room from £75.00–£81.00; double room from £90.00–£120.00
Half board per person: £95.00–£140.00 daily; £525.00–£666.00 weekly
Lunch available: 1230–1345 (last orders)

Evening meal 1900 (last orders 2145)
Bedrooms: 7 single, 9 double, 2 twin
Bathrooms: 17 en-suite, 1 private
Cards accepted: Access, Visa, Diners, Amex

339 LYTHE HILL HOTEL ≈≈≈≈ HIGHLY COMMENDED

Petworth Road, Haslemere, Surrey GU27 3BQ Tel (01428) 651251 Fax (01428) 644131

A village of buildings set in twenty acres of parkland, only one hour from London, make up Lythe Hill Hotel. The 14th-century house has five rooms, including one with an antique four-poster bed, and a large brass-bedded suite with an 'old time' clawed-feet bath. Across the courtyard, more modern bedrooms include luxury doubles with jacuzzi bathrooms, and two glorious garden suites with their own patios which overlook the lake. Two restaurants include the Auberge de France, which is oak-panelled and beamed.

Bed & Breakfast per night: single room from £93.00–£144.00; double room from £113.00–£168.00
Half board per person: £73.00–£118.00 daily; £483.00–£708.00 weekly
Lunch available: 1215–1415

Evening meal 1915 (last orders 2115)
Bedrooms: 4 single, 20 double, 8 twin, 8 family rooms
Bathrooms: 40 en-suite
Parking for 150
Cards accepted: Access, Visa, Diners, Amex, Switch/Delta

340 LAINSTON HOUSE ≈≈≈≈≈ DE LUXE

Sparsholt, Winchester, Hampshire SO21 2LT Tel (01962) 863588 Fax (01962) 776672

Magnificent, listed 17th-century William & Mary country house, set in 63 acres of parkland. Warm, friendly atmosphere with a very high standard of service and cuisine. Situated nearby are the beautiful city of Winchester, with its Cathedral and College, and many country houses and gardens.

Bed & Breakfast per night: single room £105.00; double room from £135.00–£255.00
Half board per person: £119.50–£179.50 daily; £836.50–£1256.50 weekly
Lunch available: 1145–1415

Evening meal 1900 (last orders 2200)
Bedrooms: 7 single, 16 double, 14 twin, 1 triple
Bathrooms: 38 en-suite
Parking for 96
Cards accepted: Access, Visa, Diners, Amex, Switch/Delta

341 HIGHFIELD HOUSE

〰〰〰 HIGHLY COMMENDED

Newtown Road, Awbridge, Romsey, Hampshire SO51 0GG Tel (01794) 340727 Fax (01794) 341450

Set in an unspoilt rural village in a delightful position with charming gardens. Home cooking a speciality. Close to Mottisfont Abbey (National Trust) and Hillier Arboretum. Twelve miles from Winchester and Salisbury. Fishing, golf and horse-riding can be arranged. On-site parking.

Bed & Breakfast per night: double room from
£45.00–£50.00
Evening meal 1830

Bedrooms: 1 double, 2 twin
Bathrooms: 3 en-suite, 1 public
Parking for 10

Gilbert White and Selbourne

SELBOURNE IS A VILLAGE like many another in Hampshire, with a handsome church, peaceful village green and pretty stone-built houses clustered along its main street. In the late 18th-century, however, one of its inhabitants published a book which made it hugely famous; afterwards Selbourne was seen by many as an idealised, almost paradisiacal representative of the perfect English village, surrounded and enriched by the glories of the natural world. The writer was Gilbert White. His book, *The Natural History of Selbourne*, has never been out of print since publication in 1789.

White was born in the village in 1720 and from the age of 10 lived with his family at The Wakes, now a museum (tel: 01420 511275). Later he studied at Oxford and briefly took up a fellowship there. But Selbourne apparently exerted a pull over White which he found difficult to resist and, as the years went by, he became ever more immersed in his rural existence, his increasing reluctance to leave exacerbated by appalling coach sickness.

There was little in Gilbert White's early life which prepared him for the rôle of eminent naturalist, and his passionate study of nature began as little more than a gardening hobby. Matters horticultural, however, were all carefully recorded in *The Garden Kalender*, and increasingly he documented not only the progress of his vegetables but minute and extraordinarily vivid observations concerning natural phenomena throughout the local area.

When White was in his late 40s he began to correspond with two other naturalists, Thomas Pennant and Daines Barrington. Into letter after letter, for a period of over 15 years, he poured all his remarkable observations, drawing heavily on previous journals and keeping copies of everything he wrote. Slowly, the idea of publishing the letters in book form took hold and, after a rather protracted editing and restructuring of material, *The Natural History of Selbourne* finally appeared in print.

The naturalist's home, The Wakes, has been much altered by successive owners. (There are some largely Victorian extensions, for example, now devoted to another museum celebrating the achievements of the polar explorer, Lawrence Oates.) But the old core of the house remains reasonably intact: Gilbert White's bedchamber where he produced much of his correspondence is especially well-preserved. Even his bed hangings, charmingly embroidered by his four aunts, are now in place, together with his own writing table and stool.

342 PLANTATION COTTAGE

 HIGHLY COMMENDED

Mockbeggar, Ringwood, Hampshire BH24 3NL Tel (01425) 477443

A charming 200-year-old Grade II listed cottage set in three acres of gardens and paddocks in the beautiful New Forest between Ringwood and Fordingbridge. Mockbeggar is a peaceful hamlet where wild ponies graze by the roadside, and is also within easy reach of Bournemouth, Poole and Salisbury. There are many excellent pubs and restaurants in the area, which is ideal for walking and cycling, and riding at stables close by. The guest lounge and garden are available all day.

Bed & Breakfast per night: single occupancy from £30.00–£40.00; double room from £45.00–£60.00

Bedrooms: 1 double, 1 twin
Bathrooms: 2 en-suite
Parking for 4

The Tolpuddle Martyrs

IN 1833 AGRICULTURAL WAGES in the Dorset village of Tolpuddle had fallen to seven shillings a week, considerably below the bread-line. When a further reduction looked likely, a group of local farmworkers sought the advice of the Grand National Consolidated Trades Union which, under the leadership of the social reformer Robert Owen, was much in the news. As a result, George Loveless and five other Tolpuddle men formed the Friendly Society of Agricultural Labourers hoping that by uniting they could preserve themselves and their families from 'utter degradation and starvation'. In common with members of many other trade unions, they took oaths of loyalty to their union in October 1833.

There had been a spate of rioting by agricultural labourers across southern England a few years earlier, and the local landowners (*ipso facto* the local magistrates) were keen to nip any potential trouble in the bud. They consulted friends in high places and were advised by the Home Secretary that while the act of joining a trade union was no longer illegal, there was a clause in the otherwise irrelevant Mutiny Act of 1797 that stipulated it was a crime to administer unlawful oaths.

The local squirearchy took advantage of this and in February 1834 the six men were arrested. At the March Assizes in Dorchester Crown Court they were sentenced to seven years transportation and were despatched in convict ships to Australia and put to work in penal colonies.

Even in an age of severe punishments, this was exceptionally harsh and caused an immediate outcry. In London 30,000 people attended a demonstration, and petitions for the men's release flowed in from all over the country. Eventually a new Home Secretary gave in to two years of pressure and in March 1836 the Tolpuddle Martyrs were granted a full pardon. It was many months before news reached them, and many more before they arrived home. Five were given farm tenancies in Essex and subsequently emigrated to Canada. One, James Hammett, settled back in Tolpuddle.

A tombstone (carved by Eric Gill in 1934) marks Hammett's burial place in Tolpuddle churchyard. Near the gate is an ageing sycamore under which the Martyrs met and where there is now a thatched shelter erected in their memory. Thomas Standfield's cottage, where the men took their oaths, is towards the eastern end of the main street while at the western end are six memorial cottages erected by the TUC in 1934 for the use of retired agricultural workers. The adjoining Tolpuddle Martyrs Museum (tel. 01305 848237) tells the whole story. In July each year the Labour Movement holds a commemorative rally in the village.

343 BRANDON THATCH

HIGHLY COMMENDED

Charles' Lane, Bagnum, Ringwood, Hampshire BH24 3DA Tel (01425) 474256 Fax (01425) 478452

In the heart of the New Forest, nestling between Burley and Ringwood, this delightful 17th-century thatched country house, set amidst three acres of secluded gardens and woodlands, awaits you. In this haven of peace and tranquillity, with pretty en-suite bedrooms, sitting room and breakfast room, we pride ourselves on offering unsurpassed service, looking after our guests with care and courtesy. A host of activities can be arranged, including golf, riding, cycling, badger watching, a swim in our new outdoor heated swimming pool or even a helicopter flight for that special occasion! We are a non-smoking house.

Bed & Breakfast per night: double room from
£54.00–£60.00

Bedrooms: 1 double, 1 twin
Bathrooms: 2 en-suite
Parking for 4

---

344 STOCKLANDS HOUSE

HIGHLY COMMENDED

Hilton, Blandford Forum, Dorset DT11 0DE Tel (01258) 880580 or (01258) 881188 Fax (01258) 881188

With wonderful views over the Dorset countryside, this secluded house is superbly located for the coast, sightseeing, walking or riding (paddock and stable for your horse, if required). The delightfully appointed, ground floor en-suite bedrooms have all facilities, an accomplished chef provides delicious meals, and picnics are available. The heated pool is open from May to September and golf and tennis are nearby. We specialise in pampering our guests, and a warm welcome awaits you.

Bed & Breakfast per night: single room from
£17.50–£27.50; double room from £35.00–£55.00
Half board per person: £29.50–£39.50 daily;
£196.50–£262.50 weekly
Lunch available: 1230–1400

Evening meal 1930 (last orders 2100)
Bedrooms: 1 double, 1 twin
Bathrooms: 2 en-suite
Parking for 15

---

345 SHIRLEY HOTEL

HIGHLY COMMENDED

West Lulworth, Wareham, Dorset BH20 5RL Tel (01929) 400358 Fax (01929) 400358

Just five minutes' walk from Lulworth Cove, with the magnificent Dorset coastline stretching in both directions, we are in the centre of a small thatched village. The hotel has been run by our family with care and consideration for twenty six years, and we would like to welcome you to share the relaxing atmosphere and delicious food. To complete your stay we have an indoor heated pool and spa for the exclusive use of our guests. Special breaks available.

Bed & Breakfast per night: single room from
£29.00–£31.00; double room from £58.00–£62.00
Half board per person: £41.00–£44.00 daily;
£257.75–£275.75 weekly
Evening meal 1830 (last orders 1930)

Bedrooms: 3 single, 8 double, 4 twin, 1 triple, 2 family rooms
Bathrooms: 18 en-suite, 1 public
Parking for 22
Open: February–November and Christmas
Cards accepted: Access, Visa, Diners, Amex, Switch/Delta

346 PURBECK HOUSE HOTEL

≋ ≋ ≋ HIGHLY COMMENDED

91 High Street, Swanage, Dorset BH19 2LZ Tel (01929) 422872 Fax (01929) 421194

Our enchanting country house-style hotel, which nestles in two acres of Victorian gardens, is close to the town centre and safe, sandy beaches. The hotel, which is steeped in history, boasts tessellated mosaic floors, original painted ceilings and Carrara marble fireplaces sculpted by Italian craftsmen. Our aim is to provide an oasis of relaxation and enjoyment reminiscent of a bygone era, with all of the requirements of a modern hotel.

Bed & Breakfast per night: single room from £32.00–£45.00; double room from £64.00–£90.00
Half board per person: £47.50–£57.50 daily; £320.00–£395.00 weekly
Evening meal 1900 (last orders 2100)

Bedrooms: 2 single, 9 double, 2 twin, 1 triple, 4 family rooms
Bathrooms: 18 en-suite
Parking for 23
Cards accepted: Access, Visa, Diners, Amex, Switch/Delta

347 NORFOLK ROYALE HOTEL

≋ ≋ ≋ ≋ ≋ HIGHLY COMMENDED

Richmond Hill, Bournemouth, Dorset BH2 6EN Tel (01202) 551521 Fax (01202) 299729

This luxuriously restored Edwardian hotel, situated within a minute's walk from theatres, shops, gardens and golden beaches, provides the perfect blend of friendly and efficient service to ensure a relaxing short break. The Orangery Restaurant offers international cuisine and a fine wine list. The individually-designed bedrooms, studios and suites and the dome-covered pool set in the lovely garden make this the perfect location for that special occasion. ↑ CATEGORY 3

Half board per person: 2-night breaks from £155.00
Lunch available: 1200–1430
Evening meal 1900 (last orders 2300)

Bedrooms: 9 single, 46 double, 32 twin, 8 suites/studios
Bathrooms: 95 en-suite
Parking for 88
Cards accepted: Access, Visa, Diners, Amex, Switch/Delta

348 THE BEECH TREE

≋ ≋ ≋ HIGHLY COMMENDED

2 Stuart Road, Highcliffe, Christchurch, Dorset BH23 5JS Tel (01425) 272038

A superb value guest house, offering above average accommodation, quality home cooking and a welcome which is second to none. Just five minutes' walk through the woods is the unspoilt coastline of Highcliffe-on-Sea, with outstanding views of the Isle of Wight, the Needles and Christchurch Harbour. The nearby New Forest has unlimited potential for exploring and the ancient borough of Christchurch is but a short drive away. Private luxury suite available.

Bed & Breakfast per night: single occupancy from £17.00–£20.00; double room from £34.00–£40.00
Half board per person: £25.50–£28.50 daily
Evening meal 1800 (last orders 1800)

Bedrooms: 5 double, 1 twin
Bathrooms: 6 en-suite
Parking for 7

349 CHEWTON GLEN HOTEL, HEALTH & COUNTRY CLUB 〰〰〰〰〰 DE LUXE

Christchurch Road, New Milton, Hampshire BH25 6QS Tel (01425) 275341 Fax (01425) 272310

A very warm welcome awaits you here. Great emphasis is placed on service, with the restaurant being renowned for the quality of its food and wines. All bedrooms are individually decorated, and most have a balcony or terrace with a beautiful view. The health club offers a full range of health and fitness facilities, including an indoor pool and gymnasium. Beauty therapy appointments also available. 9-hole golf course within grounds.

Bed & Breakfast per night: double room from
£205.00–£425.00
Half board per person: £160.00–£220.00 daily;
£985.60–£1355.20 weekly
Lunch available: 1230–1345

Evening meal 1930 (last orders 2130)
Bedrooms: 53 double
Bathrooms: 53 en-suite
Parking for 125
Cards accepted: Access, Visa, Diners, Amex, Switch/Delta

Clouds Hill and Lawrence of Arabia

THE NAME T.E. LAWRENCE will always be associated with the Middle East for he became internationally famous as 'Lawrence of Arabia' after his successful encouragement of the Arab revolt against the Turks during World War I. But with the war over, Lawrence was content to abandon his wanderings in distant lands. He eventually retreated to a tiny, ramshackle gamekeeper's cottage at Clouds Hill, in the depths of Dorset, which became his actual and his spiritual home.

Lawrence had first come to Dorset disillusioned with what he termed 'the shallow grave of public duty'. He had attended the peace conference at the end of the War and had acted as adviser on Arab affairs to the Colonial Office, but had found himself powerless to secure all he had hoped for the Arab cause. So, abandoning his role as peace negotiator and seeking anonymity, he had, in 1922, joined the ranks of the RAF. Soon afterwards he enlisted as a private in the Tank Corps, a move which brought him to Dorset.

While stationed at Bovington Camp, near Wareham, Lawrence began searching for a place of escape where he could work undisturbed on *The Seven Pillars of Wisdom*, his account of his Arab campaigns. The dilapidated cottage he had found on the slopes of

nearby Clouds Hill was little more than a single room when he began renting it in 1923. He repaired it, installed some simple furniture, and, when his duties allowed, spent weekends and evenings there, writing, listening to music or talking with friends, before returning to the camp to sleep. Though in 1925 he decided to rejoin the Air Force, necessitating a move from the area, he couldn't bear to relinquish the cottage. Instead he bought it, and used it as a holiday home until he left the RAF ten years later. Once retired, he intended to live permanently at Clouds Hill, and increased the living space to make a comfortable, if small, home. He spent two happy months there in the spring of 1935. Then, after posting a telegram at Bovington Camp, he lost control of his motorbike on the way home and crashed. He died in the camp hospital, aged 47.

The cottage at Clouds Hill (tel: 01985 847777), now owned by the National Trust, contains Lawrence's simple furnishings and many items of memorabilia. At Bovington's Tank Museum (tel: 01929 463953) a special display is devoted to the writer. His grave is in the churchyard at Moreton, and an effigy by his friend and sculptor Eric Kennington lies not far away at St Martin's Church, Wareham.

350 THE NURSE'S COTTAGE

〰〰 HIGHLY COMMENDED

Station Road, Sway, Lymington, Hampshire SO41 6BA Tel (01590) 683402 Fax (01590) 683402

Formerly home to the village's successive District Nurses, this cosy cottage has been lovingly refurbished in recent years by chef/proprietor Tony Barnfield to provide every possible creature comfort. The enterprising dinner menu comprises thoughtfully-prepared dishes from fresh local produce wherever possible, and the wine list (unrivalled in an establishment of this size) contains over 70 worldwide selections. Ideal touring centre for the New Forest and surrounding area, with good connections to London and elsewhere.

Half board per person: £42.50–£47.50 daily;
£245.00–£280.00 weekly
Lunch available: by arrangement
Evening meal 1830 (last orders 1930)

Bedrooms: 1 single, 1 double, 1 twin
Bathrooms: 3 en-suite, 1 public
Parking for 4
Cards accepted: Access, Visa, Amex, Switch/Delta

351 STRING OF HORSES

〰〰〰〰 HIGHLY COMMENDED

Mead End Road, Sway, Lymington, Hampshire SO41 6EH Tel (01590) 682631 Fax (01590) 682631

A secluded hotel set in four acres of grounds. Experience the luxury of individually-designed bedrooms – several with four-poster beds – each with its own fantasy bathroom and offering every facility. Intimate, award-winning candle-lit restaurant. The perfect setting for newly-weds, second honeymooners and couples. Heated outdoor swimming pool. Excellent location for horse-riding, yachting, golfing and exploring the New Forest. Regrettably, we are unable to accommodate children.

Bed & Breakfast per night: single occupancy from
£52.50–£55.00; double room from £70.00–£100.00
Half board per person: £53.95–£68.95 daily;
£340.00–£425.00 weekly
Lunch available: 1230–1330 (Sunday only)

Evening meal 1900 (last orders 2030)
Bedrooms: 7 double
Bathrooms: 7 en-suite
Parking for 24
Cards accepted: Access, Visa, Diners, Amex, Switch/Delta

352 THE HILLSMAN HOUSE

〰〰 HIGHLY COMMENDED

74 Milford Road, Lymington, Hampshire SO41 8DP Tel (01590) 674737

The Hillsman House is beautifully situated in a garden of one-and-a-half acres, with all of the splendid en-suite guest rooms enjoying views of the surrounding countryside. Avril and Victor La Breche have given every attention to detail and make sure that a full English breakfast will enhance your day whilst visiting this delightful area.

Bed & Breakfast per night: single occupancy £25.00;
double room from £46.00–£50.00

Bedrooms: 2 double, 1 twin
Bathrooms: 3 en-suite
Parking for 4

353 WHITLEY RIDGE COUNTRY HOUSE HOTEL   HIGHLY COMMENDED

Beaulieu Road, Brockenhurst, Hampshire SO42 7QL Tel (01590) 622354 Fax (01590) 622856

A small secluded Georgian country house with views overlooking open fields where ponies graze. We pride ourselves on a high standard of cuisine and this quality is also reflected in the same care we show in our rooms and the courtesy we provide in our service. Log fires burn in cooler months. Special two-night breaks available.

Bed & Breakfast per night: single room from £48.00–£60.00; double room from £82.00–£96.00
Half board per person: £47.00–£63.00 daily;
£315.00–£329.00 weekly
Lunch available: 1200–1400 (Sunday only)

Evening meal 1900 (last orders 2030)
Bedrooms: 2 single, 8 double, 3 twin
Bathrooms: 13 en-suite
Parking for 24
Cards accepted: Access, Visa, Diners, Amex, Switch/Delta

354 NEW PARK MANOR HOTEL   HIGHLY COMMENDED

Lyndhurst Road, Brockenhurst, Hampshire SO42 7QH Tel (01590) 623467 Fax (01590) 622268

The New Park Manor is a prestigious and romantic country house hotel, dating back to the 16th-century, in a wonderful setting of gardens, lawns and beautiful parkland in the heart of the New Forest. The award-winning Stag Head restaurant offers excellent, French-influenced cuisine. Log-fire ambience, quality and service with a smile. Charmingly designed en-suite bedrooms. Own equestrian centre, seasonal heated swimming pool and tennis court. Wedding receptions, conferences and all other celebrations.

Bed & Breakfast per night: single occupancy from £75.00–£115.00; double room from £110.00–£150.00
Half board per person: £65.00–£85.00 daily
Evening meal 1930 (last orders 2145)

Bedrooms: 20 double, 4 twin
Bathrooms: 24 en-suite
Parking for 40
Cards accepted: Access, Visa, Amex

355 CLOUD HOTEL   HIGHLY COMMENDED

Meerut Road, Brockenhurst, Hampshire SO42 7TD Tel (01590) 622165 Fax (01590) 622165

A perfect place to relax and unwind. Delightful country house hotel situated in an award-winning location, with superb panoramic views of the New Forest. All rooms are en-suite with TVs, hospitality trays and direct-dial telephones. Four-poster room available. Excellent service and cuisine. Ideal situation for walking, cycling and bird-watching. Mid-week breaks offered throughout the year – four nights for the price of three. Proprietor: Avril Owton – Hampshire Woman of the Year, 1995. For reservations please telephone 01590 622165.

Bed & Breakfast per night: single room £48.00; double room from £80.00–£100.00
Half board per person: £57.00 daily; £310.00 weekly
Lunch available: 1200–1430
Evening meal 1900 (last orders 2030)

Bedrooms: 3 single, 8 double, 4 twin, 1 family room
Bathrooms: 16 en-suite, 1 public
Parking for 20
Cards accepted: Access, Visa

356 WOODLANDS LODGE HOTEL

〰〰〰〰 HIGHLY COMMENDED

Bartley Road, Woodlands, New Forest, Hampshire SO4 2GN Tel (01703) 292257

Stunning and luxuriously restored Georgian country house hotel set in three acres. Beautiful, well-kept gardens open onto the New Forest. All bedrooms enjoy en-suite facilities including jacuzzi baths and separate showers. The sumptuous hand-made king size pocket-sprung beds are there to give guests the most restful of nights. The informality and total peace of the hotel makes it the ideal retreat for the stressed to comfortably unwind and spoil themselves.

Bed & Breakfast per night: single occupancy from £69.00–£99.00; double room from £99.00–£129.00
Evening meal 1900 (last orders 2030)

Bedrooms: 16 double, 1 twin
Bathrooms: 17 en-suite
Parking for 40
Cards accepted: Access, Visa

Cowes and Cowes Week

COWES IS NOT ONE TOWN but two. East Cowes is linked to (West) Cowes by a 'floating bridge' – in reality a chain ferry that conveys passengers and cars across the mouth of the Medina River. The western town was hardly more than a small collection of fishermen's shacks until Henry VIII decided to build West Cowe, a coastal fortification protecting the waters of the Solent. West Cowe now forms part of the castle-like head-quarters of the Royal Yacht Squadron, one of the eight yacht clubs that together organise Cowes Week, the landmark sailing event in the social calendar which has made Cowes the best known town on the Isle of Wight.

In typically English fashion, Cowes Week begins on the first Saturday following the last Tuesday in July. This convoluted formula means that in 1997 Cowes Week runs from 2–9 August, during which time accommo-dation is at a premium, the waters of the Solent turn into a riot of brightly coloured sails and in the town's pubs the chatter is of spinnakers, huffing and slam dunks.

Cowes Week is perhaps primarily aimed at those competing in the various races but there are several spectacles to be enjoyed even by confirmed land-lubbers. Royal patronage of Cowes Week dates back to the first half of the last century, when Prince Albert's obsession with matters nautical, together with the fact that he and Victoria had their summer residence at nearby Osborne House (tel: 01983 200022), combined to ensure that he was a regular participant. Since then George V and Prince Philip have both competed, and royalty-spotting is a popular August pastime in Cowes. The races start at 10.30 each morning and are a natural and dramatic focus of attention. Competition is open to any member of any recognised yacht club, worldwide, so some events attract large fields. Some races are fortunate enough to take place on a sunny evening, when the myriad colours of the huge sails dashing for the finishing line form a memorable sight. Soon the social events are in full swing with countless balls, parties and concerts held across the town. Most are, of course, private functions, but on the Friday evening everyone is invited to watch the spectacular fireworks display taking place at 2130 on a floating raft just off the Marine Esplanade. Innumerable vessels throng Cowes Roads (as the stretch of water by Cowes is called) and thousands watch from each side of the Solent.

357 CHINE COURT HOTEL

HIGHLY COMMENDED

Popham Road, Shanklin, Isle of Wight PO37 6RG Tel (01983) 862732 Fax (01983) 862732

Welcome to Chine Court. A truly elegant Victorian residence, lavishly furnished and decorated throughout. Standing in large grounds, it commands magnificent sea views from its elevated cliff-top position. Beautifully appointed public rooms include a large luxurious bar lounge, dry lounges and an elegant Victorian dining room offering a sumptuous five-course dinner with a full choice of traditional and continental dishes. The hotel offers peace and tranquillity and a high degree of comfort and Victorian grace and charm.

Bed & Breakfast per night: single room from £22.00–£32.00; double room from £44.00–£64.00
Half board per person: £31.00–£41.00 daily; £199.00–£260.00 weekly
Evening meal 1830 (last orders 1915)

Bedrooms: 3 single, 8 double, 6 twin, 5 triple, 4 family rooms
Bathrooms: 25 en-suite, 1 public
Parking for 24
Open: April–October

358 CELEBRATION HOTEL

HIGHLY COMMENDED

6 Avenue Road, Shanklin, Isle of Wight PO37 7BG Tel (01983) 862746

A perfect retreat for couples who are looking for somewhere very special. Ideal for celebrations or relaxing romantic breaks. Enjoy champagne breakfasts, delicious candle-lit dinners and much more. Nothing is too much trouble – ensuring a most memorable stay. The loving care and attention bestowed upon this special hotel is reflected in the quality of service – this can only be described as the hotel with the big heart! An intimate wedding and honeymoon package is available. All our bedrooms have four-poster beds.

Bed & Breakfast per night: double room from £56.00–£66.00
Half board per person: £42.50–£44.50 daily
Evening meal 1830 (last orders 1900)

Bedrooms: 8 double
Bathrooms: 8 en-suite, 1 public
Parking for 7

359 RYLSTONE MANOR HOTEL

HIGHLY COMMENDED

Rylstone Gardens, Popham Road, Shanklin, Isle of Wight PO37 6RG Tel (01983) 862806

The Manor is an excellent Victorian house set in four-and-a-half acres of mature gardens overlooking the sea, but close to Shanklin Old Village, the Chine and the beach. All rooms are individually decorated and are en-suite with TVs and hospitality trays. Some rooms have four-poster beds. If you desire a quiet haven for relaxation, personal service with superb cuisine and a comprehensive bar and wine list, then this Victorian manor is for you.

Bed & Breakfast per night: single room from £28.00–£32.00; double room from £56.00–£64.00
Half board per person: £38.00–£42.00 daily; £256.00–£284.00 weekly
Evening meal 1900 (last orders 2000)

Bedrooms: 1 single, 5 double, 3 twin
Bathrooms: 9 en-suite
Parking for 10
Open: March–October
Cards accepted: Access, Visa

360 BEAUFORT HOTEL
 HIGHLY COMMENDED

71 Festing Road, Southsea, Hampshire PO4 0NQ Tel (01705) 823707 or 0800 919237 Fax (01705) 870270

The Beaufort Hotel is situated in a quiet part of Southsea, overlooking the canoe lake, with the seafront just a one-minute walk away. All the bedrooms have recently been refurbished and individually designed to a very high standard, each with en-suite bath and shower. Delightful restaurant offering both à la carte and table d'hôte menus. Satellite TV. Licensed bar. Car park. For reservations freephone 0800 919237.

Bed & Breakfast per night: single room from £40.00–£48.00; double room from £48.00–£70.00
Half board per person: £34.00–£42.00 daily; £196.00–£270.00 weekly
Evening meal 1830 (last orders 2030)

Bedrooms: 3 single, 11 double, 2 twin, 2 triple, 1 family room
Bathrooms: 19 en-suite
Parking for 10
Cards accepted: Access, Visa, Amex, Switch/Delta

361 COCKLE WARREN COTTAGE HOTEL
HIGHLY COMMENDED

36 Seafront, Hayling Island, Nr Portsmouth, Hampshire PO11 9HL Tel (01705) 464961 Fax (01705) 464838

A delightful tile-hung cottage hotel on the seafront, with white picket fencing and a smugglers' tunnel running beneath the large garden. Lovely en-suite bedrooms facing out to sea or overlooking the swimming pool, some with four-poster and Victorian beds, all with chocolates and a decanter of Madeira. Award-winning restaurant serving French and English country cooking with home-made bread and French wines. Relax by the open log fire to the sound of the sea just a few yards away.

Bed & Breakfast per night: single occupancy from £50.00–£65.00; double room from £68.00–£98.00
Half board per person: £58.50–£68.50 daily
Evening meal 2000 (last bookings 1600)

Bedrooms: 4 double, 1 triple
Bathrooms: 5 en-suite
Parking for 9
Cards accepted: Access, Visa, Amex

362 THE BROOKFIELD HOTEL
HIGHLY COMMENDED

Havant Road, Emsworth, Hampshire PO10 7LF Tel (01243) 373363 Fax (01243) 376342

Situated in the fishing village of Emsworth, between historic maritime Portsmouth and the cathedral city of Chichester. Landscaped gardens give a peaceful setting in which to relax and unwind. Friendly, personal service and attention to detail are reflected in the Hermitage Restaurant, with its nationally award-winning wine list and use of fresh produce prepared to order.

Bed & Breakfast per night: single room from £54.00–£60.00; double room from £79.50–£90.00
Half board per person: £54.00–£59.00 daily
Lunch available: 1200–1400
Evening meal 1900 (last orders 2130)

Bedrooms: 5 single, 23 double, 12 twin
Bathrooms: 40 en-suite
Parking for 80
Cards accepted: Access, Visa, Diners, Amex, Switch/Delta

363 WHITE BARN

Crede Lane, Bosham, Chichester, West Sussex PO18 8NX Tel (01243) 573113 Fax (01243) 573113

An outstanding, unique, open plan, single-storey house with heavily timbered interior. Located in the beautiful Saxon harbour village of Bosham. Accommodation is in three delightful en-suite bedrooms with comfortable beds, colour TVs, radios and tea and coffee making facilities. Relax in the charming sitting room with a log fire on chilly evenings. Memorable dinners and breakfasts are served overlooking the pretty and colourful garden. A very warm welcome is assured.

Bed & Breakfast per night: single occupancy from £32.00–£55.00; double room from £50.00–£70.00
Half board per person: £39.00–£54.00 daily; £246.00–£341.00 weekly
Evening meal 1915

Bedrooms: 1 double, 2 twin
Bathrooms: 3 en-suite
Parking for 4
Cards accepted: Access, Visa

Fishbourne and Bignor

IN 1960, A WORKMAN digging a trench across empty pasture at Fishbourne, near Chichester, uncovered some ancient building material; the site later revealed the remains of one of the most magnificent Roman palaces anywhere in Britain. It was not the first fortuitous discovery of substantial Roman remains in the Chichester area. In 1811, a farmer ploughing fields near Bignor, just a few miles to the north-east, struck a large stone, actually a water basin from another impressive Roman villa.

Whoever once lived at Fishbourne (tel: 01243 785859) were citizens of ever-increasing wealth and importance. Excavations show the progression of the building from a modest timber construction to a vast, elaborately-decorated palace, fitted with every luxury and convenience of the time. The chief glory of Fishbourne is its mosaics. Room after room is floored with tiny tesserae, or tiles, laid during the 1st- and 2nd-centuries to create a variety of patterns, some geometric in design and austere in colour, others vivid and elaborate. The finest and most intact of the mosaics represents Cupid riding on a dolphin surrounded by exotic sea-monsters and exuberant designs of urns and tendrils. Amazingly, only a quarter of the original layout of the palace can be seen; the rest lies beneath a main road and nearby houses.

The villa at Bignor (tel: 01798 869259) was a less ostentatious residence, but between the 3rd- and 4th-centuries AD it also increased dramatically in size, perhaps to accommodate a growing extended family. Upon completion it was one of the largest villas in the country and stood upon an important site close to the military road, Stane Street. The mosaics, though less numerous than those at Fishbourne, are some of the best in the country. Laid in later centuries than those at Fishbourne, they display an interesting contrast: at Bignor the decoration is elaborate and sophisticated, showing an assured mastery of the mosaic technique. Most memorable perhaps is the lugubrious allegorical figure of winter, well muffled against the cold.

Archaeological evidence has thrown light on the fate of both buildings. Lumps of molten lead and charred timbers indicate that Fishbourne was destroyed by a terrible fire in the late 3rd-century and was never rebuilt. By contrast Bignor, it seems, was simply abandoned sometime in the 5th-century and left to moulder gently into the ground. Both are now open to the public.

364 PARK HOUSE HOTEL
≋≋≋≋ HIGHLY COMMENDED

Bepton, Midhurst, West Sussex GU29 0JB Tel (0173081) 2880 or (0173081) 3543 Fax (0173081) 5643

Beautifully situated country house hotel nestling in the South Downs, but close to Goodwood racecourse and Chichester Festival Theatre. A quiet village location and beautifully-furnished accommodation make this hotel the perfect retreat. Home-cooked nutritious and satisfying food is served in the elegant dining room. Set in nine acres of grounds with two grass tennis courts, putting and croquet lawns, 9-hole pitch and putt course and heated swimming pool. Conference facilities available.

Bed & Breakfast per night: single room from
£60.00–£75.00; double room from £110.00–£130.00
Lunch available: 1200–1400 (by arrangement)
Evening meal 2000

Bedrooms: 1 single, 4 double, 7 twin, 1 triple
Bathrooms: 13 en-suite, 1 public
Parking for 60
Cards accepted: Access, Visa, Amex, Switch/Delta

365 ABELANDS BARN
≋≋ HIGHLY COMMENDED

Bognor Road, Merston, Chichester, West Sussex PO20 6DY Tel (01243) 533826 Fax (01243) 555533

Abelands Barn is an 1850s farm building converted into a comfortable and interesting family home. It offers spacious and flexible accommodation for six guests with secure overnight parking. The Barn is situated only two miles from the Roman city of Chichester and is surrounded by magnificent countryside together with many local attractions, including Goodwood, Arundel, South Downs and the coast. The highly respected Festival Theatre is only ten minutes drive.

Bed & Breakfast per night: double room from
£45.00–£50.00

Bedrooms: 2 double, 1 twin
Bathrooms: 3 en-suite
Parking for 5
Cards accepted: Access, Visa

366 WHITE HORSE INN
≋≋≋ HIGHLY COMMENDED

The Street, Sutton, Pulborough, West Sussex RH20 1PS Tel (01798) 869221 Fax (01798) 869291

Sutton is a picture-postcard village tucked away at the foot of the South Downs. Great sensitivity has been used to bring our charming Georgian inn up to the standards expected by the discerning traveller, whilst retaining its essential character. The bedrooms are elegantly furnished, each with its own spacious bathroom. The food has a strong emphasis on traditional country cooking, enhanced by a selection of other well-chosen dishes. Log fires in the winter!

Bed & Breakfast per night: single occupancy £48.00;
double room from £58.00–£68.00
Half board per person: £43.00–£62.00 daily;
£232.00–£316.00 weekly
Lunch available: 1200–1400

Evening meal 1900 (last orders 2145)
Bedrooms: 4 double, 2 twin
Bathrooms: 5 en-suite, 1 private shower
Parking for 10
Cards accepted: Access, Visa, Diners, Amex

367 BURPHAM COUNTRY HOTEL

HIGHLY COMMENDED

Burpham, Arundel, West Sussex BN18 9RJ Tel (01903) 882160 Fax (01903) 884627

Nestling in a fold of the famous Sussex South Downs, the hotel offers the most perfect location for a "stress remedy break"! The hamlet of Burpham is totally peaceful and unspoilt and the walks are truly spectacular. The dining room offers a regularly changing menu using only the best ingredients. Swiss-born Marianne Walker and husband George – the resident owners – are justly proud of their award-winning cuisine. The comfort offered here is truly memorable.

Bed & Breakfast per night: single room from £35.00–£49.50; double room from £72.00–£79.00
Half board per person: £54.50–£58.00 daily; £381.50–£406.00 weekly
Evening meal 1915 (last orders 2045)

Bedrooms: 1 single, 6 double, 3 twin
Bathrooms: 10 en-suite
Parking for 12
Cards accepted: Access, Visa, Amex

---

368 PINDARS

HIGHLY COMMENDED

Lyminster, Arundel, West Sussex BN17 7QF Tel (01903) 882628

Pindars was designed and built by the Newmans thirty years ago, and provides them and their guests with a welcoming home, modern in comfort, antique in furnishing. There is a large garden with colourful herbaceous borders, shady trees and an outdoor swimming pool. Jocelyne loves cooking and specialises in celebration weekends for that special birthday or anniversary. Within easy driving distance are Goodwood, Petworth, Parham, Uppark, country, coast, castles, cathedrals – and gardens!

Bed & Breakfast per night: single occupancy £22.00; double room from £32.00–£42.00
Evening meal 1900

Bedrooms: 2 double, 1 twin
Bathrooms: 1 en-suite, 1 public
Parking for 6
Cards accepted: Access, Visa

---

369 THE LEONARD

HIGHLY COMMENDED

15 Seymour Street, London W1H 5AA Tel (0171) 935 2010 Fax (0171) 935 6700

Conveniently located off Portman Square, London's latest townhouse hotel has, in its short time of being open, received critical acclaim and awards. Each of the twenty suites and six bedrooms are air-conditioned and beautifully decorated with a combination of traditional furniture, both contemporary and antique, elegant fabrics and distinctive objets d'art. The bathrooms are bright and bedrooms contain everything from mini bars to satellite televisions. Professional, friendly house staff are around to provide service from concierge to 24-hour room service.

Bed & Breakfast per night: double room from £164.00–£276.00

Bedrooms: 22 double, 1 triple, 3 family rooms
Bathrooms: 26 en-suite
Cards accepted: Access, Visa, Diners, Amex, Switch/Delta

370 FIVE SUMNER PLACE HOTEL

Listed HIGHLY COMMENDED

South Kensington, London SW7 3EE Tel (0171) 584 7586 Fax (0171) 823 9962

This delightful hotel is situated in South Kensington, one of the most fashionable areas of London. The hotel itself has been sympathetically restored to recreate the ambience and style of a bygone era. Family-owned and run, it offers excellent service and personal attention. All rooms are luxuriously appointed and come with private en-suite facilities, telephone, colour television, trouser press and full buffet breakfast.

Bed & Breakfast per night: single room from £75.00–£85.00; double room from £99.00–£120.00

Bedrooms: 3 single, 10 double
Bathrooms: 13 en-suite, 1 public
Cards accepted: Access, Visa, Amex

---

371 HOTEL NUMBER SIXTEEN

 HIGHLY COMMENDED

16 Sumner Place, London SW7 3EG Tel (0171) 589 5232 Fax (0171) 584 8615

Situated in South Kensington, Number Sixteen has been created from four Victorian town houses. Offering style, elegance and seclusion, guests are encouraged to make themselves at home. There is a relaxed informality about the drawing room and the library, where everyone is invited to pour themselves a drink from the honour bar. The conservatory opens onto an award-winning garden. The comfortable well-appointed bedrooms are individually decorated with a combination of antique and traditional furnishings.

Bed & Breakfast per night: single room from £80.00–£105.00; double room from £140.00–£170.00

Bedrooms: 9 single, 24 double, 3 triple
Bathrooms: 32 en-suite, 2 private, 1 private shower
Cards accepted: Access, Visa, Diners, Amex

---

372 SELSDON PARK

HIGHLY COMMENDED

Sanderstead, South Croydon, Surrey CR2 8YA Tel (0181) 657 8811 Fax (0181) 651 6171

Set in 200 acres of Surrey countryside, historic Selsdon Park is somewhere very special. In our elegant restaurant you will enjoy the finest of food, and some of the best entertainment if you choose one of the many 'Special Event' evenings in our calendar. We also hold dinner dances every Friday and Saturday evening. But there is a lot more than that! Sports include golf, tennis, squash, keep-fit, swimming and jogging – or you could just relax.

Bed & Breakfast per night: single room from £69.00–£99.00; double room from £138.00–£198.00
Half board per person: £79.00–£109.00 daily (weekends only)
Lunch available: 1230–1430
Evening meal 1930 (last orders 2200)

Bedrooms: 40 single, 50 double, 80 twin
Bathrooms: 170 en-suite
Parking for 350
Cards accepted: Access, Visa, Diners, Amex, Switch/Delta

373 STANHILL COURT HOTEL
HIGHLY COMMENDED

Stanhill Road, Charlwood, Horley, Surrey RH6 0EP Tel (01293) 862166 Fax (01293) 862773

Built in 1881 in Scottish baronial style, this award-winning hotel is set in thirty five acres of ancient woodland with an original Victorian walled garden. Traditionally furnished, providing an intimately warm and comfortable atmosphere, with rich pine panelling evident throughout the hall, minstrels' gallery and barrel roof. Some four-poster bedrooms. Full à la carte menu and excellent wine cellar. Versatile conference facilities, function rooms to take up to 150 and an amphitheatre to seat up to 1,000 for corporate hospitality.

Bed & Breakfast per night: single occupancy £94.00; double room from £117.00–£150.00
Half board per person: £89.00–£95.00 daily
Lunch available: 1200–1430
Evening meal 1900 (last orders 2130)

Bedrooms: 12 double, 2 twin, 3 triple
Bathrooms: 17 en-suite
Parking for 150
Cards accepted: Access, Visa, Diners, Amex, Switch/Delta

374 SOUTH LODGE HOTEL
HIGHLY COMMENDED

Brighton Road, Lower Beeding, Horsham, West Sussex RH13 6PS Tel (01403) 891711 Fax (01403) 891253

A Victorian country house hotel set in ninety three acres of wooded parkland in the heart of the Sussex countryside with thirty nine individually furnished bedrooms, some overlooking the South Downs, and the excellent Camellia Restaurant presenting exquisitely beautiful dishes with a complementary extensive wine list. Leisure pursuits include clay-pigeon shooting, archery, fishing, croquet, tennis, putting, petanque and Mannings Heath Golf Club. Ideally situated for the varied local attractions; an hour from London; twenty minutes from Gatwick; an easy drive to M23/25.

Bed & Breakfast per night: single room from £130.00–£275.00; double room from £165.00–£285.00
Half board per person: £100.00–£160.00 daily
Lunch available: 1230–1400 (1500 on Sundays)
Evening meal 1930 (last orders 2200)

Bedrooms: 2 single, 26 double, 11 twin
Bathrooms: 39 en-suite
Parking for 100
Cards accepted: Access, Visa, Diners, Amex, Switch/Delta

375 CHEQUERS HOTEL
HIGHLY COMMENDED

Church Place, Pulborough, West Sussex RH20 1AD Tel (01798) 872486 Fax (01798) 872715

Situated in the heart of the local conservation area and facing out over the Arun Valley towards the South Downs, we pride ourselves upon being the quintessential small English country hotel. Built in 1548 and carefully extended and refurbished, we offer luxury en-suite bedrooms, fine food in our award-winning restaurant, a conservatory coffee shop, and ample parking. Straight outside is our 9-acre meadow for walks for you and your dog.

Bed & Breakfast per night: single room from £49.50–£54.50; double room from £77.00–£87.00
Half board per person: £46.00–£51.00 daily; £299.00–£333.00 weekly
Lunch available: 1200–1400

Evening meal 1930 (last orders 2045)
Bedrooms: 1 single, 5 double, 2 twin, 3 triple
Bathrooms: 10 en-suite, 1 private
Parking for 16
Cards accepted: Access, Visa, Diners, Amex

376 **ASPEN HOUSE**

 HIGHLY COMMENDED

13 Winchester Road, Worthing, West Sussex BN11 4DJ Tel (01903) 230584

A very warm welcome awaits you at Aspen House where we look forward to ensuring that your stay will be relaxed and comfortable. This beautifully maintained Edwardian home retains many original features. All the rooms are tastefully decorated, with numerous personal touches. A delicious freshly-cooked breakfast of your choice is served in the elegant period dining room. Although we are situated in a very quiet part of town, a wide choice of restaurants, entertainment, the sea front, and Worthing's excellent shopping centre are all a short walk away.

Bed & Breakfast per night: double room from
£44.00–£46.00

Bedrooms: 2 double, 1 twin
Bathrooms: 3 en-suite
Parking for 4

Brighton's Royal Pavilion

IN AN INFLUENTIAL 18TH-CENTURY work on the medicinal properties of seawater, one Dr Richard Russell claimed that the fishing town of Brightelmstone provided the best opportunities for the health-giving pastime of bathing. Brighton soon became a popular resort and in 1783, on the advice of physicians, George, Prince of Wales, visited the town. Four years later he instructed Henry Holland to build a 'marine pavilion', the modest neo-classical core of today's remarkable Royal Pavilion (tel: 01273 603005).

When George became Prince Regent in 1811, he decided a grander Brighton residence was required. A most dedicated patron of the decorative arts, he commissioned John Nash to 'improve' his south coast home. In 1815 Nash looked east for his inspiration, embellishing the existing building in 'Hindoo-Gothic' style.

By common consent the result is memorable; whether the flamboyant onion-domed creation was an architectural triumph is still debated. The Comptesse de Boigne called it a 'masterpiece of bad taste', though George was apparently delighted. And so he should have been, for the design of the building, now the Royal Pavilion, was carefully crafted to gratify all the King's tastes (he had become George IV in 1820). Chief among his consuming passions were good food and drink, and music. Thus the Pavilion's Banqueting Room is one of the highlights of the modern-day visitor's tour. Those enjoying royal hospitality must have been impressed, too, for the room is sumptuously decorated in gilt and crimson. Just as Nash looked to India for the exterior design, so Robert Jones, to whom the decoration of the Banqueting Room

was entrusted, looked to China. This is chinoiserie in the grand style, with dragons, lotus flowers and bamboo wherever you look.

Complementing the Banqueting Room was the kitchen. The scale of this room, refreshing in its more restrained décor, seems large, but this was just the grandest of many kitchens: there were, for example, five rooms dedicated to the creation of pastry and confectionery. Hardly surprising that the King was hugely overweight and that his apartments were moved to the ground floor since gout and dropsy had made him somewhat immobile.

The other highlight of a visit to the Pavilion is the Music Room. Perhaps even more lavish than the Banqueting Room, and again with a dominant Chinese theme, this is a monument to the interior design skills of Robert Jones's colleague, Frederick Crace. The room has been restored twice in recent years, once after a serious fire in 1975, and again in 1987 after a hurricane had sent a huge ornamental stone ball crashing through the intricate ceiling.

377 THE OLD TOLLGATE RESTAURANT AND HOTEL 〰〰〰 HIGHLY COMMENDED

The Street, Bramber, Steyning, West Sussex BN44 3WE Tel (01903) 879494 Fax (01903) 813399

In a lovely old Sussex village nestling at the foot of the South Downs, standing on the original Tollhouse site, a perfect blending of the old with the new. Award-winning, carvery-style restaurant – a well-known and popular eating spot – offers a magnificent hors d'oeuvres display followed by a vast selection of roasts, pies and casseroles, with delicious sweets and cheeses to add the final touch. Luxuriously-appointed bedrooms, including two four-posters with jacuzzi baths, and two suites.

Bed & Breakfast per night: single occupancy from
£63.95–£83.95; double room from £69.90–£89.90
Half board per person: £52.60–£62.60 daily
Lunch available: 1200–1400
Evening meal 1900 (last orders 2130)

Bedrooms: 21 double, 10 twin
Bathrooms: 31 en-suite
Parking for 60
Cards accepted: Access, Visa, Diners, Amex,
Switch/Delta

378 ADELAIDE HOTEL 〰〰〰 HIGHLY COMMENDED

51 Regency Square, Brighton, East Sussex BN1 2FF Tel (01273) 205286 Fax (01273) 220904

This elegant Regency townhouse hotel centrally situated in Brighton's premier seafront square offers, among its hallmarks, a warm welcome, friendly service and delicious food. All the bedrooms include the extras that guarantee a relaxing and comfortable stay. Brighton's extensive and diverse shopping, many restaurants, theatre, etc., are all within easy walking distance, and parking is available in the square. An ideal centre from which to explore the Sussex hinterland. Discounted leisure breaks available.

Bed & Breakfast per night: single room from
£38.00–£60.00; double room from £62.00–£75.00
Evening meal 1830 (last orders 2030)

Bedrooms: 3 single, 7 double, 1 twin, 1 triple
Bathrooms: 12 en-suite, 1 public
Cards accepted: Access, Visa, Diners, Amex,
Switch/Delta

379 ASCOTT HOUSE HOTEL 〰〰〰 HIGHLY COMMENDED

21 New Steine, Marine Parade, Brighton, East Sussex BN2 1PD Tel (01273) 688085 Fax (01273) 623733

Located in one of the most convenient central positions in Brighton, this Grade II listed building is situated in a seafront garden square close to the Palace Pier, Royal Pavilion, Theatre Royal, famous Lanes and the Brighton Conference Centre. Whether your visit is for business or pleasure, enjoy a delicious, individually-prepared English breakfast served in the elegant dining room. This excellent well-established, licensed hotel offers all the home comforts in a relaxed and welcoming atmosphere.

Bed & Breakfast per night: single room from
£20.00–£40.00; double room from £40.00–£80.00
Evening meal 1830

Bedrooms: 4 single, 6 triple, 2 family rooms
Bathrooms: 10 en-suite, 1 private shower, 1 public
Cards accepted: Access, Visa, Diners, Amex

380 ARLANDA HOTEL

HIGHLY COMMENDED

20 New Steine, Brighton, East Sussex BN2 1PD Tel (01273) 699300 Fax (01273) 600930

The Arlanda Hotel is owned by Ken and Karenza Mathews. Karenza played table tennis for England and was twice England Champion. Sport has taken Ken and Karenza to many parts of the world and they have stayed in all kinds of hotels! They use their experience to ensure that their guests are well looked after, with warmth, comfort and good food being priorities. The hotel is licensed and offers excellent accommodation close to the heart of Brighton.

Bed & Breakfast per night: single room from £18.00–£36.00; double room from £44.00–£80.00
Half board per person: £26.00–£48.00 daily
Lunch available: 1200–1400
Evening meal 1800 (last orders 2000)

Bedrooms: 4 single, 4 double, 1 twin, 3 triple
Bathrooms: 12 en-suite
Cards accepted: Access, Visa, Diners, Amex

381 SHELLEYS HOTEL

HIGHLY COMMENDED

High Street, Lewes, East Sussex BN7 1XS Tel (01273) 472361 Fax (01273) 483152

The town of Lewes, which is well known to opera lovers who attend the celebrated annual Glyndebourne Opera Festival, is nestled among the picturesque South Downs. Recently refurbished, Shelleys offers the highest standard of comfort. A short break can offer you the chance to explore some beautiful scenery, shop for antiques and visit the attractions of Brighton – about twenty minutes away – before returning to a peaceful country house hotel, renowned for its service and cuisine.

Bed & Breakfast per night: single room from £52.00–£110.50; double room from £104.00–£201.00
Half board per person: £70.00–£125.00 daily
Lunch available: 1200–1415
Evening meal 1900 (last orders 2115)

Bedrooms: 1 single, 9 double, 9 twin
Bathrooms: 19 en-suite
Parking for 25
Cards accepted: Access, Visa, Diners, Amex

382 SOUTH PADDOCK

HIGHLY COMMENDED

Maresfield Park, Uckfield, East Sussex TN22 2HA Tel (01825) 762335

A comfortable country house, beautifully furnished with an atmosphere of warmth and elegance. All rooms face south, overlooking three-and-a-half acres of mature gardens, landscaped for attractive colouring throughout the year. A peaceful setting for relaxing on the terrace, beside the fishpond and fountain or in spacious drawing rooms with log fires. Centrally located, 41 miles from London and within easy reach of Gatwick, the channel ports, Glyndebourne, Nymans, Sissinghurst and Chartwell. Good restaurants locally.

Bed & Breakfast per night: single occupancy from £32.00–£36.00; double room from £50.00–£56.00

Bedrooms: 1 double, 2 twin
Bathrooms: 1 private, 1 public
Parking for 6

383 LYE GREEN HOUSE

 DE LUXE

Lye Green, Crowborough, East Sussex TN6 1UU Tel (01892) 652018

An elegant Sussex country house offering spacious, tastefully decorated accommodation. The en-suite rooms are large and luxurious, with king-size beds for comfort. The beautiful six-acre garden was laid out in Edwardian times, with clipped yew hedges dividing the nine gardens – each with its own style, including a potager kitchen garden and some magnificent herbaceous borders. A lime walk leads to the natural ponds set in woodland. A rowing boat and fishing rods are available for relaxation.

Bed & Breakfast per night: single occupancy from £35.00–£40.00; double room from £40.00–£55.00

Bedrooms: 2 double, 1 twin
Bathrooms: 2 en-suite, 1 private
Parking for 3

---

384 THE OLD PARSONAGE

 DE LUXE

Church Lane, Frant, Royal Tunbridge Wells, Kent TN3 9DX Tel (01892) 750773 Fax (01892) 750773

This award-winning country house is peacefully situated by the church in pretty Frant village, with its two character pubs and restaurant nearby. Overlooking Lord Abergavenny's deer park on one side and the church on the other, this fine Georgian house provides superior accommodation, including luxurious en-suite bedrooms, antique-furnished reception rooms and a flower-filled conservatory where guests may relax in armchair comfort overlooking a wide, ballustraded terrace and secluded three-acre garden. A short drive from fifteen historic houses and gardens.

Bed & Breakfast per night: single occupancy from £34.00–£44.00; double room from £54.00–£64.00

Bedrooms: 2 double, 1 twin
Bathrooms: 3 en-suite
Parking for 12
Cards accepted: Access, Visa

---

385 DANEHURST

 HIGHLY COMMENDED

41 Lower Green Road, Rusthall, Tunbridge Wells, Kent TN4 8TW Tel (01892) 527739 Fax (01892) 514804

Danehurst is a charming gabled house in a village setting in the heart of Kent. Our tastefully furnished bedrooms afford you excellent accommodation and breakfast is served in our Victorian conservatory. You can also enjoy a candle-lit dinner in our elegant dining room. We would be delighted to welcome you to our home – we like to feel that once you are in our care you can relax and enjoy everything we have to offer you. Private parking is available.

Bed & Breakfast per night: single occupancy from £39.50–£45.00; double room from £59.50–£69.50
Half board per person: £58.45–£67.95 daily;
£409.15–£475.65 weekly
Evening meal 1900 (last bookings 1800)

Bedrooms: 2 double, 2 twin
Bathrooms: 4 en-suite
Parking for 5
Cards accepted: Access, Visa, Amex

386 SWALE COTTAGE

Listed HIGHLY COMMENDED

Poundsbridge Lane, Penshurst, Tonbridge, Kent TN11 8AH Tel (01892) 870738

Swale Cottage is a spacious converted barn. Hidden away at the end of a tiny country lane, it has a pretty cottage garden, climbing roses and a glorious, tranquil setting. The three beamed bedrooms are beautifully furnished and have TVs, tea and coffee making facilities and hairdryers. Prestigious awards for hospitality, comfort and cuisine. Hearty English breakfasts are served in the elegant dining room. Close to Penshurst Place, Hever, Chartwell and Tunbridge Wells. Thirty minutes drive from Gatwick. No smoking.

Bed & Breakfast per night: single occupancy from
£34.00–£44.00; double room from £52.00–£62.00

Bedrooms: 2 double, 1 twin
Bathrooms: 2 en-suite, 1 private
Parking for 7

The River Medway

RISING IN EAST SUSSEX near East Grinstead, the River Medway flows for some 70 or so miles before reaching the sea at Rochester. Its course is largely through the county of Kent, perhaps the most fertile land in England, its banks thick with apple blossom in spring. Visible through the trees once the leaves have fallen are countless half-timbered houses of breath-taking beauty. Magnificent dwellings such as those at Penshurst, west of Tonbridge, are signs both of the enduring prosperity of the area and the huge Wealden forest through which the river once flowed.

For centuries barges took timber from the forest down to the busy towns of Tonbridge, Maidstone and Rochester. Later the same barges transported weapons forged from the local iron ore. Though this trade died out long ago, the river continued to enjoy a connection with the armed services through the Royal Navy's dockyards at Chatham. The senior service left a few years ago, but the yard, now rechristened the Chatham Historic Dockyard and run as a charitable trust (tel: 01634 812551), is perhaps more welcoming to visitors.

The introduction of hops from the Continent in the 16th-century, the fertility of the soil and the pure waters of the Medway all ensured that Maidstone was at the heart of the Kentish brewing industry. The modern-day visitor can relive Medway history either at the Museum of Kent Life at Maidstone (tel: 01622 763936) or in the Guildhall Museum in Rochester (tel: 01634 848717); both have displays relating to the river.

Those with more energy might choose to appreciate this most English of countryside

from the peaceful waters of the Medway, and boats can be hired at several places along the river, including Tonbridge. For much of its length the Medway also has footpaths running along one or other bank. Indeed the entire stretch between Tonbridge and Maidstone has a path beside the water. Much of this is the old towpath, for the river was long ago canalised. West of Tunbridge Wells is the Forest Way Country Park, an abandoned railway line now devoted to the demands of the walker.

387 GROVE HOUSE

Listed HIGHLY COMMENDED

Grove Green Road, Weavering Street, Maidstone, Kent ME14 5JT Tel (01622) 738441

Attractive, detached comfortable home in quiet surroundings, with parking for six. Comfortable, double en-suite room and double and twin rooms with attractive guest bathroom. All rooms have their own colour television and tea/coffee making facilities. Easy access to motorways for London or the Channel Tunnel. Leeds Castle, Kent County Show Ground, restaurants and golf courses all nearby.

Bed & Breakfast per night: single occupancy from £20.00–£25.00; double room from £40.00–£45.00

Bedrooms: 2 double, 1 twin
Bathrooms: 1 en-suite, 1 private
Parking for 6

388 WILLINGTON COURT

 HIGHLY COMMENDED

Willington Street, Maidstone, Kent ME15 8JW Tel (01622) 738885 Fax (01622) 631790

Charming Grade II listed building, tastefully furnished and including antiques and a four-poster bed. All bedrooms have private facilities, television, hospitality tray, hairdryer, trouser press, plus extras for that touch of luxury. Guests can relax in the attractive 'Victorian' lounge. Smoking is restricted to the 'smokers' lounge, adjacent to the conservatory. Enjoy the restful and friendly atmosphere. An ideal location for visiting National Trust and other local historic properties, including nearby Leeds Castle.

Bed & Breakfast per night: single occupancy from £26.00–£34.00; double room from £40.00–£48.00

Bedrooms: 2 double, 1 twin
Bathrooms: 2 en-suite, 1 private
Parking for 6
Cards accepted: Access, Visa, Diners, Amex

389 TANYARD

 HIGHLY COMMENDED

Wierton Hill, Boughton Monchelsea, Maidstone, Kent ME17 4JT Tel (01622) 744705 Fax (01622) 741998

Tanyard is a medieval country house hotel perched on a ridge with far-reaching views across the weald of Kent. All six bedrooms have en-suite facilities and are furnished with antiques combined with modern comforts. The top-floor suite, which is heavily beamed, has a spa bath and is particularly popular. The no-smoking restaurant seats twenty eight and is in the oldest part of the building, dating from 1350. The modern English cuisine uses only fresh local produce.

Bed & Breakfast per night: single room from £60.00–£80.00; double room from £90.00–£125.00
Half board per person: £70.00–£105.00 daily; £507.50–£770.00 weekly
Lunch available: 1200–1330 (Wednesday–Friday)

Evening meal 1900 (last orders 2100)
Bedrooms: 1 single, 3 double, 2 twin
Bathrooms: 6 en-suite
Parking for 20
Cards accepted: Access, Visa, Diners, Amex, Switch/Delta

390 **HEMPSTEAD HOUSE**

 HIGHLY COMMENDED

London Road, Bapchild, Sittingbourne, Kent ME9 9PP Tel (01795) 428020

Exclusive private Victorian country house hotel, set in three acres of beautifully landscaped gardens. We extend exceptional warmth and hospitality to all our guests, offering luxurious en-suite accommodation and elegant surroundings. You can spend a memorable evening in our licensed dining room and relax in our spacious drawing rooms and conservatory. In the daytime, wander around our peaceful grounds or relax by our outdoor heated swimming pool.

Bed & Breakfast per night: single occupancy £59.00; double room £69.00
Half board per person: £52.00–£76.50 daily; £327.60–£481.95 weekly
Evening meal 1800 (last orders 2200)

Bedrooms: 5 double, 1 twin, 1 family room
Bathrooms: 7 en-suite
Parking for 10
Cards accepted: Access, Visa, Diners, Amex, Switch/Delta

391 **PRESTON LEA**

 HIGHLY COMMENDED

Canterbury Road, Faversham, Kent ME13 8XA Tel (01795) 535266 Fax (01795) 533388

This beautiful spacious house, built a century ago, was designed by a French architect and has many unique and interesting features, including two turrets, an oak-panelled hall, staircase, dining room and guest drawing room. Situated in lovely secluded gardens but by the A2, it is convenient for Canterbury, all the Channel ports, the M2 to London and beautiful countryside. Each bedroom is individually designed and all are large and sunny. A warm welcome is assured by caring hosts.

Bed & Breakfast per night: single occupancy from £30.00–£35.00; double room from £40.00–£50.00

Bedrooms: 2 double, 1 twin
Bathrooms: 2 en-suite, 1 private
Parking for 10
Cards accepted: Access, Visa

392 **THANINGTON HOTEL**

 HIGHLY COMMENDED

140 Wincheap, Canterbury, Kent CT1 3RY Tel (01227) 453227 Fax (01227) 453225

This superior Georgian bed-and-breakfast hotel, with its beautiful, spacious and tranquil accommodation, is only a few minutes' walk from the city centre and cathedral. An oasis in a busy tourist city, we invite you to relax and enjoy the comfort and facilities of this special hotel. Indoor heated swimming pool, snooker room, walled garden, bar and elegant dining room, where a delicious breakfast – to suit all tastes – is served. Convenient for the channel tunnel, ports and the historic homes of Kent.

Bed & Breakfast per night: single occupancy from £45.00–£49.50; double room from £62.00–£68.00

Bedrooms: 5 double, 3 twin, 2 family rooms
Bathrooms: 10 en-suite, 2 public
Parking for 12
Cards accepted: Access, Visa, Diners, Amex

393 WALLETTS COURT HOTEL AND RESTAURANT   HIGHLY COMMENDED

Westcliffe, St-Margarets-at-Cliffe, Dover, Kent CT15 6EW Tel (01304) 852424 Fax (01304) 853430

Walletts Court is an 'historic building of Kent' – a restored 17th-century manor house with a truly authentic sense of history. In a lovely rural setting with far-reaching views towards St. Margaret's Bay, Dover and the famous White Cliffs. The restaurant, highly acclaimed in major guides, is under the personal supervision of Chris Oakley and his family. Fresh seasonal ingredients are used in a menu with a Jacobean flavour which, together with a fine selection of wines, makes your stay a memorable experience.

Bed & Breakfast per night: single room from
£50.00–£60.00; double room from £60.00–£80.00
Half board per person: £55.00–£85.00 daily;
£350.00–£500.00 weekly
Evening meal 1900 (last orders 2130)

Bedrooms: 1 single, 7 double, 2 twin, 2 triple
Bathrooms: 11 en-suite, 1 private
Parking for 20
Cards accepted: Access, Visa, Diners, Amex,
Switch/Delta

394 OLD VICARAGE   HIGHLY COMMENDED

Chilverton Elms, Hougham, Dover, Kent CT15 7AS Tel (01304) 210668 Fax (01304) 225118

Guests are welcomed in a warm and relaxed style at our Victorian country house, elegantly furnished with lovely antiques and pictures. Situated in the peaceful Elms Vale with outstanding views, yet only minutes from Dover. The Old Vicarage provides everything for your stay to the highest standards and in spacious comfort. Large informal gardens. Log fires in winter. Secure parking. Dinner is available by arrangement. An ideal base for touring East Kent.

Bed & Breakfast per night: single occupancy from
£35.00–£40.00; double room from £50.00–£55.00
Evening meal 1930 (last orders 2100)

Bedrooms: 3 double
Bathrooms: 1 en-suite, 2 private
Parking for 10

395 LITTLE SILVER COUNTRY HOTEL   HIGHLY COMMENDED

Ashford Road, St Michaels, Tenterden, Kent TN30 6SP Tel (01233) 850321 Fax (01233) 850647

Little Silver Country Hotel is set in its own landscaped gardens. The restaurant provides an intimate, tranquil atmosphere where local produce is enjoyed, pre-dinner drinks and after dinner coffee are offered in the beamed sitting room with its log fire. Breakfast is served in a Victorian conservatory overlooking the waterfall rockery. Luxury bedrooms, tastefully and individually designed, some with four-posters and jacuzzi baths, others with brass beds. Facilities for disabled. Personal attention, care to detail, warmth and friendliness create a truly memorable experience. CATEGORY 3

Bed & Breakfast per night: single occupancy from
£62.00–£85.00; double room from £85.00–£110.00
Half board per person: £60.00–£75.00 daily;
£420.00–£525.00 weekly
Evening meal 1830 (last orders 2200)

Bedrooms: 5 double, 3 twin, 1 triple, 1 family room
Bathrooms: 10 en-suite
Parking for 50
Cards accepted: Access, Visa, Amex, Switch/Delta

396 BISHOPSDALE OAST

 HIGHLY COMMENDED

Biddenden, Ashford, Kent TN27 8DR Tel (01580) 291027 or (01580) 292065 Fax (01580) 292321

18th-century double kiln oast house of historical interest, enjoying beautiful views overlooking rural Kent. Off the beaten track but within easy reach of numerous castles, gardens, golf courses and the coast. Offering a relaxed and comfortable atmosphere, Iain and Jane, who are professional caterers, can provide breakfast or dinner in either the dining room or on the terrace. Bedrooms with all facilities and super king-size beds.

Bed & Breakfast per night: single occupancy from £32.50–£45.00; double room from £45.00–£55.00
Evening meal 1830 (last orders 2000)

Bedrooms: 3 double
Bathrooms: 2 en-suite, 1 private
Parking for 6
Cards accepted: Access, Visa, Switch/Delta

Mad Jack Fuller and his monuments

IN THE CHURCHYARD at Brightling, East Sussex, is a 25ft-high stone pyramid. Its vast bulk and whimsical eccentricity match perfectly the stature and character of its builder, 'Mad' Jack Fuller, whose grave it marks.

Between 1777 and 1834 Fuller was Squire of Brightling and the owner of nearby Rose Hill, now renamed Brightling Park (not open to the public). He was enormously fat, with a booming voice and a predilection for drink. But he was also a cultured man, a patron of both Turner and the eminent architect, Robert Smirke, and a generous benefactor to the Royal Institute of Science. In 1807 he became an MP, but his stormy political career was cut short by several episodes of unrestrained invective. Today Fuller is chiefly remembered, not for his munificence to the arts and sciences, nor his outspoken contribution to public life, but for the obsession of his later life: folly-building.

Fuller planned his tomb 24 or more years before he died. In the course of the next couple of decades at least five other eccentric, and in most cases quite useless, edifices appeared, some of which may still be seen. A short distance to the south-east of Brightling is the Tower, a mysterious gothic-looking building with a battlemented top. Another folly, the Sugar Loaf, was allegedly built to mimic the conical spire of Dallington Church: Fuller supposedly wagered that Dallington's spire was visible from his windows, but on returning home to find this was untrue,

had the Sugar Loaf erected in a single night. Surprisingly, the building actually served as a residence for many years. A 65ft-high obelisk, known as the Brightling Needle, marks the second highest point in Sussex, and may have been built to commemorate Wellington's 1815 victory over Napoleon at Waterloo.

A wealth of legends has grown up surrounding Fuller and his monuments. The most colourful relates to his tomb: it was said that Fuller directed that after his death he should be placed inside the pyramid, sitting at a table, dressed for dinner and wearing a top hat, with a bottle of claret at his elbow. Today, the door of the tomb has been replaced by a grill, and the (empty) interior is clearly visible. Fuller lies in conventional repose in the ground below, but his many unconventional monuments ensure he will never be forgotten.

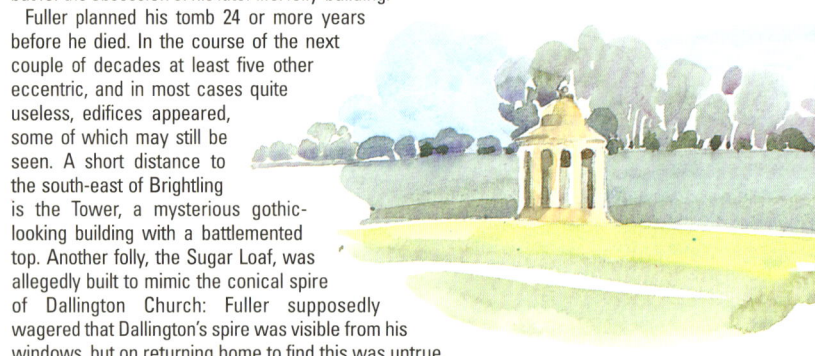

397 CRIT HALL

Listed DE LUXE

Cranbrook Road, Benenden, Kent TN17 4EU Tel (01580) 240609 Fax (01580) 241743

Crit Hall is a classic Georgian country house of great charm situated high on the Weald of Kent, enjoying wonderful views. The house is finely furnished with antiques and interesting artworks, and all bedrooms are spacious and impeccably appointed. Splendid guests' drawing room, delightful garden. Excellent breakfasts and imaginative dinners (by prior arrangement). Considerable personal attention assures every comfort and a relaxing stay. Close to Sissinghurst and numerous historic houses and gardens.

Bed & Breakfast per night: single occupancy from £30.00–£38.00; double room from £50.00–£56.00
Half board per person: £41.50–£56.50 daily; £270.00–£300.00 weekly
Evening meal 1930

Bedrooms: 1 double, 2 twin
Bathrooms: 2 en-suite, 1 private
Parking for 5
Cards accepted: Access, Visa, Switch/Delta

---

398 KENNEL HOLT HOTEL

 HIGHLY COMMENDED

Goudhurst Road, Cranbrook, Kent TN17 2PT Tel (01580) 712032 Fax (01580) 715495

Kennel Holt really is somewhere special – an Elizabethan manor house, set back three hundred yards from the road, in the heart of the Weald of Kent. Five acres of gardens ensure perfect calm, yet we are only half an hour from many historic gardens and houses, and ten minutes from Sissinghurst. Our restaurant specialises in fine fresh local ingredients, freshly prepared and imaginatively cooked. There is a wide range of wines offering wonderful value. Truly somewhere special.

Bed & Breakfast per night: single room £85.00; double room £125.00
Half board per person: from £84.50 daily; £591.50 weekly
Lunch available: by prior arrangement
Evening meal 1930 (last orders 2100)

Bedrooms: 2 single, 6 double, 2 twin
Bathrooms: 10 en-suite
Parking for 35
Cards accepted: Access, Visa, Diners, Amex, Switch/Delta

---

399 GLYDWISH PLACE

Listed HIGHLY COMMENDED

Fontridge Lane, Burwash, East Sussex TN19 7DG Tel (01435) 882869 or 0850 421732 Fax (01435) 882749

Beautiful, split-level house on a lovely wooded site, with far-reaching views for your relaxation. Large gardens with lawns and ponds on different levels, a summer house and putting green. Many different breeds of ducks, geese and pheasants. The surrounding countryside is delightful, with lovely walks and excellent pubs in the local villages. A sauna, solarium, gymnasium and games room are also available and free of charge when staying for two or more nights.

Bed & Breakfast per night: single occupancy from £20.00–£30.00; double room from £45.00–£55.00

Bedrooms: 3 double
Bathrooms: 2 en-suite, 1 private
Parking for 12

400 CONQUERORS

🌊🌊 HIGHLY COMMENDED

Stunts Green, Herstmonceux, Hailsham, East Sussex BN27 4PR Tel (01323) 832446 Fax (01323) 832446

With its commanding views over 1066 country, Conquerors was built, to the highest standards, in the 1930s. Peaceful and secluded in its parkland setting of outstanding natural beauty, Conquerors is only one mile from several old village inns and restaurants. Famous houses, castles and gardens are within easy touring distance, as are the historic towns of Hastings, Battle, Royal Tunbridge Wells, Brighton and Eastbourne. Conquerors aims to offer complete comfort in total tranquillity. ♈ CATEGORY 3

Bed & Breakfast per night: single occupancy from £20.00–£25.00; double room from £40.00–£48.00

Bedrooms: 1 double, 2 twin
Bathrooms: 2 en-suite, 1 private
Parking for 25

Walmer Castle and the Cinque Ports

ONE OF THE MANY CONSEQUENCES of Henry VIII's decision to defy papal decree by divorcing Catherine of Aragon was the construction of three Kentish castles, all within a mile or two of each other. Henry feared that the Pope's invective would persuade the French to invade, so to protect a vulnerable stretch of coastline he built the castles of Sandown, Deal and Walmer between 1538 and 1540. The invasion never materialised, but the castles took their place at the centre of English defences. Sandown is now little more than a rock garden, but Deal (tel: 01304 372762), despite taking a direct hit from a bomb in World War II, superbly demonstrates the robust defensive architecture favoured by Henry. Walmer Castle (tel: 01304 364288), by contrast, has been so domesticated that it is now the *ex officio* residence of the Queen Mother in her capacity as Lord Warden of the Cinque Ports.

Established before the Norman Conquest, the Cinque Ports (pronounced 'sink') formed a powerful confederation of Channel ports throughout the medieval period. The original five (*cinq*) towns were Hastings, New Romney, Hythe, Dover and Sandwich. The 'antient' towns' of Rye and Winchelsea were later added to their number, as were several minor ports, or 'limbs' as they came to be known. In return for providing the monarch with ships and seamen – these towns formed the backbone of England's maritime defences – the ports enjoyed certain privileges, including the lucrative right to punish miscreants by levying and keeping fines. Another right enabled fisherman of the Cinque Ports to sell their catch at Yarmouth in Norfolk without paying tax – unlike the local boats. The vitriol engendered by this changed to bloodshed in 1340 when the Yarmouth and Cinque Ports elements within the King's fleet attacked one another; 32 Yarmouth ships and 200 Yarmouth men perished. However, as the harbours of the once-flourishing ports became choked with silt (only Dover remains a working port today), so the influence of the Cinque Ports waned.

By the time the Lord Warden of the Cinque Ports took up official residence in Walmer Castle in the early 18th-century the post – and indeed the confederation – was largely symbolic. Notable Lords Warden have included William Pitt the Younger (his niece, Lady Hester Stanhope laid out the gardens), the Duke of Wellington, Winston Churchill (though he never stayed at Walmer) and the Queen Mother. Visitors to Walmer Castle (English Heritage) may be excused for thinking that the Iron Duke is still in residence, for his bedroom is (sparsely) furnished exactly as it was when he died here in 1852.

401 BEAUPORT PARK HOTEL
HIGHLY COMMENDED

Battle Road, Hastings, East Sussex TN38 8EA Tel (01424) 851222 Fax (01424) 852465

Our Georgian Country House is the jewel in a 1500-acre parkland estate, three miles from the village of Battle and a short drive to Rye. Our acclaimed restaurant offers the best of English and continental cuisine. Each bedroom overlooks our gardens and Sussex cream teas can be served in the Italian sunken garden. A nine and eighteen-hole golf course and riding stables are adjacent to the hotel.

Bed & Breakfast per night: single room from £69.00–£71.00; double room from £90.00–£95.00
Half board per person: £57.00–£65.00 daily; £342.00–£390.00 weekly
Lunch available: 1230–1400

Evening meal 1900 (last orders 2130)
Bedrooms: 4 single, 10 double, 7 twin, 2 triple
Bathrooms: 23 en-suite
Parking for 64
Cards accepted: Access, Visa, Diners, Amex, Switch/Delta

402 FLACKLEY ASH HOTEL & RESTAURANT
HIGHLY COMMENDED

London Road, Peasmarsh, Rye, East Sussex TN31 6YH Tel (01797) 230651 Fax (01797) 230510

A Georgian country house hotel, set in beautiful gardens with croquet and putting lawns, an indoor swimming pool, a leisure centre with gym, saunas, whirlpool spa and flotation tank, and beauty salon offering aromatherapy massage. Warm, friendly atmosphere, fine wines and good food. Well situated for visiting the castles and gardens of East Sussex and Kent and the ancient Cinque port of Rye. Golf, bird-watching, country or seaside walks, potteries and steam trains are some of the attractions in the area.

Bed & Breakfast per night: single occupancy from £69.00–£85.00; double room from £108.00–£124.00
Half board per person: £49.50–£69.00 daily; £299.00–£415.00 weekly
Lunch available: 1230–1345

Evening meal 1900 (last orders 2130)
Bedrooms: 21 double, 9 twin, 1 triple, 1 family room
Bathrooms: 32 en-suite
Parking for 60
Cards accepted: Access, Visa, Diners, Amex, Switch/Delta

403 PLAYDEN COTTAGE GUESTHOUSE
HIGHLY COMMENDED

Military Road, Rye, East Sussex TN31 7NY Tel (01797) 222234

On the old Saxon shore, less than a mile from Rye town and on what was once a busy fishing harbour, there is now only a pretty cottage with lovely gardens, a pond and an ancient right of way. The sea has long receded and, sheltered by its own informal gardens, Playden Cottage looks over the River Rother and across the sheep-studded Romney Marsh. It offers comfort, peace, a care for detail – and a very warm welcome.

Bed & Breakfast per night: single occupancy from £37.50–£60.00; double room from £50.00–£60.00
Half board per person: £37.00–£42.00 daily; £233.10–£264.60 weekly
Evening meal 1800 (last orders 2030)

Bedrooms: 1 double, 2 twin
Bathrooms: 3 en-suite, 1 public
Parking for 7
Open: January–December
Cards accepted: Access, Visa

404 JEAKE'S HOUSE

 HIGHLY COMMENDED

Mermaid Street, Rye, East Sussex TN31 7ET Tel (01797) 222828 Fax (01797) 222623

Jeake's House stands on the most famous cobbled street in medieval Rye. Bedrooms have been individually restored to create a very special atmosphere, combining traditional elegance and luxury with modern amenities. Oak-beamed and panelled bedrooms with brass, mahogany or four-poster beds overlook the marsh and rooftops to the sea. Vegetarian or traditional breakfast is served in the galleried former chapel where soft chamber music and a roaring fire will make your stay a truly memorable experience.

Bed & Breakfast per night: single room from
£22.50–£54.00; double room from £41.00–£59.00

Bedrooms: 1 single, 7 double, 1 twin, 2 triple, 1 family room
Bathrooms: 7 en-suite, 1 private, 2 private showers,
2 public
Cards accepted: Access, Visa

405 RYE LODGE

HIGHLY COMMENDED

Hilders Cliff, Rye, East Sussex TN31 7LD Tel (01797) 223838 Fax (01797) 223585

Premier position on East Cliff, close to the historic 14th-century Landgate, High Street shops and restaurants. De luxe rooms, all en-suite with luxurious bathrooms, remote control colour TVs, direct-dial telephones and hospitality trays. Room service with breakfast in bed as late as you like. Candle-lit dinners in the elegant Terrace Room, with delicious food and an extensive, well-chosen wine list. Tastefully furnished, where elegance is the keynote in a relaxed atmosphere with really caring service. Own car park.

Bed & Breakfast per night: single room from
£47.50–£65.00; double room from £65.00–£105.00
Half board per person: £42.50–£58.75 daily;
£295.00–£395.00 weekly
Evening meal 1930 (last orders 2130)

Bedrooms: 1 single, 10 double, 4 twin
Bathrooms: 15 en-suite
Parking for 20
Cards accepted: Access, Visa, Diners, Amex,
Switch/Delta

406 WHITE VINE HOUSE

HIGHLY COMMENDED

24 High Street, Rye, East Sussex TN31 7JF Tel (01797) 224748 Fax (01797) 223599

Tudor house at the heart of unspoilt ancient Rye, with its cobbled streets and rich history. Very comfortable bedrooms; excellent generous breakfast. Oak beams, stone fireplaces, books and paintings make this beautiful home your choice for restful days. Our tiny town garden is a tranquil haven, ideal for spending time with a favourite book and a glass of wine. Antique hunting, castles and gardens, walking, bird-watching and the coast – all close by. A non-smoking haven for grown-ups.

Bed & Breakfast per night: single occupancy from
£45.00–£100.00; double room from £86.00–£110.00
Lunch available: 1200–1600

Bedrooms: 4 double, 1 triple
Bathrooms: 5 en-suite
Cards accepted: Access, Visa, Diners, Amex,
Switch/Delta

SYMBOLS

For ease of use, the key to symbols appears on the back of the cover flap and can be folded out while consulting individual entries. The symbols which appear at the end of each entry are designed to enable you to see at-a-glance what's on offer, and whether any particular requirements you have can be met. Most of the symbols are clear, simple icons and few require any further explanation, but the following points may be useful:

ALCOHOLIC DRINKS

Alcoholic drinks are available at all types of accommodation listed in the guide unless the symbol **UL** (unlicensed) appears. However, even in licensed premises there may be some restrictions on the serving of drinks, such as being available to diners only. You may wish to check this in advance.

SMOKING

Many establishments offer facilities for non-smokers, indicated by the symbol ✄. These may include no-smoking bedrooms and parts of communal rooms set aside for non-smokers. Some establishments prefer not to accommodate smokers at all, and if this is the case it will be made clear in the establishment description in the guide entry.

PETS

The symbol 🐕 is used to show that dogs are not accepted in any circumstances. Some establishments will accept pets, but we advise you to check this at the time of booking and to enquire as to whether any additional charge will be made to accommodate them.

BOOKING CHECKLIST

When enquiring about accommodation remember to state your requirements clearly and precisely. It may be necessary or helpful to discuss some or all of the following points:

- Your intended arrival and departure dates.
- The type of accommodation you require. For example, a twin-bedded room, a private bath and WC, whether the room has a view or not.
- The terms you require, such as room only; bed & breakfast; bed, breakfast and evening meal (half board); bed, breakfast, lunch and evening meal (full board).
- If you have any children travelling with you, say how old they are and state their accommodation requirements, such as a cot, and whether they will share your room.
- Any particular requirements, such as a special diet or a ground-floor room.
- If you think you are likely to arrive late in the evening, mention this when you book. Similarly, if you are delayed on your journey

a telephone call to inform the management may well help avoid any problems on your arrival.

- If you are asked for a deposit or the number of your credit card, find out what the proprietor's policy is if, for whatever reason, you can't turn up as planned – see 'cancellations' opposite.
- Exactly how the establishment's charges are levied – see below.

Misunderstandings can easily occur over the telephone, so it is advisable to confirm in writing all bookings, together with special requirements. Please mention that you learnt of the establishment through *Somewhere Special*. Remember to include your name and address, and please enclose a stamped, addressed envelope – or an international reply coupon if writing from outside Britain. Please note that the English Tourist Board does not make reservations; you should address your enquiry directly to the establishment.

PRICES

The prices given throughout this publication will serve as a general guide, but you should always check them at the time of booking. The following information may prove useful when determining how much a trip may cost:

- Prices were supplied during the autumn of 1996 and changes may have occurred since publication.
- Prices include VAT where applicable.
- You should check whether or not a service charge is included in the published price.
- Prices for double rooms assume occupancy by two people; you will need to check whether there is a single person supplement.
- Half board means the price for the room, breakfast and evening meal per person per day or per person per week.
- A full English breakfast is not always included in the quoted price; you may be given a continental breakfast unless you are prepared to pay more.
- Establishments with at least four bedrooms or eight beds are obliged to display in the reception area or at the entrance overnight accommodation charges.
- Reduced prices may apply for children; check exactly how these reductions are calculated, including the maximum age for the child.
- Prices are often much cheaper for off-peak holidays; check to see whether special off-season packages are available.

DEPOSITS AND ADVANCE PAYMENTS

For reservations made weeks or months ahead a deposit is usually payable which will be deducted from the total bill at the end of your stay.

Some establishments, particularly the larger hotels in big towns, now require payment for the room upon arrival if a prior reservation has not been made. Regrettably this practice has become necessary because of the number of guests who have left without settling their bills. If you are asked to pay in advance, it is sensible to see your room before payment is made to ensure that it meets your requirements.

If you book by telephone and are asked for your credit card number, you should note that the proprietor may charge your credit card account even if you subsequently cancel the booking. Ask the owner what his or her usual practice is.

CREDIT/CHARGE CARDS

Any credit/charge cards that are accepted by the establishment are indicated at the end of the written description. The abbreviations used in this guide are:

Access – Access/Eurocard/Mastercard

Visa – Visa/Barclaycard

Diners – Diners

Amex – American Express

Switch/Delta – Direct debit card

If you intend to pay by either credit or charge card you are advised to confirm this at the time of booking. Please note that when paying by credit card, you may sometimes be charged a higher rate for your accommodation in order to cover the percentage paid by the proprietor to the credit card company. Again find this out in advance.

When making a booking, you may be asked for your credit card number as 'confirmation'. The proprietor may then charge your credit card account if you have to cancel the booking, but if this is the policy, it must be made clear to you at the time of booking – see below.

CANCELLATIONS

When you accept offered accommodation, including over the telephone, you are entering into a legally binding contract with the proprietor. This means that if you cancel a reservation or fail to take up all or part of the accommodation booked, the proprietor may be entitled to compensation if the accommodation cannot be re-let for all or a good part of the booked period. If you have paid a deposit, you will probably forfeit this, and further payment may well be asked for.

However, no such claim can be made by the proprietor until after the booked period, during which time every effort should be made to re-let the accommodation. It is therefore in your interests to advise the management immediately in writing if you have to cancel or curtail a booking. Travel or holiday insurance, available quite cheaply from travel agents, and some hotels, will safeguard you if you have to cancel or curtail your stay.

And remember, if you book by telephone and are asked for your credit card number, you should check whether the proprietor intends charging your account should you later cancel your reservation. A

proprietor should not be able to charge for a cancellation unless he or she has made this clear at the time of your booking and you have agreed. However, to avoid later disputes, we suggest you check whether he or she intends to make such a charge.

SERVICE CHARGES AND TIPPING

Some establishments levy a service charge automatically, and, if so, must state this clearly in the offer of accommodation at the time of booking. If the offer is accepted by you, the service charge becomes part of the contract. If service is included in your bill, there is no need for you to give tips to the staff unless some particular or exceptional service has been rendered. In the case of meals, the usual tip is 10% of the total bill.

TELEPHONE CALL CHARGES

There is no restriction on the charges that can be made by hotels for telephone calls made from their premises. Unit charges are frequently considerably higher than telephone companies' standard charges in order to defray the costs of providing the service. It is a condition of being awarded a national Crown classification that the telephone unit charges are displayed alongside the telephone. However, it may not always be clear how these compare with the standard unit charge. Before using a hotel telephone, particularly for long-distance calls, you should enquire how much extra you will be paying per unit.

SECURITY OF VALUABLES

It is advisable to deposit any valuables for safe-keeping with the management of the establishment in which you are staying. If the management accept custody of your property they become wholly liable for its loss or damage. They can however restrict their liability for items brought on to the premises and not placed in their special custody to the minimum amounts imposed by the Hotel Proprietors Act, 1956. These are the sum of £50 in respect of one article and a total of £100 in the case of one guest. In order to restrict their liability the management must display a notice in the form required by the Act in a prominent position in the reception area or main entrance of the premises. Without this notice, the proprietor is liable for the full value of the loss or damage to any property (other than a motor car or its contents) of a guest who has booked overnight accommodation.

FEEDBACK

Let us know about your holiday. We welcome suggestions about how the guide itself may be improved.

Most establishments welcome feedback. Please let the proprietor know if you particularly enjoyed your stay. We sincerely hope that you have no cause for complaint, but should you be dissatisfied or have any problems, make your complaint to the management at the time of the incident so that immediate action may be taken.

The English Tourist Board, Jarrold Publishing and Celsius cannot guarantee the accuracy of the information in this guide and accept no responsibility for any error or misrepresentation. All liability for any loss, disappointment or damage caused by reliance upon the information contained in this guide, or in the event of bankruptcy or liquidation or cessation of trade of any company, individual or firm mentioned, is hereby excluded. All establishments listed are bound by the Trades Description Acts of 1968 and 1972 when describing and offering accommodation and facilities, but we strongly recommend that prices and other details should be confirmed at the time of booking.

Details listed were believed correct at time of going to press. It is advisable to telephone in advance to check the details have not altered and to discuss any specific requirements.

CODE OF CONDUCT

All establishments appearing in this guide have agreed to observe the following Code of Conduct:

1 To ensure high standards of courtesy and cleanliness; catering and service appropriate to the type of establishment.

2 To describe fairly to all visitors and prospective visitors the amenities, facilities and services provided by the establishment, whether by advertisement, brochure, word of mouth or any other means. To allow visitors to see accommodation, if requested, before booking.

3 To make clear to visitors exactly what is included in all prices quoted for accommodation, meals and refreshments, including service charges, taxes and other surcharges. details of charges, if any, for heating or for additional services or facilities available should also be made clear.

4 To adhere to, and not to exceed, prices current at time of occupation for accommodation or other services.

5 To advise visitors at the time of booking, and subsequently, of any change, if the accommodation offered is in an unconnected annexe, or similar, or by boarding out, and to indicate the location of such accommodation and any difference in comfort and amenities from accommodation in the main establishment.

6 To give each visitor, on request, details of payments due and a receipt if required.

7 To deal promptly and courteously with all enquiries, requests, reservations, correspondence and complaints from visitors.

8 To allow an English Tourist Board representative reasonable access to the establishment, on request, to confirm that the Code of Conduct is being observed.

Index

Index